CONSTITUENT ASSEMBLY OF INDIA

CONSTITUENT ASSEMBLY OF INDIA

Springboard of Revolution

(SECOND EDITION)

SHIBANIKINKAR CHAUBE

MANOHAR
2022

First published 1973
Second edition, 2000
Reprinted 2022

ISBN 978-81-7304-365-9 (Pb)
ISBN 978-81-7304-356-7 (Hb)

Published by
Ajay Kumar Jain *for*
Manohar Publishers & Distributors
4753/23 Ansari Road, Daryaganj
New Delhi 110 002

Printed and bound by CPI Group (UK) Ltd, Croydon, CRo 4YY

Dedicated
to the memory
of my father

Contents

Preface to the Second Edition

The first edition of this book was published after 25 year of India's Independence. In the fifty-fourth year of Independence it is somewhat satisfying to note that the Constitution still works, almost a unique achievement for a constitution framed in the wake of World War II.

The expert body set up by the Union government in January 2000 to review the working of the Constitution and to suggest amendments will do well to remember that no constitution in the world—that is to say, the lasting ones—was drawn up in a perfectly democratic way or has been perfect. Hence the need for amendments. But the longevity of a constitution itself is proof to the fact that the constitution suits the people well. Secondly a constitution is not a programme of the people, but a record of their achievements. Finally, every constitution has an integrity of its own which should not be weakened by thoughtless tampering of its particular segments.

The present edition has been revised in order to bring the central thesis of the book into sharper focus, to take stock of the numerous amendments that have been made and to clip the appendix in view of recent global changes. The purpose of the appendix that appeared in the first edition was to drive home a point which needs to be stated.

Although, historically, a constituent assembly has been found to be the product of a liberal bourgeois revolution, the Constituent Assembly of India was a *part* of such a revolution, and not its fulfilment. It was conceived to be the culmination of a process of devolution of power from the British Crown in Parliament within the dominion framework. In overstepping its limits the Assembly had to pay the price of partition for the sake of a centralized polity. That polity had all the ingredients of a liberal bourgeois democracy with a welfarist edge.

Such a statement goes beyond the description of India as a post-colonial state. That description is chronological and not categorical. Of course the Constitution did not describe India as a capitalist state. No constitution does so; the standard argument is that political democracy is ideologically neutral. At the end of the twentieth century there is little doubt that the Indian state has developed into a capitalist state.

Delhi — S.K. CHAUBE

30 June 2000

Preface to the First Edition

The late Dr Dhirendranath Sen, former Surendranath Banerjee Professor of Political Science in Calcutta University, first provoked the author to undertake a study of the constituent assemblies of the major countries of the world in historical contexts. After Dr Sen's sudden death, Dr Ramesh Chandra Ghosh, Centenary Professor of Public Administration in the same university, kindly consented to guide the author's research. On his advice a specific case-study of the Constituent Assembly of India was chosen. The shift appeared to be minor but immensely rewarding, for the author has been able not only to view the Constituent Assembly as the product of a particular historical situation, but also to gain some insight into the constitutional system of India.

As to the first point, the Constituent Assembly of India was born at the climax of an incomplete, though painless, national democratic revolution. The price of liberty it attained was partition of British India. But the end of the separate existence of feudal India was a positive achievement of the revolution. A study of the decision-making process in the Constituent Assembly, in the second place, helps clear the hedges that have already grown around the Constitution.

This volume is a revised version of the thesis entitled 'Constituent Assembly of India and the Indian Constitution', on the merit of which Calcutta University conferred Doctorate of Philosophy on the author. The appendix furnishes a brief comparative perspective. An epilogue has been added.

Shillong
15 May 1973

S.K. CHAUBE

Introduction

The purpose of this book is to examine the basic concepts of the Indian Constitution in their historical context. No other method has been found as suitable for the purpose as the study of the Indian Constituent Assembly, the relevance of which was pointed by C.H. Alexandrowicz in 1957:

> Whereas the American Constitution was framed more than 160 years ago, the Constitution of India came into force only recently, in 1950. Those who framed the Constitution enjoy at the same time undisputed national leadership, and the needs for adjusting the Constitution, in accordance (with) or in spite of the intentions of the founder fathers, to new conditions of life are still non-existing. Quite to the contrary, it is the Constitution which is intended to bring about social and economic reform. Moreover, whereas recorded evidence as to the intentions of the constitution-makers in the United States has by now been fully exploited, Indian constitutional lawyers seem hardly to have acquainted themselves with the Constituent Assembly debates. . . . Whereas new contributions to the understanding of the intentions of the original framers of the American Constitution and its amendments are not likely to be forthcoming, all contributions in this respect may have still to be made in India, in the first instance, by academic lawyers whose task it is to explore thoroughly the background of the Constitution.[1]

The task is admittedly difficult. It involves a study of the constitutional progress as well as the political struggle of India, leading to the establishment of the Constituent Assembly, and also its problems. The mind and working of the Assembly will be better understood in the setting than through any mechanical analysis. The developments in Indian politics, even during the prolonged working of the Constituent Assembly, form a part of this setting no less vital than the collective political and socio-economic background of the members of the Constituent Assembly. It is also to be remembered that the collection of a vast store of data from the constitutions of other countries formed the comparative background of the Indian Constitution.

The libraries utilized for the preparation of the book are the National Library, Calcutta; the National Archives Library, New Delhi; the Library of the Lok Sabha; the Library of the All-India Congress Committee; the

[1] C.H. Alexandrowicz, *Constitutional Developments in India*, p. 17.

Assam Legislative Assembly Library; the Library of the Indian Council of World Affairs; and the Archives of the Ministry of Law, Government of India. A number of Constituent Assembly members have been interviewed. The greatest help came from B. Shiva Rao, a Constituent Assembly member and brother of the late B.N. Rau, who has compiled select documents on the constitution-making which were made available to this author in manuscript.[2] The author has also received help from various political parties and leaders. He is thankful to all the persons and authorities mentioned above.

[2] The work has since been published under the title *The Framing of India's Constitution*, 5 vols., 1966-8.

PART I

CHAPTER 1

The Indian Problem

We have distinctly maintained that representative government, in its western sense, is totally inapplicable to the Indian empire and would be uncongenial to the traditions of eastern populations; that Indian conditions do not admit of popular representation; that the safety and welfare of the country must depend on the supremacy of British administration; and that supremacy can, in no circumstances, be delegated to any kind of representative assembly.

Lord Minto on 25 January 1910[1]

The comment on the reformed Imperial Legislative Council of India, under the Indian Councils Act of 1909, sums up the typical British scepticism about India's political future. Paradoxically, the reforms of 1909 are regarded as the first instalment of, or at least the first step towards, representative government in India. The scepticism persisted until the first world war accelerated the pace of history and radically altered the Indian situation. The liberal government of England recognized the reality and Montagu declared in the House of Commons, on 20 August 1917, the policy of 'increasing association of Indians in every branch of administration and gradual development of self-governing institutions with a view to the progressive realization of responsible government of India as an integral part of the British empire'.[2]

In place of a system of 'absolute government' the Montagu-Chelmsford Reforms granted the Indians 'an increasing share in the administration of the country and increasing opportunities of influencing and criticizing the government'.[3] The offer, as embodied in the Government of India Act, 1919, was a slight improvement on the British policy since 1858. There was no promise to the Indians of a constitution of their own choice. The only significant innovation in the act was a partially 'ministerial' government in the provinces (dyarchy).

[1] Anil Chandra Banerjee, *Indian Constitutional Documents*, vol. 2, p. 224.

[2] A.B. Keith, *Speeches and Documents on Indian Policy, 1750-1920*, vol. I, pp. 133-4.

[3] *Montagu-Chelmsford Report*, p. 1. Tej Bhadur Sapru (*The Indian Constitution*, pp. 3-4), however, regarded the 1919 reforms as a continuation of the policy followed since 1858.

By the time the Indian Statutory (Simon) Commission submitted its Report in October 1929, the federal idea had become popular as a compromise between the nationalist demand for a united India and the demands of the Muslim League and the native princes for 'safeguards' and 'independence'. The federal scheme took a concrete shape at the Round Table Conference and, supplemented by the Communal Award and further modified by the Poona Pact, formed the basis of the Government of India Act, 1935.

Until the beginning of the Second World War, therefore, British schemes for constitutional reform in India were confined to the grant of responsible government within the British empire and under British supervision. And the major obstacle to the grant of responsible government was considered to be the so called Indian problem, by which the British constitutionalists referred to the organic heterogeneity of the Indian community and the reluctance of the princes to sacrifice their rights and status. The core of the Indian problem was, however, unmistakably considered to be the Hindu-Muslim communal rivalry reflected in the Congress League differences on the political future of India. As Reginald Coupland wrote, 'of cardinal importance was not the division between British India and Indian India . . . but the conflict between the Congress and the Muslim League, more strictly, the Hindu-Moslem schism which that conflict reflects'.[4]

The Communal Problem

And what was the nature of this schism? F.K. Khan-Durrani, an unofficial theoretician of the Muslim League, regarded the question as 'wholly political': 'The Hindus claim the right of majority-rule. Majority-rule means Hindu raj. Muslims cannot agree to it. . . . There can be no peace or agreement between the two nations unless and until the major community abandons the dream of Hindu raj.[5]

Growth of this 'political question' is, however, generally explained by the apprehension of the Muslims who were not only numerically much weaker than the Hindus, but also had been lagging behind the Hindus in the march to progress. To most of them, Congress was exclusively a Hindu affair.

On the other hand, the growing influence of the Congress and the attention paid to it by the government were a lesson Moslems could not miss. Once more, it

[4] Reginald Coupland, *The Constitutional Problem in India*, part III, p. 16.
[5] F.K. Khan-Durrani, *The Meaning of Pakistan*, pp. 62-3.

seemed, they were in danger of being left behind. The knowledge that a new instalment of 'reforms' were under consideration spurred them to action, and, since most of the leaders were unwilling to make common cause with the Congress, a separate political organization of Indian Moslems was created—the Indian Moslem League.[6]

In an apparently neutral mood A.B. Keith narrated the effect of the 'reforms' of 1919: 'Another unhappy feature of the operation of the reforms was the inevitable impetus given to sectarian strife. It was obvious to Hindus and Muslims alike that the change in the form of government meant the possibility of securing effective domination by legal means; especially in the case of Bengal and the Punjab where numbers are fairly balanced.'[7]

In his 'restatement' on India, Coupland, however, admitted that the British 'had deliberately widened' the Hindu-Muslim schism.[8] Positive encouragement to separation in the constitutional set-up indeed started with the Morley-Minto Reforms (1909) which granted separate electorates to the Indian people with the first instalment of responsible government. The Montagu-Chelmsford Report considered the system as repugnant to democracy but, in view of 'the promises given and renewed by secretaries of state and viceroys',[9] recommended its retention and even extension. The Government of India Act, 1919, gave separate electorates to Muslims, Sikhs, Indian Christians, Anglo-Indians and Europeans. Among the Hindus, the non-Brahmins of Madras and Marhattas in Bombay had reservation of seats in their respective provincial legislatures. Provision was made for nomination of depressed-class Hindus to ensure them adequate representation.

The Simon Commission (1928) recommended the continuation of separate electorates for Muslims, Sikhs, Anglo-Indians and Europeans. Reservation of seats was recommended for the depressed classes and Indian Christians (the latter had so long enjoyed separate electorate). Also recommended was the abolition of reservation for the non-Brahmins of Madras, though reservation for Marhattas was allowed to stay. The Commission commented that the separate representation of the communities and special interests was 'the most noticeable feature of the Indian electoral system'.[10] The Government of India Act, 1935, extended the franchise to

[6] Coupland, *The Constitutional Problem in India*, part I, p. 33.

[7] A.B. Keith, *A Constitutional History of India, 1600-1935*, pp. 286-7.

[8] Coupland, *India—A Restatement*, p. 69.

[9] *Report on Indian Constitutional Reforms*, p. 150.

[10] *Report of the Indian Statutory Commission*, vol. I, p. 200.

cover about 15 per cent of the population, but retained and further extended the system of separate electorates to a total of 18 categories.[11]

The Tribal Pockets

A major part of the Indian problem consisted of India's tribal population which required special treatment and protection of the government. Since 1870 the British rulers adopted a policy of isolation for the tribes. The Government of India Act, 1919, empowered the Governor-General to declare any area of a province as a 'backward tract' and exclude it from the scope of ministerial administration. The power was extensively used. On the recommendation of the Indian Statutory Commission, the Government of India Act, 1935, established the excluded and partially excluded areas with these tracts.

On the eastern and north-western frontiers of British India lived certain tribes with whom effective contact was maintained through the provisions of the Foreign Jurisdiction Order in Council of 1902, up to the enforcement of the Government of India Act, 1935 which defined such areas as 'tribal areas' within 'India', but not in 'British India' (in Section 311).

On the effects of their isolation, which had been 'in force for a number of years now', the Subcommittee on the Excluded and Partially Excluded Areas (other than Assam), appointed by the Advisory Committee of the Constituent Assembly wrote that 'the benefits which the areas have derived from it are not particularly noticeable'.[12] The position of the excluded and partially excluded areas in Assam was in certain ways more difficult, because of the predominance of Christians in these areas. Yet, in political terms, out of 1585 seats in the provincial legislatures only 24 were reserved for the backward tribes by the 1935 Act. No reservation for them was provided in the Central Legislative Assembly.[13]

[11] The communities and interests were the following: men—(1) general; (2) reservation for the scheduled castes; (3) in Bombay, reservation for Marhattas; (4) backward areas and tribes (including those of Assam); (5) Sikhs; (6) Muslims; (7) Anglo-Indians; (8) Europeans; (9) Indian Christians; (10) commerce, industry, mining and plantation; (11) landholders; (12) universities; (13) labour; women—(14) general; (15) Sikhs; (16) Muslims; (17) Anglo-Indians; (18) Indian Christians.

[12] *Constituent Assembly Debates* (henceforth *CAD*), vol. VII, p. 153.

[13] *Report of the Scheduled Areas and Scheduled Tribes Commission* (*1960-61*), pp. 13-30.

THE STATES PROBLEM

Since Queen Victoria's pronouncement in 1858 guaranteeing the integrity of the Indian states, the British government developed a relationship with the princely states, based upon a policy of enlightened self-interest. The princes gained protection from external attacks and internal rebellions and a guarantee that their rights over their subjects would be respected. The British Crown, which became the paramount power, was in charge of their foreign affairs and relation with other states. The subjects of those native states were the subjects of the rulers who had no jurisdiction over the British nationals living in the state.

But for the fact of a common link with British India through the Governor-General and a feudal background, the 566 native states had virtually no unity among themselves. 'But', as Coupland says, 'if there was very little unity between the states themselves, they were bound to share to some extent in the unity imposed by the force of circumstances on India as a whole.'[14] The economic development of India, which steadily gathered strength since the nineteenth century, inevitably affected the domestic life of the states, involving their peoples in innumerable ways in a common Indian economy, and breaking their artificially created isolation.

At the first Round Table Conference in London, the states were prepared to join a federation independent of British control, though for a transition period that independence might be modified by the existence of limitations. 'It was felt that by such an attitude it would be possible to secure in framing the constitution a much stronger position for the states than mere numbers would give them, and that, at the same time, they would be able in non-federal matters to secure freedom from intervention by the crown except on definite and agreed grounds.'[15] British Indian politicians at the first Round Table Conference initially welcomed with enthusiasm the idea of making a common cause with the princes against British control. Those conservative elements of Indian leadership saw no harm in having in the representatives of the princes an assured strength of conservatism. 'It was only gradually that it came to be realized by the more advanced of moderate politicians that the princes were engaged essentially in the business of securing a definite position whence they could defy the introduction of any form of democracy in their dominions,

[14] Coupland, *The Constitutional Problem in India*, part I, p. 17.

[15] Keith, *A Constitutional History of India*, p. 296.

and that they would act rather as a support for British control than as furthering Indian autonomy.'[16]

When the scheme of federation was released, however, the rulers of states raised a series of objections against the bill. Later it seemed impossible to secure the participation of the princely states in the federation.[17] The Congress was meanwhile suspected by the princes of intending to swallow the princely rights.

The Indian Struggle

The Indian political struggle *vis-à-vis* the communal problem has a chequered history. The post-Mutiny national movement came, almost automatically, under the leadership of the English educated, and that too predominantly Hindu middle class. At the outset the leadership believed in 'constitutional' devices and wavered sometimes between 'home rule' and 'self government within the British empire' and sometimes between 'self government' and 'dominion status' until 1930, when the goal of 'complete independence' was announced from its only political platform—the Indian National Congress. The Congress, which was organized as a gathering of Indian leaders and intellectuals to discuss 'social matters' on a friendly footing, turned into a political body before long and, almost side by side with it, a separatist Muslim organization began to grow and advise the Indian Muslims to dissociate themselves from the Congress movement. Following the partition of Bengal there was the first tremendous national upsurge in 1905-6 which had an anarchist wing and, unfortunately, a Hindu revivalist outlook. In the next year the Muslim League and the Hindu Sabha were set up. Inevitably, the main challenge to the Congress came from the Muslim League.

The Lucknow Pact of 1916, having accepted the system of separate electorates, consolidated Congress-League amity which produced the Khilafat movement. The Congress at the Nagpur session of 1920 converted itself into a mass party, adopted the goal of swaraj and launched a satyagraha. The moderates left the Congress, formed the Liberal Party and decided to cooperate in the working of the Montford reforms.[18] When Gandhiji withdrew the movement many Congressites, especially the young radicals, were upset.

[16] Ibid., p. 297.

[17] Section 6 (7) of the 1935 Act enabled the princely states to join the federation any time within 20 years of its establishment.

[18] For the moderates' role in the Montford reforms, see S.R. Mehrotra's article in *Politics and Society in India*, ed. C.H. Philips, pp. 80-3.

On 1 January 1923, however, the moderates within the Congress organized the Swarajya Party and planned to enter the legislatures with a view to 'mending or ending' the reforms. The Gandhian leadership reluctantly permitted their programme. The Swarajists had a great success over the Liberal Party, who anyhow were their precursors. On 5 February 1924, the liberals moved a resolution in the Central Legislative Assembly recommending to the government revision of the 1919 Act so as to secure for India dominion status and full provincial autonomy. Motilal Nehru, leader of the Swarajya Party, moved an amendment to the resolution calling for 'a Round Table Conference to recommend a scheme of full responsible government for India'.[19] The amended resolution was passed with a great majority, though the government raised several points of objection to the demand for dominion status or responsible government for India. These objections were answered by Nehru then on the floor of the Assembly and later in All-Parties Report (1928).

In March 1927, the Muslim leaders met in Delhi under the then moderate Leaguer, Jinnah, to demand joint electorate with reservation of seats in legislatures for Muslims. In December 1927, the League conference in Calcutta, dominated by Jinnah and the Ali brothers, resolved to boycott the Simon Commission, as the Congress had done. The extremist in the Muslim League, on the other hand, decided to cooperate with the Simon Commission. Jinnah's position in the League's leadership became difficult. A split in the Muslim League was impending. The nationalists gradually dissociated from it.

Indian feelings being hurt due to the appointment of the Simon Commission, the All-Parties Conference met in Delhi, in February-March 1928 and appointed a committee to draft a constitution for India purely by Indian efforts under chairmanship of Motilal Nehru. In its report, submitted to the All-Parties Conference at the end of August the same year, the Nehru Committee looked forward to a free India wherein parties would be formed on socio-economic rather than religious and communal basis. The contemporary communal question, they thought, resolved itself to 'the questions of electorates, the reservation of seats, the separation of Sind and the form of government in the North-West Frontier Province and Baluchistan'.[20] The committee, therefore, rejected the claim for separate electorates and recommended reservation of seats in the legislatures of the Muslim-minority provinces and the centre. The NWFP

[19] Pattabhi Sitaramayya, *The History of the Indian National Congress*, vol. 1, p. 268.

[20] All-Parties Conference, *Report of the Committee Appointed by the Conference to Determine the Principles of the Constitution* (Nehru Report), p. 30.

and Baluchistan were recommended full provincial status. The question of Sind's separation from Bombay was not solved. Demanding merely dominion status, the committee rejected the idea of 'independence' pressed by the young Congress radicals.

As the first contribution of Indians to the growth of constitutionalism, the Nehru Committee recommended a constitution based on a federal structure with the participation of princely states, maximum autonomy being granted to the units. 'Devolution of provincial autonomy was', however, 'carried no further than the Act of 1919 had carried it.'[21] But the greatest failure of the Nehru Committee lay in its inability to deal with the new turn of politics of the League, which meanwhile had parted company with the All-Parties Conference. In May 1928, Jinnah left for England. Soon the League Council met at Lahore and decided to boycott the Nehru Committee. Jinnah returned in October and opposed the Nehru Report in the All-Parties Convention in Calcutta in December 1928. The split was complete subsequently. In 1930 the League first heard from its president, Iqbal, the plan for a Muslim homeland.

After the expiry, on 31 December 1929, of the Congress ultimatum that was issued at its Calcutta session in December 1928 over the Nehru report, the Congress met at Lahore in 1930. The mighty growth of the left forces in the Congress was recognized when Gandhiji nominated Jawaharlal Nehru in his place as the Congress president. The demand for complete independence was passed and the Congress resolved to start civil disobedience under the sole leadership of Gandhiji.

With the Gandhi-Irwin Pact of 5 March 1931, the first phase of satyagraha was over, to the dissatisfaction of the leftists. Gandhiji, however, secured nothing by joining the second Round Table Conference from the MacDonald government which had already faced a crisis on the home front. On his return to India, Gandhiji was arrested; the second phase of civil disobedience movement started in 1932 and collapsed before long. It was not until the Second World War that the Congress could launch another mass movement.

Democratic Movement in the States

The nationalist programme in the states consisted in the movement for democratization of the states' administration and securing the people's rights. The programme was inaugurated in 1927 with the establishment

[21] Coupland, *The Constitutional Problem in India*, part I, p. 94.

of the States & People's Conference with the purpose of 'attainment of responsible government for the people in the Indian states through representative institutions under the aegis of their rulers'.[22] This aim was endorsed by the Indian National Congress, with which the Conference was affiliated in 1928. The Nehru Committee, while welcoming the participation of the princely states in the federation of India, clearly told the princes that such participation 'would necessitate, perhaps in varying degrees, a modification of the system of government and administration prevailing within their territories'.[23] 'The commonwealth shall exercise the same rights in relation to, and discharge the same obligations towards, the Indian states, arising out of treaties or otherwise, as the Government of India has hitherto discharged.'[24] In 1929, the Congress demanded that the states be brought into line with the rest of India through the introduction of responsible government and social reforms.

The Congress policy towards the states suffered from a contradiction. Liberation movement in 'Indian' India was essentially linked with the movement for democratic institutions and liquidation of all foreign and feudal vested interests in the states. On the other hand, the Gandhiite leadership of the Congress was eager to form a broad national front in which the big and small feudal interests and the bourgeoisie would take part along with the common mass of people. This attitude of the Congress, in the later days, promoted, on the one hand, revolutionary tendency among the people of some states, such as Kashmir, Mysore and Travancore and, on the other, suspicion among the princes about the intention of the Congress about their rights and interests.

At the second Round Table Conference, Gandhiji claimed that the Congress represented the states' people as well as the British Indian people. But Coupland comments that the statement 'was not intended to be pressed to its logical conclusion'.[25] So far the Congress had identified itself with the reforms in the states only in spirit and not in action. Direct intervention by the Congress organization in states' affairs was still regarded unwise.

[22] See V.P. Menon, *The Story of the Integration of the Indian States*, p. 22.

[23] All-Parties Conference, *Report of the Committee*, p. 83.

[24] Ibid., p. 122.

[25] Coupland, *The Constitutional Problem in India*, part II, p. 4.

CHAPTER 2

Constituent Assembly as the Answer

Revival of Constitutionalism

In the midst of widespread frustration over the Communal Award and the collapse of the civil disobedience movement, lead came from the Congress moderates who revived the Swarajya Party (May 1934) with the aim of council entry and, for the first time, demanded a constituent assembly 'representative of all sections of the Indian people' to frame an acceptable constitution as 'the only method of applying' the principle of self-determination of India.[1]

When the AICC met at Patna on 18-19 May 1934, 'On the one hand, there was a large body of opinion still extant which did not conceal its antipathy to council work. On the other, there was the steadily growing Socialist Party, which without sharing Gandhian ideals with the Congress, nevertheless stood foursquare against council-entry.'[2] A day earlier, Patna had heard the president of the first All-India Socialist Conference, Narendra Deva, condemn 'the policy of alternating between direct action in a revolutionary situation and constructive or legislative work according to one's temperament'.[3]

The significance of the Patna decision of the Congress Working Committee lay in the calling off of civil disobedience, permission of council entry and the first ever demand for a constituent assembly. Meeting at the request of the Congress parliamentary party to formulate the Congress policy on the Communal Award, the Working Committee could 'neither accept nor reject' it, but, in the teeth of opposition from Madan Mohan Malaviya and M.S. Aney and the scepticism of Gandhiji,[4] resolved that:

[1] *The Indian Annual Register* (henceforth *IAR*), 1934, vol.. I, p. 279.

[2] Sitaramayya, *The History of the Indian National Congress*, vol. I, p. 572.

[3] *IAR*, 1934, vol. I, p. 340. Later, the Congress Working Committee issued a strong warning against 'loose talks' on class war, without naming the socialists.

[4] Malaviya and Aney moved an amendment in the AICC meeting in October 1934, demanding the outright rejection of the Communal Award, vide, *IAR*, 1934, vol. II,

The White Paper (which) in no way expresses the will of the people of India, has been more or less condemned by almost all Indian political parties and falls far short of the Congress goal if it does not retard the progress towards it. The only satisfactory alternative to the White Paper is a constitution drawn up by a constituent assembly elected on the basis of adult suffrage or as near it as possible with the power, if necessary, to the important minorities to have their representatives elected exclusively by the electors belonging to such minorities.[5]

The Congress adopted the new strategy of 'constitutionalism' evidently at the failure of mass struggle. Yet, the difference between the Swarajists and the Congress demands for a constituent assembly was too important to go unnoticed. The Swarajists wanted the constituent assembly to be 'representative of all sections', whereas the Congress wanted it to be elected on 'adult franchise'. The Congress found in this instrument of numerical democracy a convenient alternative to seeking compromise with the arrogant stand of the Muslim League and the princes. It was an attempt to circumvent, through an appeal to the Indian masses, the hurdle of the 'Indian problem'. At the Bombay Conference in October 1934, faith was reasserted in Gandhiji's leadership as he retired from the Congress. Malaviya, having made another unsuccessful bid to persuade the Congress to abandon its non-committal attitude and neutrality towards the Communal Award, left it to form the Congress Nationalist Party.

The Reforms of 1935

The rejection of the Government of India Act, 1935, was merely consequential to the Bombay stand of the Congress. The Lucknow Congress of April 1936 declared that 'no constitution imposed by outside authority and no constitution which curtails the sovereignty of the people of India and does not recognize their right to shape and control fully their political and economic future can be accepted'. In the opinion of the Congress such a constitution 'must be based on the independence of India as a nation' and could only be framed by a constituent assembly elected on the basis of adult franchise or a franchise approximating it as nearly as possible.[6]

The Lucknow Congress left the question of acceptance of office to be decided by the AICC at the proper time and resolved to contest the ensuing

pp. 251-2. Also see Gandhiji's statement on 19 November 1939 for his early opinion about the demand for constituent assembly.

[5] *IAR*, 1934, vol. I, p. 300.

[6] *Indian Constitutional Documents*, vol. IV, p. 71.

provincial elections. In March 1937, the All-India National Convention of Congress Legislators repeated the demand for the withdrawal of the 1935 Act 'so that the people of India may frame their own constitution'.[7] Congress success in the elections was impressive. The AICC, on 18 March 1937, demanded the withdrawal of the 1935 Act in view of the overwhelming popular endorsement of the Congress stand and decided to form provincial ministries.[8]

The Muslim League was not quite happy with the White Paper. On 2 April 1934, the All-India Muslim League Council resolved to accept the Communal Award so far as it went until a substitute was agreed upon by the various communities and, on that basis, expressed its readiness for cooperation with other communities and parties to secure such future constitution for India as would be acceptable to the country.[9] In accepting the Communal Award, as Jinnah said, the League wanted 'to make sure that any national demand which they join to put forward on behalf of the country will incorporate the safeguards which Muslims consider to be a minimum'.[10]

In the newly elected Central Legislative Assembly the Congress members moved a request to the government not to proceed further with the implementation of the White Paper scheme. The resolution was passed with an amendment moved by Jinnah, (1) accepting the Communal Award 'as far as it goes' until a substitute was agreed upon by the various communities concerned, (2) criticizing the provincial autonomy in detail, but not in principle, and (3) denouncing the all-India plan for federation as 'fundamentally bad' and 'totally unacceptable' and demanding a prompt effort to bring about the establishment of fully responsible government in British India along.[11]

Except on the question of Communal Award, the Muslim League stood very close to the Congress. Welcoming the 24th session of the All-India Muslim League at Bombay on 11-12 April 1936, Currimbhoy Ebrahim said, 'unity is the bedrock of nationhood, as it is also the essence of all religions. And no constitution, however advantageous from our point

[7] Ibid., p. 72.

[8] Ibid., pp. 73-4.

[9] *IAR*, 1934, vol. I, p. 318.

[10] Ibid., p. 319.

[11] A Congress amendment on the first part of Jinnah's amendment for neutrality over the Communal Award was defeated by the united strength of the government, nominated and League members. When Jinnah's amendment was voted in two parts, Congress members remained neutral on the first and supported the second part. The whole resolution was then passed by the united Congress and League strength. See *IAR*, 1935, vol. I, p. 287.

of view, can work well or survive in the absence of intercommunal goodwill and harmony.'[12] Jinnah, moving the resolution on the 1935 constitution, advised Indians to do with it what the Germans had done with the Treaty of Versailles. The resolution accepted the Communal Award and the provincial scheme and rejected the federal part as 'most reactionary, retrograde, injurious and fatal to the vital interests of British India *vis-à-vis* Indian states'.[13] Jinnah insisted that the communal issue should be solved by Indians and asked for new talks with the Congress. Both the Congress and the League, however, decided to participate in the provincial governments under the new act. The Congress won a majority in most of the provinces. In July 1937, the Congress Working Committee decided to accept office. A bitter Congress-League conflict immediately arose out of the Congress decision to form 'homogeneous' ministries in the provinces where it had majority and isolate the League through the development of 'mass contact'.

The League Offensive

In his presidential address to the Lucknow session of the All-India Muslim League, in October 1937, Jinnah charged the Congress leaders of 'alienating Mussalmans of India by pursuing a policy which is exclusively Hindu'.[14] He sharply criticized the Congress demand for a constituent assembly as 'the height of ignorance':

> A Constituent Assembly can only be called by a sovereign authority and from the seat of power.... Who is to constitute the electorates on the basis of adult franchise, and how many representatives will be chosen by these electorates constituted on the basis of adult franchise, and what will happen to the minorities in such constituencies, and what will the electorates understand, and how will they make their choice of their special body of men with final authority and power to frame the constitution of this great subcontinent?[15]

Intensification of the States' Movement

Since the formation of the provincial ministries, demand arose within the Congress for closer integration of the states with India and helping the growth of democratic movements therein. The AICC, in October 1937,

[12] *IAR*, 1936, vol. I, p. 296.
[13] Ibid., p. 295.
[14] *The Indian Constitutional Documents*, vol. IV, p. 100.
[15] Ibid., pp. 102-3.

passed a strong resolution. At Haripura, in February 1938, a softer resolution was passed demanding 'the same political, social and economic freedom in the states' as in the rest of India. 'The purna swaraj or complete independence, which is the objective of the Congress, is for the whole of India, inclusive of the states, for the unity and the integrity of India must be maintained in freedom as in subjection.' The only kind of federation that was acceptable to the Congress was one in which 'the states participate as free units, enjoying the same measure of democratic freedom as the rest of India'.[16]

The resolution stressed, however, that 'the burden of carrying on the struggle for freedom must fall on the people of states'. Yet it was more activist than the earlier ones. Meanwhile a popular movement was continuing in Mysore. 'The partial success' of the people of Mysore, said Gandhiji, had inspired 'a new mission of liberty' in other states.[17] Movements developed elsewhere. On 8 December, Gandhiji acclaimed the awakening of the people in one state after another and declared that there was no half-way house between the total extinction of the states and their acceptance of fully responsible government. Finally, he gave a warning that the Congress might be compelled to abandon its policy of non-interference and advised the rulers 'to cultivate friendly relation with an organization which bids fair in the future, not very distant, to replace the paramount power—let me hope, by friendly arrangement'.[18] Yet, in April 1940, Gandhiji joined issue with the socialist leader, Jayaprakash Narayan, when he ruled out a settlement in which the princes will have effaced themselves. He wrote that he could

> only conceive a settlement in which the big states will retain their status. In one way this will be far superior to what it is today; but in another it will be limited so as to give the people of the states the same right of self-government within their states as the people of other parts of India will enjoy. They will have freedom of speech, a free press and pure justice guaranteed to them.[19]

The Second World War

The 1935 Act, in its federal part, was paralysed by the opposition of the Congress and the League on the one had and of the princes on the other. In some provinces the local parties took over the government. In most,

[16] *IAR*, 1938, vol. I, pp. 299-300.
[17] *Harijan*, 17 September 1938.
[18] Ibid., 8 December 1938.
[19] Ibid., 20 April 1940.

Congress took up the responsibility after initial hesitation and, after a short period of rather successful working, gave it up during the Second World War.

On 18 October 1939, Viceroy Lord Linlithgow stated that the British aim in the war, as far as it concerned India, was 'to further the partnership between India and the United Kingdom within the empire to the aim that India may attain her due place among the great dominions'. The Act of 1935 was open to amendment 'in the light of Indian views', only 'at the end of the war'.[20] On 22 October, the Congress Working Committee considered the Viceroy's statement and found it 'unsatisfactory'.[21] Following the resolution, all Congress ministries in the provinces resigned.

Controversy over the Constituent Assembly

On 19 November 1939, Gandhiji came all out in support of the Constituent Assembly in the *Harijan*. 'Hard facts have made me a convert', he wrote, as he was convinced that 'the constituent assembly provides the easiest method of arriving at a just solution of the communal problem. Today we are unable to say with mathematical precision who represents whom. . . . But the constituent assembly will represent all communities in their exact proportion'. The constituent assembly alone could produce a constitution indigenous to the country and truly and fully representing the will of the people. 'Undoubtedly such a constitution will not be ideal, but it will be real'.

In its resolution on the war, on 18 September 1939, the League Working Committee demanded a review of 'the entire problem of India's future constitution de novo in the light of the experience gained by the working of the present provincial constitution of India and the developments that have taken place since 1935 or may take place hereafter'.[22] It also asked for an assurance from the British government that no constitutional advance of India should be made without the consent and approval of the All-India Muslim League.[23]

On 14 December 1939, Jinnah made a vitriolic attack on Gandhiji's 'sudden affection' for a constituent assembly, 'which, in the present condition of India, will mean a second and larger edition of the Congress'. He stressed that

[20] *Indian Constitutional Documents*, vol. IV, pp. 121-7.

[21] Ibid., p. 112.

[22] Ibid., p. 118.

[23] Ibid., p. 120.

a truly representative assembly presupposes that in order faithfully to express the judgment of the people it can only be constituted if you have a fully developed public opinion, an electorate educated and experienced, free from superstition and capable of judging the vital political issues affecting the country, and not, as India stands today, composed of castes, creeds, superstitions and provincial jealousies, quite apart from the main division of British India and the Indian states.[24]

Almost simultaneously, on 23 December 1939, a very similar attack on the demand for a constituent assembly came from the astute British jurist, Maurice Gwyer.[25] In a article in *Time and Tide*, London, on 19 January 1940, Jinnah warned that if the Congress demand for the right of framing India's constitution through the constituent assembly was conceded the 'inevitable result' would be a totalitarian Hindu state.[26]

Complete Independence

The year 1940 would prove fateful for India. In early 1940, the Viceroy visited Nagpur and Bombay and initiated a new move for constitutional settlement that would include the Muslim League, the princes and the scheduled castes. On 5 February, he met with Gandhiji who insisted on the expediency of a constituent assembly. No common ground was found. After his talk with Gandhiji, the Viceroy met Jinnah who 'was clear that it was out of the question to go straight to dominion status, or anything approaching it'.[27]

On 28 February, the Congress Working Committee met a Patna and decided to propose only one resolution in its Ramgarh session (19-20 March 1940) demanding 'nothing short of complete independence' and a constituent assembly. It anticipated another civil disobedience movement under Gandhiji's leadership, following withdrawal of Congress ministries.[28] The passing of the draft resolution by the Congress Working Committee was strongly resented by the Muslim League and the moderates.[29] The Ramgarh resolution, according to V.P. Menon, made the Viceroy 'turn his back on the Congress' as 'with the Congress in opposition, Lord Linlithgow felt that he should not alienate Muslim opinion

[24] Ibid., pp. 140-2.

[25] Maurice Gwyer, Convocation Address to Benares Hindu University, 1939.

[26] *IAR*, 1940, vol. I, pp. 304-5.

[27] V.P. Menon, *The Transfer of Power*, p. 78.

[28] Ibid., p. 80.

[29] Loc. cit.

or rub Jinnah the wrong way'.[30] The Viceroy met Jinnah on 13 March. Only 10 days after this interview the famous demand for 'independent states of Pakistan' for the Indian Muslims was adopted by the League in its Lahore session.[31]

Promise of a Constituent Assembly

With an offer to expand the Viceroy's Executive Council two categorical announcements of constitutional significance were made in the Viceroy's statement of 8 August 1940:[32]

(1) The British government could not contemplate the transfer of their present responsibilities to any system of government whose authority was directly denied by large and powerful elements in India's national minorities. This statement, having conveyed a strong assurance to the 'powerful' minorities of India—especially the Muslim League—bore an ominous significance for the Indian National Congress.

(2) Framing of the constitutional scheme for India would be 'primarily the responsibility of Indians themselves'. Therefore, the British government would 'assent to the setting up after the conclusion of the war with the least possible delay of a body representative of the principal elements in India's national life in order to devise the framework of the new constitution'.

The August offer was definitely the first British official admission that constitution making in India was primarily a business of the Indians. The nature of this transfer of responsibility was, however, kept vague. There was no precise definition of the 'representative' body. It is therefore difficult to read in this statement an assurance of a constituent assembly. At the same time, the promise was conditioned by 'the due fulfilment of the obligations with Great Britain's long connection with India has imposed upon her'.

The appearance of Japan in the war made Churchill send the Cripps Mission. The main offer of the Mission was embodied in the draft declaration of Stafford Cripps,[33] which held out the promise of steps to

[30] Ibid., p. 84.

[31] *IAR*, 1940, vol. I, pp. 311-12.

The Pakistan idea, however, vaguely remained on paper until, within two years, the Cripps Mission recognized it as a distinct possibility.

[32] *Indian Constitutional Documents*, vol. IV, pp. 150-1.

[33] *IAR*, 1942, vol. I, pp. 220-1.

'be taken for the earliest possible realization of self-government in India'. The proposals enunciated (1) dominion status and not independence for India with freedom to terminate her relationship with the commonwealth in future, (2) a federation with right of non-accession for any province or state, (3) transfer of responsibility to Indian hands subject to a treaty with the British government covering the rights of religious and racial minorities and other matters, and (4) new relationship of the Government of India with the states and the non-acceding provinces. The mission also proposed the setting up after the war of a constituent assembly representative of all sections of Indians, elected by a single electorate made of the entire membership of the lower houses of provincial legislatures. This new body would be, in strength, about one-tenth of the electoral college. Also, the Indian states would be invited 'to appoint representatives in the same proportion to their total population as in the case of representatives of British India as a whole, and with the same powers as British Indian members'.

The Cripps plan was rejected by the Congress mainly because it was 'a postdated cheque' on a bank that appeared very shaky at the time. But the political significance of the Cripps proposal lies in that it was the first clear promise of a constituent assembly as well as the first British official hint at a partition of India.

The Cripps Plan and the League

The hint was immediately picked up by the Muslim League. It declared that the right of the non-accession of provinces was a concession to them. Yet the Cripps statement was disapproved also by the Muslim League, which said:

> In the draft declaration a constitution-making body has been proposed with the primary object of creating one Indian union. So far as the Muslim League is concerned, it has finally decided that the only solution of India's constitutional problem is the partition of India into independent zones; and it will, therefore, be unfair to the Mussalmans to compel them to enter such a constitution-making body, whose main object is the creation of a new Indian union.[34]

The right of non-accession of provinces was not able to satisfy the League as the existing provincial boundaries were 'arbitrarily fixed'. On 16-20 August 1940, the General Council meeting of the All-India Muslim

[34] *Indian Constitutional Documents*, vol. IV, pp. 171-2.

League reiterated its regret that the Cripps proposals 'merely recognized the possibility of establishing Pakistan, through the provision for non-accession, but conceded practically the full Congress demand through the promise of a constituent assembly and the right of secession of India from the British commonwealth.[35] Obviously, the League wanted to clinch the issue before the constituent assembly was born.

THE COUPLAND PLAN

It was mainly because the proposals of the Cripps Mission did not find favour in India, that Reginald Coupland, who had come to India in 1941 and was included in the Cripps Mission in March 1942, offered his suggestions on the constitution of India. On the demand for a constituent assembly Coupland was strongly critical: 'It is taken for granted that all Indian patriots want it. But in fact it s only the Congress that wants it. The minority parties—the scheduled castes, for instance, as much as the Moslem League—do not.'[36] As 'the very essence of the Moslem revolt is its rejection of "numerical democracy", the very idea of a Constituent Assembly', he held, 'belongs to a period before the communal schism had become so difficult to bridge as it is now'.[37] His chief emphasis was on the rule of unanimity rather than the rule of majority in the matter of constitution making. And for all practical purposes the rule of unanimity would mean agreement on all major issues between the Congress and the League. 'For drafting the constitution the Congress scheme for a great constituent assembly directly elected on all-India basis seems inappropriate'.[38] A small constituent assembly, where all communal questions could be directly thrashed out, was, therefore, more desirable than a big one.

A large amount of provincial autonomy and a centre with limited powers formed the central idea of Coupland's solution: 'The strength of Moslem "nationalism" necessitates a "weak" centre or none'.[39] Also, in view of the reluctance of the native princes to part with their powers and privileges, he endorsed the federal idea, while hoping that some understanding would be reached with the princes.

[35] *IAR*, 1942, vol. II, p. 254.

[36] *The Constitutional Problem in India*, part III, p. 33.

[37] Ibid., pp. 34-5.

[38] Ibid., p. 181.

[39] Ibid., p. 182.

Coupland was the first Briton to introduce the idea of 'regional government' as a compromise between Indian unity and the demand for Pakistan. However, Coupland suggested that 'the principle of regional demarcation should be economic, not political', based on a 'river-basin scheme. India would be divided into four regions, in two of which Hindus would predominate and in two Moslems'.[40]

[40] Loc. cit.

CHAPTER 3

Birth of the Constituent Assembly

THE CABINET MISSION PLAN

The Coupland plan directly influenced the Cabinet Mission, which came to India in March 1946 and took no time to realize that the whole constitutional problem of India boiled down to the communal question. The Cabinet Mission held a conference at Shimla to bring about an understanding between the Congress and the Muslim League. Since the effort failed, the Cabinet Mission 'decided that immediate arrangements should be made whereby Indians may decide the future constitution of India'.[1]

While noting the widespread desire for a united India, the Cabinet Mission was conscious of 'the very real Muslim apprehensions' about 'a purely unitary India, in which the Hindus with the greatly superior numbers must be a dominating element'.[2] Hence the Mission proposed a federation within which provinces would have full autonomy subject only to a minimum of central powers, such as on foreign affairs, defence and communications. They, however, rejected the Congress plan under which the provinces could, if they wished to, take part in economic and administrative planning on a large scale, cede to the centre optional subjects in addition to the compulsory ones, as 'apart from the difficulty of working such a scheme, we do not consider that it would be fair to deny to other provinces, which did not desire to take the optional subjects at the centre, the right to form themselves into a group for a similar purpose. This would indeed be no more than the exercise of their autonomous powers in a particular way.'[3]

The union should embrace both British India and the states, and should deal with the subjects of foreign affairs, defence and communication; and should have the powers necessary to raise the finances required for these subjects. The residual powers were to belong to the provinces and the states. 'The union should have an executive and a legislature constituted

[1] Cabinet Mission's Statement, 16 May 1946, para 3.

[2] Ibid., para 12.

[3] Ibid., para 13.

from British Indian and states' representatives. Any question raising a major communal issue in the legislature should require for its decision a majority of the representatives present and voting of each of the two communities. . . .'[4]

Formula of a Constituent Assembly

Two very significant suggestions made in this paragraph were that

(1) 'Provinces should be free to form groups with executives and legislatures, and each group could determine the provincial subjects to be taken in common'.

(2) 'The constitutions of the union and of the groups should contain a provision whereby any province could, by a majority vote in the legislative assembly, call for a reconsideration of the terms of the constitution after an initial period of ten years and at ten-year intervals thereafter.'

While indicating the formation of the constitution-making machinery, the Cabinet Mission felt that the most satisfactory method of its composition would be an election based on adult suffrage. But, as it would involve unwarranted delay, it felt that 'The only practicable alternative is to utilise the recently-elected provincial legislative assemblies as the electing bodies.' In order to provide proportionate equality of representation to the communities the Cabinet Mission had the plan:

(a) to allot to each province a total number of seats proportional to its population, roughly in the ratio of one to a million, as the nearest substitute for representation by adult suffrage;

(b) to divide this provincial allocation of seats between the main communities in each province in proportion to their population;

(c) to provide that the representatives allotted to each community in a province shall be elected by the members of the community in its legislative assembly'.[5]

The Cabinet Mission took an important decision when, for these purposes, it recognized 'only three communities in India: "general", Muslim and Sikh, the "general" community including all who were not Muslims or Sikhs. As the smaller communities would, upon the population basis, have little or no representation since they would lose the weightage

[4] Ibid., para 15.

[5] Ibid., para 18.

which assures them seats in the provincial legislatures,' paragraph 20 of the Plan made the provision for an advisory committee of the constituent assembly on the 'right of citizens, minorities and tribal and excluded areas', containing 'full representation of the interests affected', in order 'to report to the union constituent assembly upon the list of fundamental rights, the clauses for the protection of minorities and a scheme for the administration of tribal and excluded areas, and to advise whether these rights should be incorporated in the provincial, group or union constitution'. The elections would be in the following order (see Table 3.1).[6]

In order to represent the chief commissioners' provinces there would

TABLE 3.1: REPRESENTATION OF THE PROVINCES IN THE CONSTITUENT ASSEMBLY

Section A

Provinces	*General*	*Muslim*	*Total*
Madras	45	4	49
Bombay	19	2	21
UP	47	8	55
Bihar	31	5	36
Central Provinces	16	1	17
Orissa	9	0	9
Total	167	20	187

Section B

Provinces	*General*	*Muslim*	*Sikh*	*Total*
Punjab	8	16	4	28
NWFP	0	3	0	3
Sind	1	3	0	4
Total	9	22	4	35

Section C

Province	*General*	*Muslim*	*Total*
Assam	7	3	10
Bengal	27	33	60
Total	34	36	70

Chief Commissioners' Province	4
Total for British India	296
Maximum for Indian states	93
Total	389

[6] Ibid., para 19.

be added to section A the two members representing Delhi and Ajmer-Merwara in the Central Legislative Assembly and a member to be elected by the Coorg Legislative Council. A representative from British Baluchistan would be added to section B. The grand total of the assembly's strength would thus be 389.

A temporary difficulty arose on the proposal that as a part of the 'general' community the Europeans living in India (mainly Bengal and Assam) should have a separate representation. Thus, while for Indians there would be roughly one representative for one million of population, the Europeans of Bengal and Assam, numbering 21,000, would have 7 representatives in the Constituent Assembly. After a protest, on 14 June 1946, from Maulana Azad, the Congress president, the Europeans themselves waived their claim to such representation.

Grouping

The most controversial part of the Cabinet Mission plan, however, turned out to be rules of procedure providing that after a preliminary meeting of the assembly, where the office bearers and the committees would be elected, the members would divide up into three sections as laid down above, frame the provincial constitutions and, if necessary, the group constitutions, and then reassemble to frame the union constitution. It would be open to a province to come out of a group in which it had been placed as soon as the new constitutional arrangements would come into operation. Such a decision could be taken by the new constitution. A revision of the group or union constitution could be sought by a province after ten years of working of the arrangement.

By a peculiar twist of logic the Cabinet Mission created a paradoxical situation. Taking the cue from Coupland, the Cabinet Mission anticipated a weak central government for India with only powers on foreign affairs, defence and communications, and opposed voluntary surrender of provincial subjects to the centre on administrative reasons. But it was conscious of the need for cooperation among all or a group of Indian provinces. Strangely enough, the Cabinet Mission found the second type of cooperation (among a group of provinces) more feasible and even desirable. Its whole scheme, thus, became neither 'province-oriented', nor 'centre-oriented' but 'group-oriented'.

In the union constituent assembly, on the other hand, resolutions varying from the provisions of paragraph 15 or raising any major communal issue would require a majority of the representatives of each of the two major communities present and voting. The chairman of the assembly was to decide which, if any, of the resolutions raised major communal issues and would, if so requested by a majority of the representatives of either of the major communities, consult the federal court before giving his decision. Thus, grouping and communal voting made it possible for the Muslim League to ensure that the union centre was not too strong. The League could achieve the substance of Pakistan if it could but utilize majority in sections B and C to secure strong group constitutions and provincial opinion. 'Indeed, His Majesty's government was back where it had started; the issue was Pakistan versus a united India, and it was on this issue that the battle still raged', writes V.P. Menon.[7]

Political literature of the time expressed surprise as to when and how the idea of grouping did strike the Cabinet Mission. 'The Cabinet delegates appeared to have been careless in the use of the words referring to their "grouping" proposal,' wrote the *Indian Annual Register* commentator.[8] On 6 May 1946, the Congress president Maulana Azad had actually written to Pethick-Lawrence that the Congress representatives to the talks 'were feeling mystified and disturbed at the vagueness of our talks and some of the assumptions underlying them'. 'Repeated references', were made to 'groups of provinces' 'functioning together'. He complained that grouping had not been so far discussed by 'us'.[9]

Congress Apprehensions

Compulsory grouping was something which Congress could not swallow. With a rather exaggerated apprehension, the Congress went to the extent of asserting that once the group imposed its constitution on a province it would not be possible for any reluctant province to opt out of the group. As a result, suggestions that the groups, in the absence of any alternative, could be accepted for the time being were ignored by the Congress.

On 24 May, the Congress Working Committee in a resolution demanded that the provinces should, in the first instance, have the right to make their choice 'whether or not to belong to the section in which they are placed'.[10] The Cabinet Mission, in reply, made a statement on 25 May 1946 pointing out that the Congress interpretation did not accord with the

[7] V.P. Menon, *The Transfer of Power*, p. 326.
[8] *IAR*, 1947, vol. I, p. 103.
[9] Ibid., 1946, vol. I, p. 117.
[10] Ibid., p. 163.

delegation's intentions.[11] 'The reasons for the grouping of the provinces are well known, and this is an essential feature of the scheme and can only be modified by agreement between the parties.' The statement of the Cabinet Mission also made it clear that the scheme stood as a whole, i.e. to be accepted or rejected in toto and that the provinces could not leave the groups, whatever their wishes, until after a constitution had been established and brought into operation and elections had taken place.

The Cabinet Mission plan, in essence, was thus not a recommendation, but an award, transfer of power being conditional upon its acceptance. Over and above, the British Parliament maintained the supreme right of veto on any constitution framed by the constituent assembly in view of its solemn obligations to the minorities and the princes. The constituent assembly that was proposed by the Cabinet Mission was, therefore, anything but a sovereign body like the Philadelphia Constitutional Convention of 1787 or the French National Assemblies which framed the constitutions of France after the revolutions of 1789 and 1848. In any way, 'the machinery devised by the Cabinet Mission differed materially from the constituent assembly the Congress had in view'.[12]

An Indo-British Treaty

While sending the Cripps Mission, Churchill had referred, on 11 March 1942, in the House of Commons, to 'certain lesser matters arising out of our long association with the fortunes' of the Indian empire. The Cripps Mission anticipated an Indo-British treaty 'for the protection of the racial and religious minorities'[13] of India as a condition of transfer of power. The Cabinet Mission also felt the need for a treaty (paragraph 22) 'to provide for certain matter arising out of the transfer of power'. The British government's view in September 1945 was that such a treaty would deal with: (1) defence, (2) the conduct of foreign relations, (3) financial obligations between the United Kingdom and India, (4) relations with the Indian states, and, possible, (5) minority rights and protection of the services. Such a treaty, as B.N. Rau held, could be signed not with the constituent assembly, but with a provisional government.[14]

[11] Ibid., p. 164.
[12] D.N. Sen, *Revolution by Consent?* p. 166.
[13] Shiva Rao, *The Framing of India's Constitution: Select Documents*, vol. I, p. 127.
[14] B.N. Rau's Note, *India's Constitution in the Making*, 1963, pp. 414-16.

The Cabinet Mission, however, overlooked the possibility that, given favourable circumstances, it would not be impossible for the Government of India to leave the commonwealth and discard all treaty obligations.

The Cabinet Mission and the States

From the Cabinet Mission of the princes demanded the lapse of paramountcy and their freedom to stay out of the union, forming a confederation of their own without interference from British India.[15] It was made clear by the Cabinet Mission that

> with the attainment of independence by British India, whether inside or outside the British commonwealth, the relationship which has hitherto existed between the rulers of the states and the British crown will no longer be possible. Paramountcy can neither be retained by the British crown nor transferred to the new government.[16]

The Cabinet Mission left the details of this issue to future negotiations between the new government and the states, but laid down 'that the states should be given in the final constituent assembly appropriate representation' which would not exceed ninety-three. The method of selection 'will have to be determined by consultation. The states would in the preliminary stage be represented by a negotiating committee.'[17]

On 22 May, the Cabinet Mission released a 'Memorandum on States' Treaties and Paramountcy'[18] which recalled that the British government had declared that if the succession government or governments desired independence, no obstacle would be placed in their way. The effect of these announcements was that all those concerned with the future of India wished her to attain a position of independence within or without the British commonwealth. During the interim period, which must lapse before the coming into operation of a new constitutional structure, paramountcy would remain in operation, and would not be transferred to an Indian government. The princes were advised to conduct negotiations with the Government of India in regard to the future regulation of matters of common concern, specially in the economic and financial fields. Since such negotiations would occupy a considerable period of time, and since

[15] V.P. Menon, *The Story of the Integration of the Indian States*, p. 62.

[16] Cabinet Mission's Statement, para 14.

[17] Ibid., para 19 (ii).

[18] *IAR*, 1946, vol. I, pp. 210-11.

some of them might well be incomplete when the new structure would come into being, an understanding between the states and those likely to control the succession government or governments would be necessary, so that the interim arrangements could continue until new agreements were completed.

Initial Congress Attitude

To the Congress, the Cabinet Mission plan was not much better than the Cripps plan of 1942. The independence that had been promised was hedged in by too many restrictions. The constituent assembly would have the semblance but not the reality of a sovereign body. And the union and the provinces would be at the mercy of certain arbitrary groupings of provinces. The scheme had almost all the defects of an India divided on a communal basis without even the redeeming feature of a full-fledged scheme of Pakistan, which would have made the provincial units homogeneous and sovereign. The liberty granted to the princely states was dangerous for the growth of Indian integration and would only perpetuate feudal exploitation. The union government, without control over currency, banking, custom and planning, would be too weak to direct the economic progress of the nation under modern industrial conditions.

In the jungle of restrictions, reservations, safeguards and the balancing of one interest against another, it was difficult for the Congress to visualize a clear and complete picture of a free, independent and democratically united India. The Working Committee of the Congress on 25 June 1946 decided that, 'The limitation of the central authority as contained in the proposal, as well as the system of grouping of provinces, weakened the whole structure and was unfair to some provinces such as the North-West Frontier Province and Assam and to some of the minorities, notably the Sikhs.' The Committee disapproved of this, but felt that, taking the proposal as a whole, there was sufficient scope for enlarging and strengthening central authority and for fully ensuring the right of a province to act according to its choice in regard to grouping.

While raising objections against certain other things like non-nationals (Europeans) taking part in constitution-making, the Committee decided that the Congress should join the proposed constituent assembly.[19] The peculiar Congress attitude can be understood only when one remembers how much hope it had placed on the constituent assembly. In the AICC

[19] Pattabhi Sitaramayya, *The History of the Indian National Congress*, p. ccxxiii.

session of 6-7 July 1946, when the Congress Socialist offered a determined opposition to the Cabinet Mission plan, the Congress leadership called for the intervention of Gandhiji. Azad emphasized that 'by accepting the constituent assembly proposal, we shall lay at rest one of the longest standing problems', as Muslim League's acceptance of the Cabinet Mission's proposals implied a 'united India and one constituent assembly with one central government'.[20]

It should be pointed out that there were some differences between the constituent assembly that was proposed by the Cripps Mission and the constituent assembly that was set up under the Cabinet Mission plan. The Cripps Mission had proposed that the size of the constituent assembly should be one-tenth of the size of its electorate. Thus the total membership of the provincial legislative assemblies being 1585, the strength of the constituent assembly under the Cripps Mission scheme would not exceed 159. The Cabinet Mission, on the other hand, proposed a representation of 292, from British India exclusive of the three chief commissioners' provinces and British Baluchistan (whose total representation would be 4). Secondly, the Cripps Mission had proposed a single electoral college comprising all provincial assemblies to elect the constituent assembly. The Cabinet Mission would have the constituent assembly elected by several electorates, made up of the provincial assemblies.[21]

Yet, like the Cripps Mission, the Cabinet Mission rejected the expedience of universal adult suffrage as it would lead to a 'wholly unacceptable delay in the formation of the new constitution' and had the constituent assembly elected by the provincial legislative assemblies which themselves had been elected under the Government of India Act, 1935, according to which not more than 15 per cent of Indians had the right to vote.

So far as the electoral provisions were concerned, the constituent assembly was, therefore, made up of men who represented the relatively propertied section of Indians. The political developments in India, however, had led to an overwhelming victory of the Congress in most provincial legislatures in elections that took place in early 1946 and its consequent predominance in the constituent assembly. The Congress, therefore, did not seriously object to this part of the Cabinet Mission scheme or even the formula of proportional representation.

[20] *IAR*, 1946, vol. II, pp. 135-41.

[21] In the first fortnight of July elections in British India were completed.

Classification of Membership

The following was the relative position of parties among the British Indian representatives to the Constituent Assembly, when it first met.[22]

Out of 296 members from British India, 75 were effectively Leaguers (all Muslims), there being five non-League Muslims. In section A, Rafi Ahmed Kidwai won a Muslim seat from UP with a Congress ticket. The other Congress Muslim (in a general seat) in section A was Asaf Ali, the one member from Delhi. In section B, out of 23 Muslims three were non-Leaguers, two with Congress tickets (from NWFP—Abul Kalam Azad and Abdul Ghaffar Khan) and one Unionist (from the Punjab).[23] In section C, 35 Muslim members were Leaguers, one from Krishak Proja Party (A.K. Fazlul Huq ,whose difference with the League was difficult to trace). Fifteen members were women of whom there were Muslims, all Leaguers. The age of the members ranged from 25 to 75.

The Congress position was sound in section A with 164 seats out of a total of 190 while the Muslim League had 19 seats. In section B the League captured 19 seats, whereas 10 went to Congress, three each to Panthik Akali and the Unionist Party (Punjab). In section C, the League and Krishak Proja Party got 36 seats, though Assam returned a Congress majority (7:3). The independents numbered seven in section A and one in section B. In section C, one seat went to the Communist Party and one to the Scheduled Castes Federation.

Congress Position *vis-à-vis* the Constituent Assembly

On 20 May 1946, Azad, as Congress president, wrote to Pethick-Lawrence asserting the independence of the proposed constituent assembly.

> That the assembly itself, when formed, will in my Committee's opinion be a sovereign body for the purpose of drafting the constitution unhindered by any external authority, as well for entering a treaty. Further that it will be open to the assembly to vary in any way it likes the recommendations and procedure suggested by the Cabinet Delegation.[24]

The reply of Pethick-Lawrence was quite precise:

> We think the authority of the constituent assembly and the procedure which it is intended to follow are clear from the statement. Once the constituent assembly is

[22] Figures based on *IAR*, 1946, vol. II, and *The Hindusthan Year Book*, 1947.

[23] The one representative of Shahid Jirga (Baluchistan) was with the Muslim League.

[24] *IAR*, 1946, vol. I, p. 161.

TABLE 3.2: PARTIES, COMMUNITIES AND INTERESTS IN THE CONSTITUENT ASSEMBLY

Hindus (excluding Scheduled Caste Hindus)	
Congress	156
Unionist	1
Communist	1
Landlord	3
Commerce and Industry	2
Total	163
Scheduled Castes	
Congress	29
Scheduled Castes Federation	1
Unionist	1
Total	31
Muslims	
Muslim League	73
Congress	3+1 (general)
Krishak Proja	1
Unionist	1
Sahid Jirga (Baluchistan)	1
Total	80
Anglo-Indians	
Congress	3
Indian Christians	
Congress	6
Parsis	
Congress	3
Backward Tribes	
{ Congress	4 }
{ Independents	2 }
Total	6
Sikhs	
Congress	1
Panthik Akali*	3
Total	4
Total for British India	296

*On 10 July 1946, the Pratinidhi Panthik Board, the representative Sikh organization, in a meeting under the presidentship of Col. Niranjan Singh Gill, unanimously decided to boycott the Constituent Assembly unless and until Punjab was partitioned. They joined the Constituent Assembly only after an assurance from the Congress of sympathetic support to its cause, given in August 1946.

TABLE 3.3: COMPARATIVE POSITION OF PARTIES IN THE PROVINCIAL ASSEMBLIES

Group		Congress General	Nationalist Muslim	ML	HMS	SCF	CPI	Others
A	Bihar	98	5	34	0	0	0	15
	Bombay	125	0	30	1	0	2	17
	CP and Berar	92	0	13	1	0	0	6
	Madras	165	0	29	0	0	2	19
	UP	153	7	54	0	0	0	14
	Orissa	47	0	4	0	0	1	8
B	NWFP	30	2	17	0	0	0	1
	Punjab	51	0	73	0	0	0	51
	Sind	18	4	27	0	0	0	11
C	Assam	58	3	31	0	0	0	16
	Bengal	86	0	113	1	1	3	46

Source: Figures based on *IAR*, 1946, vol. I, pp. 230-1.

formed and working on this basis, there is naturally no intention to interfere with its discretion or to question its decisions. When the constituent assembly itself has completed its labour, His Majesty's Government will recommend to Parliament such actions as may be necessary for the cession of sovereignty to the Indian people, subject only to the provisions which are mentioned in the statement and which are not, we believe, controversial, namely adequate provision for the protection of minorities and willingness to conclude a treaty to cover matters arising out of the transfer of power.[25]

The resolution of the Congress Working Committee of 24 May 1946 raised the same points and received the same reply, which was not acceptable to the Congress. The attitude of the Muslim League to this particular question is not clear from this correspondence.[26] It is, however, obvious that protection of the League's interests was one of the major objectives of the limitation imposed on the constituent assembly that was likely to be dominated by the Congress. And, in spite of the express Congress desire to flout the limitations of the Cabinet Mission scheme, none of them was relaxed by the British government.

The greatest Congress mistake, however, lies not in the fact that it wanted to turn the constituent assembly into a sovereign body, but its growing belief that the assembly was actually sovereign. It fell to Jinnah

[25] Cabinet Mission's Statement, 22 May 1946, ibid., p. 162.

[26] W. Ivor Jennings, *The Constitutional Problems in Pakistan*, pp. 8-9.

to repeatedly hammer the point that under the Cabinet Mission plan the constituent assembly was a greatly circumscribed machinery, for that was his greatest bargaining asset. On 27 July 1946, at the meeting of the League, Jinnah said:

> It is no use imagining things. The constituent assembly is not a sovereign body. Either we accept this view or not. If we accept the view that it is not a sovereign body, the only honourable course open to us is to treat it for what it is. It is an assembly summoned by the Viceroy, who has been appointed by the British government. It is not going to be a sovereign body by a statement or show of bravado.[27]

The most significant point about the status of the constituent assembly is that it was convened not by any national provisional government but by the British government who regarded it merely as a conference of the delegates of the major political parties in this country. This was exactly what Reginald Coupland had suggested a few years earlier, though recommending a smaller size. The restrictions were imposed on the constitution-making body obviously on the assumption that, unless guided by the British, the Indian communities would fail to arrive at any agreed formula regarding the constitution. The limitations on the powers of the constituent assembly to change the composition and procedure of work and even give its own interpretation to the clauses of the Cabinet Mission's statement could be disregarded only when complete communal harmony was reached. Until then any attempt of the parties to modify any of the provisions of the Cabinet Mission plan was destined to be unsuccessful as the British Parliament still retained the right to veto over the transfer of power. The procedure of constitution-making in India was thus intended to be similar to that in Canada and Australia where, notwithstanding the people's approval of the constitutions, their legal authority was sanctioned by the British Parliament. Transfer of power was conditional upon the acceptability of the constitution to the League as well as the British government.

[27] *IAR*, 1946, vol. II, p. 167.

CHAPTER 4

Constituent Assembly *versus* Interim Government

Scope of the Interim Government

'While the constitution-making proceeds the administration of India has to be carried on. We attach the greatest importance, therefore, to the setting up at once of an interim government having the support of the major political parties.'[1]

The scope of the interim government was only 'to carry on the administration of British India until such time as a new constitution can be brought into being'.[2] At the Shimla Conference between the Cabinet Mission and the Indian leaders (5-12 May 1946), negotiations for replacing the Viceroy's Executive Council by an interim ministry of fourteen members (six Congress nominees including a Schedule Caste Hindu member, five League nominees and three representative members of other communities to be nominated by the Viceroy) were held. The major point of Congress-League difference on which the talks failed was the Congress insistence on its right to nominate two nationalist Muslims from its own quota. Acceptance of the demand by the League would raise the Muslim strength to seven in a fourteen-member cabinet.

Congress-League Tussle

Jinnah, however, had a different plan. If on the eve of the transfer of power, which was then only a matter of time, the Muslim League failed to be recognized as the sole representative of Indian Muslims, it would suffer a tremendous strategic defeat. The effect of the interim government on permanent decisions over the future of India was realized by all. On 16 June 1946, the Viceroy issued invitations to fourteen Indians 'to serve as members of the interim government, on the basis that the constitution-

[1] Cabinet Mission's Statement, 16 May 1946, para 23.

[2] Ibid., para 3.

making will proceed in accordance with the statement of May 16th'.[3] Five of them belonged to the upper-caste Hindu community and were members of the Congress. One Scheduled Caste member was also a Congressite. Five Muslim members were Leaguers. One representative each from the Sikh, Parsi and Indian Christian communities belonged to no party. The Scheduled Castes still being considered a minority community, party was sought to be established between the caste-Hindu Congressites and the Muslim Leaguers as the sole representatives of the Muslims of India.

That was unacceptable to the Congress. The parity between the Congress as an upper-caste Hindu organization and the Muslim League as the sole Muslim organization was considered as essentially unjust. The Congress also wanted the inclusion of a nationalist Muslim. Besides, the Parsi member, N.P. Engineer, who was an official, was not considered by the Congress as a representative Parsi. Therefore the Congress Working Committee rejected, on 25 June, the interim government plan, but accepted the long-term plan of the constituent assembly. But then it objected to the grouping arrangement, as it considered the plan to be unjust to the Congress-majority provinces of Assam and NWFP and to the Sikh minority of the Punjab.[4]

Subject to certain conditions the Muslim League was ready to join the interim government. When the Congress refused to join, the Muslim League wanted to form the interim government even without the Congress. The Cabinet Mission and the Viceroy evidently found no sense in having such an interim government. On 29 June, Lord Wavell announced the formation of a caretaker government for the time being. The elections to the constituent assembly were held in July 1946 in spite of opposition from the League. The League, however, took part in the elections.

On 6-7 July, the AICC approved the 26 June resolution of the Working Committee and elected Jawaharlal Nehru, in a press statement, categorically announced that the Congress had no intention to abide by the grouping arrangement proposed by the Cabinet Mission. He also said that the Congress had only agreed to join the constituent assembly and regarded itself free to change the Cabinet Mission plan as it thought best.[5] The statement has been considered unfortunate by many but it was consistent with the hitherto enunciated stand of the Congress which had

[3] *IAR*, 1946, vol. I, pp. 170-1.

[4] Ibid., pp. 175-6.

[5] *Indian Constitutional Documents*, vol. II, pp. 232-3.

misread the Cabinet Mission's mind in Pethick-Lawrence's letter of 22 May 1946.[6]

Jinnah, who had already been angered by the Viceroy's unwillingness to form the interim government with Muslim members chosen by only the Muslim League, reacted immediately. He issued a statement that the statement by the Congress president demanded a review of the whole situation.[7] The League Council met at Bombay on 27-30 July and, withdrawing the acceptance of the Cabinet Mission scheme as a whole, called for 'direct action'. The League blamed the Viceroy for going back on his promise and insisting on the participation of the Congress in the interim government, even though the Congress, by putting several conditions on the Cabinet Mission plan, had virtually rejected it. The League also emphasized that the Congress had only agreed to join the constituent assembly which it considered as a sovereign body. The League was afraid of the brute majority of the Congress in such a constituent assembly, which would result in the suppression of minority interests.[8]

Formation of the Interim Government

The Viceroy renewed his effort to form an interim government on 22 July, granting the Congress freedom to nominate six members (including a Scheduled Caste Hindu). The Muslim League would nominate its five members. Three other members (a Parsi, a Sikh and an Anglo-Indian) would be nominated by the Viceroy. Distribution of portfolios would be decided after the parties agreed to join. Such an interim government, the Viceroy was sure, would enjoy the status of a dominion government with least interference by the British government. The Viceroy would welcome a convention, if freely agreed to by the Congress, that major communal issues would be settled by the assent of both the major parties.

Jinnah rejected even this offer as it was not based on Congress-League parity and as he apprehended that the Congress would not follow the 'convention' of respecting minority interests in a cabinet under its dominance. On 8-10 August 1946, the Congress Working Committee accepted the offer of the interim government and evasively repeated their acceptance of the Cabinet Mission plan 'in its entirety'.[9] The Viceroy immediately requested the Congress president, Jawaharlal Nehru, to form

[6] See, for instance, Abul Kalam Azad, *India Wins Freedom*, p. 155.

[7] *Indian Constitutional Documents*, vol. IV, pp. 237-9.

[8] Ibid., pp. 241-4.

[9] *IAR*, 1946, vol. II, p. 105.

the interim government. Nehru sought the cooperation of Jinnah who objected to the status of the interim government. Unless it was another version of the Viceroy's Executive Council, the position was unacceptable to the League.[10] No agreement could be reached between Nehru and Jinnah.

Hence came the Direct Action on 16 August 1946, which immediately resulted in a series of communal riots all over the country. In the midst of this situation the personnel of the interim government was announced on 24 August. Most of the members were Congressites, three members belonged to the Sikh, the Indian Christian and the Parsi communities. Of the Congress members one was a Scheduled Caste Hindu, three were nationalist Muslims. Two seats remained vacant. A communique said that the Viceroy's Executive Council had resigned. It also stated that five seats would be allotted to the Muslim League whenever it agreed to join the government.[11]

On the same day, Wavell, in a radio broadcast, desired that the work of the constituent assembly should begin as early as possible, stressing that

> assurances have been given to the Muslim League that the procedure laid down in the statement of May 16th regarding the framing of provincial and group constitutions will be faithfully adhered to; that there can be no question of any change in the fundamental principle proposed for the constituent assembly in paragraph 15 of the Cabinet Mission's statement or of a decision on any main communal issue without a majority of both the major communities; and that the Congress is ready to agree that any dispute of interpretation may be referred to the federal court . . . that the Muslim League will reconsider their decision not to take part in the plan.[12]

Nehru, in a broadcast on 7 September 1946, a few days after joining the interim government, said that Congress was 'perfectly prepared to and have accepted the position of sitting in sections which will consider the question of formation of groups', and that 'we do not look upon the constituent assembly as an arena for conflict or for the forcible imposition of one viewpoint over another'.[13]

The League's Participation in the Interim Government

There passed some time, however, before the purport of Nehru's latest statement and its inconsistency with the statement of 10 July became clear. On 2 September the interim government took office; and negotiations

[10] Nehru-Jinnah Correspondence, *IAR*, 1946, vol. II, p. 222.

[11] *The Statesman*, 25 August 1946.

[12] *IAR*, 1946, vol. II, p. 229.

[13] Quoted by Sitaramayya in *The History of the Indian National Congress*, vol. II.

with the League continued. On 13 October Wavell was able to persuade the League to join the interim government. Three Congress members having resigned, five Leaguers joined the interim government on 22 October 1946. After some bargaining the portfolios were redistributed.

The effort of the Viceroy to have a coalition government was in the hope that a long period of its working might have some healing effect on the strife-torn country. But the position contained some constitutional anomalies. So far as the interpretation of the Cabinet Mission plan was concerned, 'neither the Congress accepted the standpoint of the Cabinet Mission in respect of grouping nor did the Cabinet Mission give up its point of view'.[14] Until the day of its acceptance of office no Congress resolution or statement did suggest that the Congress had accepted the interpretation of the Cabinet Mission. While the Viceroy invited the Congress to form the interim government, it must be assumed that he was aware of the position and invited the Congress in spite of it. On the other hand, when the Muslim League joined the interim government, it did not cancel its Bombay resolution of 29 July, which had rejected the Cabinet Mission plan in toto.

Yet the move was a judicious one on the part of the Viceroy, who hoped that joint working of the two parties might lead to some understanding between them. In such a situation the covering of the constituent assembly had naturally to be postponed until December. But then difficulty arose out of the Congress eagerness to convene the constituent assembly as early as possible and the persistent refusal of the Muslim League to participate immediately in any long-term project. In a letter to Jinnah, written on 6 October, Nehru hoped that if the League finally decided to join the interim government, it would simultaneously decide to join the constituent assembly. On 7 October, Jinnah replied emphasizing that the question of the long-term plan should stand over until a better and more conducive atmosphere was created and agreement was reached on points of difference. Wavell wrote to Nehru on 23 October:

> I have made it quite clear to Mr. Jinnah . . . that the Muslim League's entry into the interim government is conditional on the acceptance of the schemes of the cabinet delegation contained in the statement of 16 May and explained in the statement of 25 May and that he must call his council at an early date to agree to it.[15]

[14] N.C. Roy, *Towards Framing the Constitution of India*, p. 173.
[15] *IAR*, 1946, vol. II, p. 281.

He also wrote that Jinnah had agreed to join the constituent assembly as well as the interim government. Jinnah, however, on 26 October, the day before the League joined the interim government, told the press that he had 'never for a single moment conveyed to the Viceroy anything by way of assurances or otherwise, except that the long-term plan could only be considered and decided by the Council of the All-India Muslim League'.[16]

In the Cabinet Mission's statement on 16 May the interim government plan was not integrally connected with the long-term plan of constitution-making. The interim government was necessitated because 'while the constitution-making proceeds, the administration of India has to be carried on'. The integral connection of the interim government with the constitution-making body was, like the interpretation of the 'grouping' clause, an afterthought. It was assumed only when the Viceroy issued his invitation on 16 June. Ever since the Muslim League took office the Congress pressure on the Viceroy for the former's participation in the constituent assembly increased. The Congress forgot that the 16 May statement had not been and could not be, accepted by itself in toto.

Summoning of the Constituent Assembly

On 20 November, a government press note said that it had been finally decided that the preliminary meeting of the constituent assembly would be held at New Delhi on 9 December. On the same day, the correspondence between the Viceroy and Jinnah was released to the press. The Viceroy had written to Jinnah on 5 November asking him to hold the meeting of the League Council at an early date to consider the acceptance of the 16 May statement. He wanted to know from Jinnah what assurance he needed. Jinnah in reply reminded him that the Congress had not so far accepted the 16 May statement in toto, as in all official documents and statements the Congress leaders expressed their reservations about the grouping clause. As the Congress had not budged from its position, it would be 'futile' for him to summon the meeting of the League Council.[17]

On the same day, invitation was issued to all members of the constituent assembly to attend its session. Jinnah declined the invitation. On 21 November 1946, Nehru addressed the Meerut session of the Congress and reiterated the 'two basic principles' of the formation of the interim

[16] *The Statesman*, 27 October 1946.

[17] *Indian Constitution Documents*, vol. IV, pp. 257-8.

government. They were 'firstly, that it should work as a team, and, secondly, that Muslim League could only join it if it accepted the long-term plan'. He held that the League had 'accepted both the principles although Mr Jinnah used roundabout phraseology, but now the League say that the interim government is neither a cabinet nor a coalition and that the Muslim members form a separate bloc'. For the first time, however, Nehru appeared pessimistic about the constituent assembly:

> Mr Jinnah has tried to get the constituent assembly postponed sine die. If it is so postponed now, it may be said to be postponed for ever. I am not enamoured of this constituent assembly, but we have accepted it and should make the best use of it for our benefit. I do not expect that this will be the last constituent assembly. When our freedom becomes ampler we shall have another constituent assembly.[18]

On the eve of the convocation of the constituent assembly, Prime Minister, Attlee made a last-moment bid to resolve the deadlock by inviting the Congress, League and Sikh leader, along with Wavell, to London for talks. Nehru, Liaqat Ali and Baldev Singh went to London, but the talks failed. Nehru returned on 8 December and said:

> The main point about the constituent assembly has been that it is as self-governing and self-determining body and any kind of imposition from outside will not be welcomed. It has been our purpose all along to make the constituent assembly as representative as possible of all groups in the country, but if some people unfortunately keep away, this cannot be allowed to stop the functioning of the constituent assembly as a whole.[19]

On 6 December, the British government, at the failure of the London talks, issued a statement reiterating 'the view that the decisions of the sections should, in absence of an agreement to the contrary, be taken by a simple majority vote of the representatives in the sections'.[20] The British government noted that though this view had been accepted by the Muslim League, the Congress had put forward a different view, asserting that the true meaning of the statement, read as a whole, was that the provinces had the right to decide both as to grouping and as to their own constitution.

The British government reasserted 'that the statement of 16 May means what the Cabinet Mission have always stated was their intention. This part of the statement, as is interpreted, must therefore be considered an essential part of the scheme of 16 May'. It was hoped by the British

[18] *The Statesman*, 22 November 1946.
[19] Ibid., 9 December 1946.
[20] *IAR*, 1946, vol. II, pp. 301-2.

government, however, that other questions of interpretation might be submitted to the federal court with the consent of both the parties. On the matter immediately in dispute, the British government urged the Congress to accept the view of the Cabinet Mission in order that a way might be opened for the Muslim League to reconsider its attitude.

> If, in spite of their reaffirmation of the intention of the Cabinet Mission, the constituent assembly desires that this fundamental point should be referred for a decision to the federal court, such a reference should be made at a very early date. It will then be reasonable that the meetings of the sections of the constituent assembly should be postponed until the decision of the federal court is known.

Finally, the British government made it clear that, 'should the constitution come to be framed by a constituent assembly in which a large section of the Indian population had not been represented, His Majesty's Government could not, of course, contemplate—as the Congress have stated they would not contemplate—forcing such a constitution upon the unwilling parts of the country'.

The paradox of the Cabinet Mission plan was that the groups did not admit of either a communal veto or a provincial veto prescribed for the constituent assembly as a whole. The British government, however, did not show any inclination to sort it out or to postpone the holding of the assembly. The Congress now took a position which complied with the 16 May statement, but not with the statement of 25 May of the Cabinet Mission and thus pointed out the contradiction between the two. The Congress was ready to the extent of sitting in sections but was opposed to the enlisting of a province in any group, for constitutional and administrative purposes, wherein the province would consider its interests unsafe. Joining a group, thus, still remained an open question for the Congress. Under such circumstances, further postponement of the convening of the constitution-making body and a trial to the working of the interim government meanwhile, for a rather long duration, was perhaps the only alternative. This might not necessarily mean the postponement of the transfer of power, for a free national government was a better authority to convene the constituent assembly. By all estimates it is recognized that the convening of the constituent assembly without the League was ill-timed.

CHAPTER 5

Constituent Assembly *versus* the Muslim League

The Constituent Assembly Meets

On 9 December 1946 the Constituent Assembly met in the Constitution Hall, New Delhi, at 11 of the clock in the morning. According to the programme set by the Congress Experts Committee, J.B. Kripalani, Congress president, proposed the name of Sachchidananda Sinha, the seniormost member of the Constituent Assembly, for the temporary chairmanship of the Assembly. The chairman took his seat with perfect dignity and immediately started business. He read three congratulatory messages from abroad, gave his ruling on an election dispute concerning the member from Baluchistan and nominated Frank Anthony as his deputy. B.N. Rau read out Sinha's address. A total of 207 members presented their credentials on the same day.

On the next day a resolution was moved by Jawaharlal Nehru, and seconded by Govind Ballabh Pant, proposing the provisional adoption of Central Legislative Assembly rules and standing orders until permanent rules were framed. It was passed after some discussion. So was passed another resolution confirming the existing organization of the Constituent Assembly office pending final decision of the Assembly.

Controversial Move

The first controversial subject that was taken up by the Constituent Assembly was a resolution on the Committee on Rules of Procedure of the Constituent Assembly moved by Kripalani.[1] Regarding the scope of the rules, Kripalani said that the original draft had included the words 'sections and committees', but he dropped them as they were 'superfluous'. 'The Assembly rules included the rules for sections and committees'.[2]

[1] *Constitutional Assembly Debates* (hereafter *CAD*), 10 December 1946, vol. I, p. 22.
[2] Loc. cit.

That the reference to sections and committees was not just 'superfluous', and had been dropped out of a special consideration, was found, when Suresh Chandra Banerjee and Syama Prasad Mookerjee of Bengal respectively moved and seconded an amendment to the resolution proposing the addition of the words 'sections and committees'. Mookerjee argued that

> when the sectional assemblies will meet each may frame its own rules of procedure. The question may then arise whether the Constituent Assembly as such had the authority to frame rules of procedure for the sections at all. Reference has then to be made to the resolution which gave authority to the Rules Committee to frame rules and then the only mention which will be found will be that this committee was appointed to frame rules of Procedure of the Assembly. If your intention is that the Rules Committee will also frame rules for the sections, why not say specifically 'including sections and committees', so that there may not be any ambiguity or doubt whatsoever when sections start doing their work.[3]

When, in view of the general support of the House to the amendment, Nehru advised Kripalani[4] to accept it, M.R. Jayakar, the liberal Hindu Mahasabha leader, elected from Bombay on a Congress ticket, opposed the amended resolution. He said:

> Remember the word 'sections'. You are asked by express terms to legislate for them in advance of their future formation. Remember 'sections' include 'B' and 'C' sections. Remember further that in 'B' and 'C' sections there is likely to be—almost certainly to be—a preponderance of a certain group of men who are not present here today and who may be present at the date when these sections begin to function. That group of men are not present here today under a feeling of suspicion, if not hostility. Would you like to legislate for them in advance at this stage, or would you not let the matter remain where it is, namely, that as the word 'Assembly' prima facie would include 'sections' no rules can be framed by sections 'A', 'B' and 'C' which are in conflict with the rules of the Assembly? . . . Remember that this group of men is not present here today and is, besides, watching these proceedings with jealousy and suspicion to discover whether you are taking anything out of their hands and deciding it finally in advance of their arrival? If you do so may it not interfere with their future arrival here in a friendly and trustful atmosphere?[5]

[3] Ibid., p. 23.
[4] Ibid., p. 26.
[5] Ibid., p. 27.

The Assembly—A Sovereign Body?

The resolution, as amended, was carried. The next day, on 11 December 1946, the Committee for Rules of Procedure was elected without contest. On the same day Rajendra Prasad, then a member of the interim government, was elected permanent chairman of the Constituent Assembly. In reply to the congratulatory speeches of the members of the Constituent Assembly he made a speech, the following portion of which is significant:

> This Constituent Assembly has come into being with a number of limitations, many of which we will have to bear in mind as we proceed. But it must also be borne in mind that the Assembly is a sovereign body and is fully competent to conduct its proceedings in the manner it chooses to follow. I also believe that it is competent to break the limitations attached to it at its birth.[6]

Nehru spoke in the same vein while, in the next meeting of the Assembly, on 13 December 1946, he moved the resolution on 'Aims and Objectives' and said:

> You all know that the Constituent Assembly is not what many of us wished it to be. It has come into being under particular conditions and the British government has a hand in its birth. They have attached to it certain conditions. We accepted the State Paper which may be called the foundation of this Assembly after serious deliberations and we shall endeavour to work within its limits. But you must not ignore the source from which the Assembly derives its strength. We have met here today because of the strength of the people behind us and we shall go as far as the people—not of any particular group but the people as a whole—shall wish us to go. We should, therefore, keep in mind the passions that lie in the hearts of the masses of the Indian people and try to fulfil them.
>
> I am sorry, there are so many absentees. We shall have to be careful that we do nothing which may cause uneasiness in others or goes against any principles. . . . It is, at the same time, manifest that when a great country starts to advance, no party or group can stop it. This house, although it has met in the absence of some of its members, will continue functioning and try to carry out its work at all costs.[7]

The Objectives Resolution

The Constituent Assembly declared its firm and solemn resolve to proclaim India as an independent sovereign republic and draw up for her future governance a constitution for a union of the territories of British India,

[6] Ibid., p. 49.
[7] Ibid., pp. 55-6.

the Indian states, and such other parts of India as were outside British India and the states as well as such other territories as were willing to be constituted into the independent sovereign India. Therein the said territories, whether with their existing boundaries or with such others as might be determined by the Constituent Assembly and there after according to the law of the constitution, would possess and retain the status of autonomous units together with residuary powers.

The sovereignty of the constitution would be derived from the people who would secure justice, equality and freedom. 'Adequate safeguards shall be provided for minorities, backward and tribal areas, and depressed and other backward classes'. The constitution would maintain the integrity of the territory of the Republic and the law of civilized nations.[8]

On 16 December 1946, the first speaker on the Objectives Resolution, M.R. Jayakar, moved an amendment seeking an adjournment of the consideration of the Objectives Resolution. His point was that

> within the limits of the power which the Cabinet Mission's statement of 16 May accords to this preliminary meeting, it cannot validly lay down any fundamentals, however sketchy they may be, of the constitution. That must wait until we meet in the sections and the provincial constitutions have been prepared. At that stage, the two other parties, the Muslim League and the Indian states, are expected to be present. . . . We are no doubt a sovereign body as you, Sir, very rightly remarked but we are sovereign within the limitations of the Paper by which we have been created. We cannot go outside those limitations except by agreement and, the two other parties being absent, no agreement can be thought of.[9]

His amendment, in a way, challenged the orderliness of Nehru's resolution. But as the latter had already been moved, the chairman allowed both the resolution and the amendment to be discussed.[10] This resulted in a long-drawn debate which ended only when the chairman, on 21 December, declared the postponement of consideration of the Objectives Resolution until the resumption of the Assembly after the Christmas recess.

A number of forces operated behind this postponement. There was strength in Jayakar's argument which was vindicated by the great lawyer representative of the depressed classes, B.R. Ambedkar. It was realized by everybody except the diehards that, in spite of the solemn character of

[8] Ibid., p. 57. Undoubtedly, the Objectives Resolution was a precious document of the democratic aspirations of a newly freed people. Yet it was basically a political document and had no economic outlook.

[9] Ibid., p. 70.

[10] Ibid., p. 72.

the Objectives Resolution, its adoption would put an additional hurdle in the effort of persuading the League to join the Assembly. Also, as V.P. Menon notes, the suggestion was 'backed outside the house by Sir Sultan Ahmed, Constitutional Adviser to the Chamber of Princes and the Dewans of Hyderabad, Travancore, Mysore and Bikaner'.[11]

The Working Committee's Stand

The Congress Working Committee was in session at Delhi from 8 to 22 December 1946 to consider the statement of the British government on 6 December. On 23 December, the Working Committee issued a statement pointing out that the several governmental statements of the period were clearly in addition to and variation of the Cabinet Mission's statement of 6 May 1946, on which the whole scheme of the Constituent Assembly was based. It said that, according to the 16 May statement, the provinces were intended to be autonomous, subject to the union controlling certain specified subjects. Paragraph 19 laid down inter alia the freedom for sections to meet, for decisions to be taken as to whether groups should be formed or not and for any provinces to elect to come out of the group in which it might have been placed. Already, in their resolution of 24 May 1946, the Working Committee had pointed out what appeared to be the divergence between the basic principles and the procedure suggested, in that a measure of compulsion was introduced which infringed the basic principles of provincial autonomy. The Congress made it clear that their objection was not to provinces entering sections but to compulsory grouping and the possibility of a dominating province framing a constitution for another province entirely against the wishes of the latter.

The Working Committee then cited a letter dated 15 June 1946, from the Viceroy to the president of the Congress, in which the Viceroy had assured the latter that the statement of 16 May did not make grouping compulsory and that it left the decision to the representatives of the provinces concerned, sitting together in sections. Considering the 6 December statement as both 'an addition to and an interpretation of' the earlier statement, the Working Committee regretted that the British government's intervention, long after the members of the Constituent Assembly had been elected, 'has created a new situation which is full of peril for the future'. The Working Committee was still of the opinion that 'the

[11] V.P. Menon, *The Transfer of Power*, p. 331.

interpretation put by the British government in regard to the method of voting in the sections is not in conformity with provincial autonomy'.[12]

The Working Committee thus rightly pointed out the ever-changing interpretation by the British government of the grouping clause. But one serious political problem was already obvious to everybody. Unless the grouping clause was accepted by the Congress with the Anglo-League interpretation, the League was definitely not joining the Constituent Assembly. And if the League did not join the constitution-making body, could it live up to its purpose? In any case, though the Cabinet Mission plan left enough scope for provinces to step out of the groups, the Congress leaders at that time thought that such opting out would be difficult, after elections were held according to the plan, if not entirely impossible. Nevertheless, the Congress Working Committee, in its earnestness to get the participation of the League in the Constituent Assembly, left the decision to the AICC and requested the Congress representatives of the Constituent Assembly to postpone consideration of important issues to a subsequent meeting.

Rules of the Assembly

On 21 December, the Report of the Committee on Rules of Procedure was presented by K.M. Munshi.[13] The Committee recommended that the permanent chairman of the Constituent Assembly would be called the president. He would fix the dates of its meetings (Rule 8), and 'be the guardian of the privileges of the Assembly, its spokesman and representative and its highest executive authority' (Rule 27/3).

In all matter relating to the procedure of the conduct of business, the decision of the chairman would be final. Provided that when a motion raised an issue which is claimed to be a major communal issue, the chairman shall, if so requested by a majority of the representatives of either of the major communities, consult the federal court before giving his decision (Rule 23).

Rule 23-A provided that the functions of the Advisory Committee, referred to in paragraphs 19 and 20 of the statement of the Cabinet Mission, would be to initiate and consider proposals and to make a report to the Assembly upon fundamental rights, clauses for the protection of minorities and the administration of tribal and excluded areas, 'and it shall be the

[12] *IAR*, 1946, vol. II, pp. 126-9.
[13] *CAD*, vol. I, p. 167.

exclusive function of the Assembly to take decisions upon such reports and further to decide the question of the incorporation of these rights in the appropriate part of the Constitution'.

Rule 59 laid down the application of the principle of proportionate representation in all elections to the Constituent Assembly.

Rule 62 provided that the provisions of these rules would apply *mutatis mutandis* to the sections and the committees of the Assembly.

Rule 63 (1) provided that before the settlement of the constitutions of the union and the provinces and the decision on the formation of groups, the provincial legislatures would be given an opportunity to express their views on the drafts of such constitutions and on the question of formation of a group constitution.

Nothing was mentioned about summoning the Assembly, which, evidently, remained the Governor-General's prerogative. However, there would be no dissolution 'except by a resolution assented to by at least two-thirds of the whole number of members of the Assembly' (Rule 7). The limitation on the powers of the Assembly is apparent from the fact that it was for the Governor-General to change the name of the chairman to that of the president or surrender the power of dissolution by the issue of the India (Provisional Constitution) Order on 14 August 1947.

The AICC Stand

The resolution of the Working Committee on December 1946 was considered in the AICC meeting in Delhi on 5 January 1947 which declared that a reference to the federal court of the communal issues arising in the Constituent Assembly 'has become purposeless and undesirable owing to the recent announcements made on behalf of the British government. A reference could only be made on an agreed basis, the parties concerned agreeing to abide by the decision given.'

The AICC was firmly of the opinion that the constitution of a free and independent India should be framed by the people of India on the basis of as wide an agreement as possible. There must be no interference whatsoever by any external authority and no compulsion on any province or part of a province by another province. The AICC realized and appreciated 'the difficulties placed in the way of some provinces, notably Assam, Baluchistan, Sind and the NWFP and the Sikhs in the Punjab, by the British Cabinet's scheme of 16 May 1946, and more especially by the interpretation put upon it by the British government in their statement of 6 December 1946'. The Congress could not be a party to any such compulsion or imposition against the will of the people concerned. Yet anxious for the satisfactory progress of constitution-making, the AICC agreed 'to advise action in accordance with the interpretation of the British government in regard to the procedure to be followed in the section', but stressed 'that this must not involve any compulsion on a province and that the rights of the Sikhs in the Punjab should not be jeopardised. In the event of any attempt at such compulsion, a province or a part of a province has the right to take such action as may be deemed necessary in order to give effect to the wishes of the people concerned.'[14]

The AICC resolution was evidently a modification of the earlier stand of the Congress and it was passed against severe opposition from a substantial minority including the Congress Socialists. Yet it would really mean nothing more than Congress agreement to sit in the preliminary meetings of the sections, with the reservation of the right of provinces to leave a section meeting in case of any coercion or compulsion. It also reserved the right for a part of a province and for the Sikhs of Punjab to secede in similar cases.

Following this resolution, Gopinath Bardoloi, prime minister of Assam, declared on 7 January that Assam was 'prepared to sit in sections in the Constituent Assembly, but Assam demands exactly what the Muslim League demands from the union centre. If the Muslim League has apprehensions about the union centre forcing its brutal majority in grouping with Bengal'.[15] Simultaneously, demands among the Sikhs of Punjab and the Hindus of Bengal were growing for partition of the provinces.

Second Session of the Assembly

The next meeting of the Constituent Assembly was scheduled on 20 January 1947. But the Muslim League, having no intention to join it, fixed its Working Committee meeting on 29 January. When the second session of the Assembly started, the debate on the Objectives Resolution continued. Jayakar said that as the Muslim League had not so far shown any intention of joining the Constituent Assembly, it was no use further holding up the Objectives Resolution. Nehru wound up the debate on 22 January. He regretted the delay, but considered it justified, 'because we have always balanced two factors. One, is the urgent necessity of reaching our goal,

[14] *IAR*, 1947, vol. I, pp. 114-15.
[15] Ibid., p. 27.

and the other, that we should reach it in proper time and with as great unanimity as possible'. However, 'there has been waiting enough'. the Objectives Resolution was carried unanimously.[16]

The second session also disposed of some routine work like setting up of the Steering Committee, Advisory Committee on Minorities, Tribal Areas and Fundamental Rights, Business Committee, and Union Powers Committee, electing Harendra Coomer Mukherjee as the vice-president[17] and passing the budget of the Assembly. A letter from the only communist member, Somnath Lahiri, complaining that his house had been suddenly searched by the police damaging his papers and notes relating to the Assembly, was read. The vice-president ruled that he had nothing to do with it.[18]

Looking for a United India

While proposing the formation of the Committee on subjects assigned to the union centre, Rajagopalachari said on 25 January 1947 that if one thing is more clearly decided in His Majesty's Government's statement than anything else, it is this, that there shall be only one sovereign state in India. It has been decided clearly beyond all possibility of doubt that a division of India into two sovereign states is not to be thought of in this connection. This explains many of the things we are doing and will remove many of the misunderstandings that are likely to arise. . . . If the League comes in, they come in on an express understanding that India shall be only one sovereign state, abandoning their separatist policy. . . . Let us give them ample time to come.[19]

The Congress, thus, took the sovereignty of the Constituent Assembly for granted and decided to make use of it. The League Working Committee met at Karachi from 31 January to 1 February 1947 and gave the Congress a rebuff by resolving that the Congress had destroyed the foundations of the Cabinet Mission plan and no possibility of compromise was left.

With regard to the Congress contention that 'if a constitution comes to be formed by a Constituent Assembly in which a large section of the Indian population had not been represented, such constitution would not

[16] *CAD*, vol. II, p. 305.

[17] On 16 July 1947, H.C. Mukherjee and V.T. Krishnamachari were finally elected permanent vice-presidents of the Assembly.

[18] *CAD*, vol. II, pp. 304-41.

[19] Ibid., p. 333.

be forced upon any unwilling parts of the country', the League alleged that the AICC resolution

> completely distorts the meaning and application of this principle and makes this an excuse to instigate a section of the population of Assam, the North-West Frontier Province, the Sikhs and even Baluchistan to revolt against the decision that might be taken by the relevant sections sitting as a whole and by simple majority vote. In the opinion of the Working Committee of the All-India Muslim League, the subsequent decision of the Assam Provincial Congress not to abide by the procedure laid down for sections and its reiteration that the constitution for Assam shall be framed by her own representatives only is a direct result of this instigation and is a step taken by Assam Congressmen in collusion with all-India leaders of the Congress.

The League Working Committee also objected to the proceedings of the Constituent Assembly, particularly to the passing of the Objectives Resolution in the League's absence. The Objectives Resolution was fundamental to the future constitution, as it 'speaks of a republic of "union", functions and power vested in the "union" or as are inherent or implied in the union and resulting therefrom, and talks of present boundaries, states and present authorities, the residuary powers, powers being derived from the people, minority rights and fundamental rights'.

The League had objection to the appointment of several committees including the Advisory Committee, referred to in paragraph 20 of the statement of the Cabinet Mission and the passing of the rules of procedure, particularly rule 63, through which sections were sought to be controlled. The appointment of the Union Powers Committee, before the setting of the group constitutions, was regarded as violative of Cripps's interpretation of the Cabinet Mission plan issued on 25 May 1946.

It was clear to the League that

> the Constituent Assembly in which only the Congress party is represented has taken decisions on principles and procedures some of which exceed the limitations imposed by the statement of 16 May on the Constituent Assembly's functions and powers at the preliminary stage and which further impinge upon the powers and functions of the sections. By taking these decisions in the Constituent Assembly and by appointing a packed committee consisting of individuals chosen by the Congress, the Congress has already converted that truncated Assembly into a rump and something totally different from what the Cabinet Mission's statement has provided for.

The League reasserted that the proposals of 16 May could only be given effect to and carried out if the two major parties agreed to accept them. The Congress had not accepted them at any stage although the

Muslim League had accepted, by their resolution, the statement of 16 May 1946, as far back as 6 June 1946. But, in view of the fact that the Congress refused to accept the proposals in toto and unequivocally, the Muslim League had to withdraw its acceptance on 29 July 1946. Finally, they declared that 'the elections to and thereafter the summoning of the Constituent Assembly, in spite of strong protests and most emphatic objections on the part of the Muslim League, were ab initio void, invalid and illegal as not only the major parties had not accepted the statement but even the Sikhs and the Scheduled Castes had also not done so and that continuation of the Constituent Assembly and its proceedings and decisions are ultra vires, invalid and illegal and it should be forthwith dissolved.[20]

The League Intransigence

There was, at the same time, not the slightest intention, on the part of the League, to make the interim government a success. While taking part in the interim government the Congress had decided to work under a system of collective responsibility. But, from the very day the Muslim League entered the government, it refused to work as a team with the Congress. Leaguers never attended the cabinet meetings except on invitation from the Viceroy. That is to say, the Muslim League was determined to reduce the interim government to the Viceroy's executive council. Abul Kalam Azad describes the League's attitude as: 'They were in the government and yet against it. In fact they were in a position to sabotage every move we took.'[21]

The biggest controversy arose in respect of two important portfolios: Home, held by Vallabhbhai Patel, and Finance held by Liaqat Ali. They came to a head-on clash when Liaqat Ali, in his budget proposals, suggested a 25 per cent tax on all business profits of more than one hundred thousand rupees. 'This was interpreted', says V.P. Menon, 'in Congress circles as an attempt to penalize the Hindu capitalists (who largely financed the Congress) and to bring about dissension among the right wing and the socialist group within the Congress party.'[22]

Liaqat Ali's move was undoubtedly very clever and intended to expose the weakness of the Congress in regard to its rich patrons. Abul Kalam

[20] *IAR*, 1947, vol. I, pp. 149-51.

[21] Abul Kalam Azad, *India Wins Freedom*, p. 175. Also, see Rajendra Prasad, *Autobiography*, pp. 196-7.

[22] *The Transfer of Power*, p. 348.

Azad noted that 'Sardar Patel and Sri Rajagopalachari in particular were violently opposed to his budget'.[23] It was Mountbatten's first job, after arrival, to solve this deadlock. Under such a strained relationship it was but natural that there would be a parting of the ways. Already in the Congress the demand had risen that unless the League entered the Constituent Assembly, it must quit the interim government. On 12 February 1947, Nehru addressed a letter to the Viceroy demanding resignation of League members from the interim government. Two days later Vallabhbhai Patel, in a press conference, announced the Congress decision to withdraw from the interim government if the League members were allowed to remain in it.[24] The wheel had turned full circle. All prospects of Congress-League collaboration were unceremoniously buried.

[23] *India Wins Freedom*, p. 176.
[24] Menon, *The Transfer of Power*, pp. 335-7.

CHAPTER 6

Constituent Assembly and Partition

HINT AT PARTITION

The final refusal of the League to join the Constituent Assembly created a critical situation. If the League members were asked to resign from the interim government, it would have serious consequences. If the Congress was allowed to resign, on the other hand, there might be a disaster. It was also not possible for the British to hold on to power much longer. Already, the Congress Socialists and the communists had declared their hostility towards the Cabinet Mission's proposals.

On 20 February, Prime Minister Attlee, therefore, made a vital statement on the floor of parliament. He regretted that there were still differences among the Indian parties which were preventing the Constituent Assembly from functioning as a fully representative body, though the British government desired to hand over their responsibility to authorities established by a constitution approved by all parties in India in accordance with the Cabinet Mission's plan. 'The present state of uncertainty is fraught with danger and cannot be indefinitely prolonged. His Majesty's Government wish to make it clear that it is their definite intention to take the necessary steps to effect the transference of power to responsible Indian hands by a date not later than June 1948.'[1] But, if it should appear that such a constitution would not have been worked out by a fully representative assembly before that time, the British government would have to consider 'to whom the power of the central government in British India should be handed over, on the due date, whether as a whole to some form of central government for British India . . . or in such other way as may seem most reasonable and in the best interests of the Indian people'.

Although the final transfer of authority would not take place until June 1948, preparatory measures were to be taken in advance. As the first of such measures, Attlee announced the termination of the war-time appointment of Wavell and the appointment of Mountbatten 'who will be entrusted

[1] *IAR*, 1947, vol. I, pp. 142-3.

with the task of transferring to Indian hands responsibility for the Government of India'.

If the Cabinet Mission's plan was based on the 'regionalism' of Coupland, the 20 February 1947 statement of Attlee had something fundamentally common with the Cripps plan in that both these plans anticipated a partition of the country in the event of a disagreement between the major parties of India. Yet other questions remained. In respect of the states, British policy was to give them freedom to bargain their own position in the new dominion. The British government wanted to 'negotiate agreements in regard to matters arising out of the transfer of power with representatives of those to whom they propose to transfer powers'. Such 'matters' included 'the British commercial and industrial interests in India' which, they hoped, could 'look forward to a fair field for their enterprise under the new condition'.[2]

Congress Determination

The Congress, nevertheless, was determined to go on with the constitution-making. As events moved inevitably towards a climax, communal tension grew in the country.

Within a fortnight the non-League ministry of the Punjab fell and Governor's rule was imposed. Under such circumstances, the Congress Working Committee met to make the last bid for achieving the League's cooperation in view of Attlee's statement on 20 February 1947. In this meeting, held on 6-8 March 1947, the Working Committee passed a few resolutions emphasizing the voluntary character of the Constituent Assembly and inviting the cooperation of the League in the constitution-making.[3] The League still marked time until the controversy on Liaqat Ali budget made feelings too bitter for any possibility of reconciliation. In April 1947, demands for partition of Bengal and the Punjab were put forward by most of the non-Muslim parties.[4] While Jinnah bitterly opposed the move for partition of the provinces, Rajendra Prasad, in a press statement from New Delhi, said that if there was to be a partition of India, it should be as complete and thorough as possible, including the partition of Bengal and the Punjab.[5]

[2] Loc. cit.

[3] *Indian Constitutional Documents*, vol. IV, pp. 282-3.

[4] *IAR*, 1947, vol. I, pp. 238 and 245.

[5] Ibid., pp. 246-7.

Third Session

The third session of the Constituent Assembly was due to start on 25 April 1947. Meanwhile, at the Governors' conference on 15 April Mountbatten gave out the definite intention of partitioning the country if no solution was soon found.[6] Therefore partition became almost inevitable, and the subsequent interparty discussions were all based on this assump-tion. Nehru's statement at the All-India States People's Conference, held from 18 to 20 April 1947, was by far the last official invitation of the Congress to the League to join the constitution-making body. Nehru said there that though representatives of Indian states and the Muslim League had not entered the Assembly, despite frequent invitations, the door was still open for the League. But he wanted to make it clear that the Assembly would go ahead with the task of framing a constitution.[7]

On the opening day of the third session of the Constituent Assembly, while submitting the first report of the committee on Union Powers, N. Gopalaswami Ayyangar requested a postponement of consideration of the report, as he thought that, in view of further political developments, the report might need overhauling in future. He also wanted to submit at a later date a supplementary report.

The major factors which compelled him to plead for time were:

> The coming in of the Muslim League is not yet officially ruled out. There is still a possibility of their coming in, though the probability is perhaps very small. Should this possibility materialise, it would be only just and reasonable that the debate on so important a subject, as the subjects and powers to be assigned to the union centre, should be held in a house which contains a full representation of the Muslim League. Whether they will come in or not will be definitely known before the June-July session this Assembly. . . .

Then, Sir, there are the Indian states—a number of representatives of Indian states have joined us today but there is a very large number still to come in. . . . Thirdly, Sir, there is the question of the present political conversations. The decisions on those conversations will be available in all probability before we meet again in the June-July session.[8]

[6] *The Statesman*, Calcutta, 16 April 1947.

[7] *IAR*, 1947, vol. I, p. 211.

[8] *CAD*, vol. III, p. 381.

Partition Decision

Mountabatten, on the other hand, was only too eager to arrive at a prompt solution of the 'Indian problem'. But his talks with the party leaders, particularly with Jinnah and his colleagues, convinced him that there was no prospect of an agreed solution and that an alternative plan for the transfer of power had to be found and implemented without loss of time, in order to ease the growing political tension. 'Thus', as Menon observes, 'within six weeks of his arrival and after constant and ceaseless effort, Lord Mountbatten had produced a plan which marked the first stage towards the transfer of power.'[9] 'After full consultation with Indian political leaders', Mountbatten declared on 3 June 1947 that the British government was formulating the new plan, though it had 'no intention of attempting to frame any ultimate constitution for India' which was 'a matter for the Indian themselves'. The plan did not preclude 'negotiations between communities for a united India'. Yet, 'any constitution made by this [Constituent] Assembly cannot apply to those parts of the country which are unwilling to accept it'.[10] Partition was, therefore, inevitable by implication, though negotiation for a united India was not ruled out.

In order to ascertain the wishes of the people of Bengal and the Punjab, the plan provided that the representatives of the Muslim-majority districts and the representatives of the other districts to the provincial legislative assemblies would sit separately to decide whether the provinces would be partitioned. If even one part of a particular provincial legislature decided in favour of partition, the province would be partitioned. If both the parts agreed to remain united they would decide to which Constituent Assembly they would belong. The legislative assemblies of Sind and British Baluchistan would also, at special meetings, decide which Constituent Assembly they would join. The British government considered the position of NWFP as 'exceptional'.

> Two of the three representatives of the province are already participating in the existing Constituent Assembly. But it is clear, in view of its geographical situation and other considerations, that if the whole or say part of the Punjab decided not to join the existing Constituent Assembly, it will be necessary to give the North-West Frontier Province an opportunity to reconsider its position.

So, there would be a referendum in that province.

In the predominantly non-Muslim province of Assam the Sylhet district

[9] V.P. Menon, *The Transfer of Power*, pp. 353-7.

[10] *IAR*, 1947, vol. I, pp. 143-6.

had a majority of Muslims. In case of a decision for partition of Bengal, Sylhet would get a referendum to choose whether it would or would not join the Muslim part of Bengal. If Sylhet, along with the contiguous Muslim-majority areas of adjoining districts, were to join 'Eastern Bengal', the rest of Assam would continue in the Constituent Assembly.

Consequences of Partition

Consequent upon the possible partition, the number of representatives to which each area would be entitled was as indicated in Table 6.1

In accordance with the mandates given to them, the representatives of the various areas would either join the existing Constituent Assembly or form a new Constituent Assembly. British policy in respect of the Indian states remained as under the Cabinet Mission's plan. It was proposed to introduce legislation shortly to implement the transfer of power on the basis of dominion status, the dominion(s) having the right to opt out of the commonwealth.

The most important change introduced by the 3 June plan in the working of the Constituent Assembly was the abolition of the communal veto. So far as the communal question was concerned, the Constituent Assembly of India could work independently. The Constituent Assembly was thus promoted to the status of a really free body, though its authority would still apply to the states only to the extent of their negotiated acceptance of it. Transfer of power remained subject to an agreement between the British government and the successor authority or authorities on matters arising out of the transfer of power.

Acceptance of the 3 June declaration involved the partition of the country, consequent upon the splitting up of the Constituent Assembly into two parts, Sind, Baluchistan and , after a referendum on 20 July 1947 which was boycotted by the Khudai Khidmatgar Party, the North-West Frontier Province went wholly to Pakistan. The Punjab, Bengal and Assam

TABLE 6.1: NUMBER OF REPRESENTATIVES FOR THE PARTITIONED PROVINCES

Province	*General*	*Muslim*	*Sikh*	*Total*
Sylhet district of Assam	1	2	0	3
West Bengal	15	4	0	19
East Bengal	12	29	0	41
West Punjab	3	12	2	17
East Punjab	6	4	2	12

TABLE 6.2: POSITION OF THE PARTIES (BRITISH INDIA)

Section A		
1. Congress	164	(general 163, Muslim 1)
2. Muslim League	19	(Muslim)
3. Independent	7	(general)
Total	190	
Section B (East Punjab)		
1. Congress	7	(general 6, Sikh 1)
2. Muslim League	4	(Muslim)
3. Akali	1	(Sikh)
Total	12	
Section C (Assam & West Bengal)		
1. Congress	21	(general)
2. Muslim League	6	(Muslim)
Total	27	

TABLE 6.3: INTEGRATED PARTY POSITION IN THE CONSTITUENT ASSEMBLY (THREE SECTIONS)

1. Congress	192
2. Muslim League	29
3. Akali	1
4. Independent	7
Total	229

Source: Compiled from contemporary newspapers.

(after a referendum in Sylhet on 14 July 1947) were divided. This brought down (East) Punjab's representation to the Indian Constituent Assembly to 6 general, 4 Muslim and 2 Sikh and (West) Bengal's representation to 15 general and 4 Muslim. On 22 July 1947, by a government press-note, the Governor-General fixed the representation of Assam minus Sylhet (a part of which remained with Assam) at 6 general and 2 Muslim.

New elections took place in West Bengal, East Punjab and Assam. All general seats in West Bengal and Assam went to the Congress and some sitting members were dropped. The only communist member, Somnath Lahiri, lost his seat. B.R. Ambedkar returned from Bombay, with a Congress ticket, in the vacancy caused by the resignation of Jayakar. All Muslim seats of Bengal went to the Congress. The other Sikh seat went to the Akali party. The four Muslim seats went to the League. In the new house, the total strength of British Indian representatives came down to 229.

A New Assembly

The die was cast. On 5 July 1947, a joint meeting of the Union Constitution Committee and the Provincial Constitution Committee decided that the limitations imposed by the 16 May 1946 statement 'on the form of the constitution and the procedure to be followed in the Constituent Assembly' no longer existed. 'Consequent changes in the rules of procedure should be carried out.' Every attempt should be made to form the basic parts of the Constitution before the middle of August 1947, by which time the Constituent Assembly would also become the Union legislature. Indeed, after the middle of August, the Constituent Assembly would distinctly maintain its dual role. Finally, 'the position of the states' representative, when it began to function as the Union Legislature, should be examined'. A special subcommittee of nine members was also set up to examine the necessity of changes in the Objectives Resolution.

On 7 June 1947, however, another joint meeting of the two committees, with Rajendra Prasad in the chair, decided that the 3 June 1947 statement had not altogether invalidated the Cabinet Mission plan. Yet the centre-unit relation was now made alterable. The grouping scheme also could be modified. On 12 July 1947, the special subcommittee decided that the Objectives Resolution did not require any change, at least not immediately. It was never changed.[11]

Participation of the League's Rump

On 14 July 1947, when the fourth session of the Constituent assembly started, 23 Muslim League members took seats. Deshbandhu Gupta (Delhi), who had earlier replaced Asaf Ali, asked whether the League members still subscribed to the two-nation theory. He demanded that as a sovereign body the Constituent Assembly should not permit a member, who subscribed to the two-nation theory and not to the Objective Resolution, to sign the register. He wanted the ruling of the president, who did not consider it a matter of ruling, but a matter of right of one who had been elected.[12]

The president in his opening address referred to the changes that had followed the 3 June declaration. Sri Prakasa wanted a ruling of the president on the position resulting from the new elections:

[11] Minutes of the joint meeting of the Union and the Provincial Constitution Committees. B. Shiva Rao, *The Framing of India's Constitution*, vol. II, pp. 606-8.

[12] *CAD*, vol. IV, p. 535.

We were told that once the Constituent Assembly was elected, neither any changes would be made in its constitution nor could any outsider have any authority or control over it. It appears to me that all these changes have taken place according to the statement of the Viceroy—a proceeding which is improper, unjust, illegal and contrary to the rules.[13]

Sri Prakasa, obviously, regarded the Viceroy bound by the rules of the Assembly. The president admitted that the changes were the result of the Viceroy's statement and the consequent action taken by him:

But I believe that everyone has consented to these changes being made and so also have we done. The question of invalidity, therefore, does not arise. Moreover, now no one from among the members who had been formerly elected and have now lost their membership has submitted any petition against the termination of his membership. The newly elected members are members of this Assembly and shall continue to take part in its proceedings.[14]

On the same day, presenting a further report of the Order of Business Committee, K.M. Munshi spoke of the 'many and momentous changes' that had occurred due to the 3 June plan. He described the 16 May plan as 'the parricide's bag which was invented by ancient Roman law' out of which India had got released at last!

We have no sections and groups to go into, no elaborate procedure as was envisaged by it, no double majority clause, no more provinces with residuary powers, no opting out, no revision after ten years and no longer only four categories of powers for the centre. We, therefore, feel free to form a federation of our choice, a federation with a centre as strong as we can make it, subject of course to this that the Indian states have to be associated in this great task on a footing of the four categories of power and such further powers as they choose by agreement to cede to the centre. Therefore, Sir, I personally am not at all sorry that this change has taken place.[15]

Under the recommendation of the Order of Business Committee, Rules of Procedure of the house were amended in order to drop all references to sections and groups. On 25 July, the Assembly passed Sri Prakasa's resolution validating all elections to the Assembly since the acceptance of the 3 June plan.[16] It was only now that the Constituent Assembly, for all practical purposes, became independent.

[13] Ibid., p. 541.

[14] Ibid., p. 542.

[15] Ibid., pp. 544-5. Munshi personally regarded it a 'fundamental error' to look upon the Muslim as a political minority. K.M. Munshi, *Pilgrimage to Freedom*, p. 62.

[16] Ibid., p. 567.

TRANSFER OF POWER

The Indian Independence Bill was introduced in the British Parliament on 4 July 1947 in order to create two 'independent dominions', making a technical departure from the Statute of Westminster, which had merely provision for dominions. The Act defined the Indian Constituent Assembly as the Constituent Assembly, 'the first sitting whereof was held on the ninth day of December, nineteen hundred and fortysix', modified by the exclusion of the members representing the territories due to go to Pakistan.[17]

Section 6, subsection 1 of the Act provided that, 'The legislature of each of the new dominions shall have full power to make laws for that dominion, including laws having extraterritorial operation.' This would necessarily imply that no law and no provision of any law made by the legislature of either of the new dominions would be void or inoperative on the ground of its repugnance to the law of England, or to the provisions of any act of the British Parliament, including the Indian Independence Act itself, or to any order, rule or regulation made under any such act. The powers of the dominion legislatures would include the 'power to repeal or amend any such act, order, rule or regulation insofar as it is part of the law of the dominion' (section 6, subsection 2).

Subsection 3 of section 6 gave unlimited power of assent to the Governor-General 'in His Majesty's name to any law of the legislature of that dominion'. Disallowance by His Majesty or reservation for His Majesty's signification of a law would no longer apply in case of the two dominions. It was in this respect that the Indian Independence Act was a definite improvement on the Statute of Westminster. No law of the British Parliament and no order-in-council passed after 15 August 1947 would be automatically operative in the dominions (subsections 4 and 5).

This unlimited legislative competence of the Assembly would cover constitutional legislations for the dominions (section 8, subsection 1). Subsection 2 of section 8 provided that 'except in so far as other provision was made by or in accordance with a constituent law', enacted by the Constituent Assembly of the dominion, 'each of the new dominions and all provinces and other parts thereof shall be governed as nearly as may be in accordance with the Government of India Act, 1935'. The provisions of the 1935 Act, and the orders-in-council, rules and other instruments made thereunder would, so far as applicable, and subject to any express

[17] See B. Shiva Rao, op. cit., vol. I, pp. 539-55.

provisions of the Indian Independence. Act, and with such omissions, additions, adaptations and modifications as might be specified in orders of the Governor-General, have effect accordingly. This meant that, so long as the Constituent Assembly did not interfere, the Governor-General-in-Council was competent to make alterations, adaptations, modifications, etc., of the Government of India Act, 1935, in order to run the administration.

According to proviso (b) of the section, these powers of the Governor-General would in no way imply the control of Parliament over the dominion legislatures. Proviso (c) removed the power of the Governor-General and Governors to act in individual discretion. Also proviso (c) laid down that 'the powers of the federal legislature or Indian legislature under that act (i.e. Government of India Act, 1935), as in force in relation to each dominion, shall in the first instance be exercisable by the Constituent Assembly of the dominion in addition to the powers exercisable by that Assembly under subsection 1 of this section'. The ordinary legislative authority of the dominion was thus also vested in the Constituent Assembly. On the whole, the total legislative functions and authorities of the successor government were vested in the Constituent Assembly.

A New Governor-General

Section 5 of the Indian Independence Act provided that there would be a Governor-General for each or both of the dominions,'who shall be appointed by His Majesty for the purposes of the government of the dominion'. What was missing in the section was the declaration of the earlier dominion constitutions that the executive power of the government would continue to be vested in the British monarch, on whose behalf the Governor-General's assent to every legislation was a formal necessity but could not be withheld at his discretion (section 8, proviso [e]). In fact, every ordinary legislation was placed before him for his assent, which was given. But a big question mark was put against the constituent legislations. The British commonwealth legality has made no distinction between 'constituent' and 'ordinary' legislations. Apparently, the British Parliament thought that the assent of the Governor-General was necessary.[18] But the Congress had made up its mind not to seek the

[18] Jennings, *The Constitutional Problems in Pakistan*, p. 24.
Elsewhere, Jennings writes that the Indian Independence Act was 'more complicated'

Governor-General's assent to the Constitution. Jennings critically comments:

The main principles of the Indian Independence Act, 1947, never came under the scrutiny of the Indian court, but a traditional interpretation of the act was adopted, based upon the concept laid down in correspondence between the Indian National Congress and the Cabinet Mission that the Constituent Assembly was a 'sovereign body'.[19]

Section 9 of the Indian Independence Act asked the Governor-General to make, by order, such provision as appeared to him to be necessary or expedient for bringing the provision of the act into effective operation. Such powers would, however, lapse on 31 March 1948, unless earlier terminated by the Constituent Assembly. Accordingly, the Governor-General, on 14 August 1947, passed the India (Provisional Constitution) Order, 1947, providing for various omissions, additions, adaptations and modifications to the Government of India Act, 1935, and the India (Central Government and Legislature) Act, 1946, with effect till 'other provision is made by or in accordance with a law made by the Constituent Assembly'. The same order also omitted, in the said acts, all references to the expression, 'in his discretion', 'acting in his discretion' and 'exercising, his individual judgment'. The Governor-General ceased to be part of the dominion legislature through an adaptation of the Government of India Act, 1935, by the India (Provisional Constitution) Order, 1947, and abandoned the power of dissolution. Thus, the Governor-General turned himself, on 15 August 1947, into a mere constitutional head of the country and the Constituent assembly became a full-sovereign legislature.

End of Stigmas

According to section 7(1-a) of the Indian Independence Act all British administrative responsibilities in British India were disposed of. Section 7(1-b) declared, in respect of the Indian states, that 'the suzerainty of His Majesty lapses, and with it, all treaties and agreements in force at the date of the passing of this act between His Majesty and the rulers of

than the Statute of Westminster as it created the two separate countries of India and Pakistan, provided them with interim constitutions, authorized their constituent assemblies to enact permanent constitutions and gave their legislatures the same powers as the dominion parliaments had under the statute of Westminster. Ivor Jennings, *The British Commonwealth of Nations*, pp. 193-4.

[19] Jennings, *The Constitutional Problems in Pakistan*, p. 23.

Indian states, all functions exercisable by His Majesty existing at that date towards Indians states and the rulers thereof, and all powers, rights, authority of jurisdiction exercisable by His Majesty at that date in or in relation to Indian states by treaty, grant, usage, sufferance or otherwise'. Under section 7(1-c) the British government also shed its responsibilities in respect of the tribal areas. But all existing agreements, with the rulers and persons having authority in the tribal areas, relating to 'customs, transit and communication, posts and telegraph, or other like matters' would continue to be in effect 'until the provisions in question are denounced', or 'are superseded by subsequent agreements'.

Under other provisions of the Act, British armed forces had to be, withdrawn completely by the end of February 1948. During the period between 15 August 1947 and 28 February 1948, if any British military personnel was to serve in the Indian Army, it would be, by the Independence Act, exempt from the law governing Indian forces. The Indian forces were to be divided under the supervision of a Joint Defence Council headed by Mountbatten.

The Government of India agreed to pay compensation to British officers leaving India and regular remunerations and other privileges to those serving in India. On the other hand, the British government agreed to pay back India's huge sterling balances. All these claims were settled by the Indo-British Financial Agreement on 14 August 1947.

Till 31 March 1948, the Governor-General-in-Council passed four 'amendment orders' on his Provisional Constitution Order of 14 August 1947. In all, the Constituent Assembly made six extra constituent legislations after March 1948. The Government of India Act, 1935 (with its adaptations under the Indian Independence Act, 1947), was amended four times by 1949. On 25 May 1947, the India (Central Government and Legislature) Act, 1946, was amended and, on 17 September 1949, the Privy Council's jurisdiction over the Indian courts was abolished. The Constituent Assembly also ratified, on 16 June 1949, the Commonwealth Prime Minister's Declaration on 27 April 1949. (This was necessary in view of the resolution of the Assembly about the Objectives of the Constitution which aimed at constituting India into a sovereign republic.) None of the constituent legislations were placed for the Governor-General's assent. They were authenticated by the President of the Constituent Assembly.

CHAPTER 7

A Sovereign Body

Assumption of Power

In order to make the transfer of power 'smooth' and utilize Mountbatten's services in the transition period the Congress leadership proposed that Mountbatten would continue as the Governor-General of India for some time. This led to an interesting discussion in the Constituent Assembly.

On 31 July 1947, the concluding day of the fourth session, while the programme for Independence Day was announced by the president, Mahavir Tyagi objected to the proposal of 'inviting' Mountbatten to take up the governor-generalship of India. He said:

> Can you not kindly spare this house the part of the programme according to which we are required to invite Lord Mountbatten to be our Governor-General in future; because this House has never discussed that question; nor has the House passed so far any resolution, nor agreed to the idea, of Lord Mountbatten being the Governor-General of India?[1]

He later explained that he was not recording any objection on behalf of the House to the acceptance of Lord Mountbatten as the Governor-General of India.

> That thing has already been done. What I was suggesting was that you had better drop the idea of going through that item of programme in which, you say, on behalf of this House, Lord Mountbatten was to be invited to accept the governor-generalship. I think he has already done it and this formality may better be given up, because the House has never discussed the issue and if, without the House having considered this issue, he is invited this will be too formal and in my opinion slightly unfair. . . .[2]

Most of the members were, however, reluctant to discuss the question. Finally, they authorized the president to chalk out the programme for Independence Day celebrations. On 14 August at 11 p.m. the Constituent

[1] *CAD*, vol. IV, p, 1045.
[2] Ibid., p. 1046.

Assembly met and decided upon the formalities of the transfer of power. As the clock struck twelve, the president and members stood up and took the pledge of service to India and her people. Then the president proposed 'that it should be intimated to the Viceroy that—

(1) The Constituent Assembly has assumed power for the governance of India, and
(2) The Constituent Assembly of India has endorsed the recom-mendation that Lord Mountbatten be Governor-General of India from 15 August 1947 and that this message be conveyed to Lord Mountbatten by the President and Pandit Nehru.'[3]

On 15 August Mountbatten addressed the Constituent Assembly, after reading out a historic royal message of greetings to the Constituent Assembly of India.

The significance of Mountbatten's own speech lies in his acceptance of the status of a constitutional head 'devoted wholly to the furtherance of India's interests'. He was honoured that the Assembly had endorsed the invitation originally made to him by its leaders to remain the Governor-General. He hoped that, as the Assembly leaders had selected 31 March 1948 'as the end of what may be called the interim period', he would be released in April.[4]

New Status of the Constituent Assembly

On 20 August 1947, Mahavir Tyagi, K. Santhanam and other members raised the question of the status of the Assembly after the transfer of power in respect of its ordinary legislative and constituent functions. Consequently, on the same day, the president appointed a committee consisting of G.V. Mavalankar, Husain Imam, P.D. Tandon, B.R. Ambedkar, Alladi Krishnaswami Ayyar, Gopalaswami Ayyangar and B.L. Mitter 'to consider the Indian Independence Act, the adaptations of the Government of India Act, 1935, the rules and standing orders in force in the Constituent Assembly, etc., and report on the procedural matters'.[5]

On 29 August 1947, Ambedkar submitted the report of the committee which, according to him, made five recommendations:

[3] Ibid., vol. V, p. 10.
[4] Ibid., pp. 15-20.
[5] Ibid., pp. 29, 57.

Its first recommendation is that it is open to the Constituent Assembly to function as legislature and that it should function as such; (2) that while functioning as legislature it should adopt the rules of the Legislative Assembly as far as possible with necessary amendments; (3) the necessary amendments should be made under the orders of the President of the Constituent Assembly; (4) the work of the Constituent Assembly as a constitution-making body and as an ordinary legislature should be separated and should be considered in separate sessions to be held on separate days; (5) the power of prorogation would vest in the President and not in the Governor-General as found in the Adaptation of the Government of India Act.[6]

In the debate that followed, Ambedkar, speaking in reply to a question by Lakshmikanta Moitra, assured the House that 'we have got the power to change the adaptations. The Government of India Act with its adaptations is not entirely binding on us in the sense that a change is not beyond our purview. If the House, on a reconsideration of the matter, finds that certain adaptations ought to be changed, it would be possible to undertake that provision.' He also said that there was a theoretical possibility of conflict between the President of the Constituent Assembly and the Speaker of the legislature but that could be avoided in practice. The Constituent Assembly would work in the dual capacity so long as constitution-making was not completed.[7]

The business of the Assembly as a constitution-making body should be clearly distinguished from its normal business as the dominion legislature, and different days or separate sittings on the same day should be set apart for the two kinds of business. Suitable provision should be made in the rules of the Constituent Assembly for the elections of an officer to be designated the Speaker to preside over the deliberations of the Assembly, when functioning as the dominion legislature. The power of summoning the Assembly for functioning as the dominion legislature and proroguing it should vest in the president. Ministers of the dominion government, who were not members of the Constituent Assembly, should have the right to attend and participate in its work of constitution-making though, until they became members of the Constituent Assembly, they should not have the right to vote. Necessary modifications, adaptations and additions should be made by the President of the Constituent Assembly to the rules and standing orders of the Indian Legislative Assembly to bring them into accord with the relevant provisions of the Government

[6] Ibid., p. 310, Report in pp. 289-91.

[7] Ibid., pp. 329-30.

of India Act, 1935, adapted under the Indian Independence Act, 1947.[8]

In view of the report, therefore, the House passed a resolution moved by K.M. Munshi to the effect that the Assembly's functions would be:

(a) to continue and complete the work of constitution-making which commenced from 9 December 1946, and

(b) to function as the dominion legislature until a legislature under the new constitution came into being.

These changes were brought into effect by the Governor-General through the India Provisional Constitution (Second Amendment) Order, passed on 6 October 1947.

Membership Increased

During the sixth session of the Constituent Assembly, representation from West Bengal and East Punjab was increased. On 27 January 1948, Ananthasayanam Ayyangar proposed that, as West Bengal's representation had been fixed by the 3 June statement at 19 (15 general and 4 Muslim), on the basis of a border that afterwards was changed by the Boundary Commission, she became entitled to a representation of 21 members (16 general and 5 Muslim). The House therefore decided upon the election of 2 more members (1 general and 1 Muslim) from West Bengal. In spite of its assumed competence to do so, the House did not drop the principle of communal elections.[9]

On the same day Giani Gurumukh Singh proposed that, as East Punjab's representation to the Constituent Assembly had been fixed by the 3 June declaration at 6 general, 4 Muslim and 2 Sikh seats, on the basis of a boundary that afterwards was revised by the Boundary Commission and as the population composition of East Punjab was changed due to the two-way migrations of people, she became entitled to a representation of 8 general and 4 Sikh members.[10]

The President added on this point that the case of East Punjab had come up before the Steering Committee which appointed a subcommittee to examine the question. The subcommittee suggested this increase of the general and Sikh representation though it did not suggest the reduction of the Muslim representation as the four existing Muslim members of the

[8] Ibid., p. 331. Munshi indeed made it clear that the power to summon the Assembly for constitution-making also would belong to the president.

[9] Ibid., vol. VI, p. 3.

[10] Ibid., p. 5.

TABLE 7.1: FINAL POSITION OF PARTIES IN POST-PARTITION (FORMER) BRITISH INDIA

Section A		
Congress	164	(general 163, Muslim 1)
Muslim League	19	(Muslim)
Independent	7	(general)
Total	190	
Section B (East Punjab)		
Congress	10	(general 8, Sikh 2)
Muslim League	0	(4 Muslim seats vacant)
Akali	2	(Sikh)
Total	12	
Section C (Assam and West Bengal)		
Congress	23	(general 22, Muslim 1)
Muslim League	6	(Muslim)
Total	29	
Consolidated Party Position in the three sections		
Congress	197	(general 192, Muslim 5)
Muslim League	25	(Muslim)
Akali	2	(Sikh)
Independent	7	(general)

Constituent Assembly from Punjab had long been keeping absent.[11] The House passed this resolution too. Thus, representation from the Indian mainland to the Constituent Assembly rose to 235. All newcomers, save one Sikh, belonged to Congress. The four Muslim seats from East Punjab were never filled up.

Jennings on the Status of the Assembly

Some interesting legal controversies have been raised by Jennings in respect of the status of the Constituent Assembly. The Assembly started functioning from 15 August 1947 on what he calls two traditional 'interpretations' of the Indian Independence Act:

(1) The Constituent Assembly was in reality functioning in two parts—the constituent, for 'making provisions as to the Constitution' and the legislative as per the Government of India Act as adapted for

[11] Ibid., p. 9.

India, as a dominion legislature. 'In other words, a distinction was drawn out, not as section 8 specified, between the "constituent powers" and "legislative powers" but between the constituent body and the legislative body'.

(2) The constituent part was a sovereign body. 'So far as is known, nobody explained whether this sovereignty was obtained because it was exercising the powers of the legislature of the dominion under section 6 or it derived its powers independently from section 8'. India, thus, proceeded on the assumption that the Governor-General's assent was necessary for the acts of the dominion legislature and not of the Constituent Assembly. Sovereignty of the Constituent Assembly, he sarcastically notes, 'was an act of faith and indeed hope, with the Congress' which had the deepseated 'tradition of *Albion perfide*'.[12] Jennings concludes,

> Politically, no doubt, it was admitted that the special task of the Constituent Assembly was to frame a constitution, but the act did not say so. For the purpose of making provision as to the constitution, the Constituent Assembly had the powers of the legislature of the dominion. It might not frame a constitution at all. Had the Government of India Act been suitably amended either by Lord Mountbatten under section 9 or by the Constituent Assembly in the exercise of its powers under section 6, the Assembly might have been dissolved and the Government of India Act, as adapted, become the permanent constitution of the dominion. . . . The greatest difficulty was, however, in finding out where the 'sovereignty' of the Constituent Assembly came from. If it was because it was for the time being endowed with the powers of the legislature of the dominion, the rest of the argument did not seem to follow.[13]

It may be noted that of the two dichotomies pointed out by Jennings, though the first may genuinely appear to be a lawyer's puzzle, it does not warrant the conclusion that 'the Constituent Assembly might not frame a constitution at all'. As a matter of fact, the Independence Act did neither identify the dominion legislature (section 6 [1]) with the Constituent Assembly (section 8 [1]) nor set up a dominion legislature apart from the body that had been functioning as the Constituent Assembly since the introduction of the Cabinet Mission Plan. It was only be the India (Provisional Constitution) Order that the powers of the dominion legislature were made exercisable by the Constituent Assembly. When Henderson, the Under-Secretary for India, replied in the British Parliament

[12] W. Ivor Jennings, *The Constitutional Problems in Pakistan*, p. 24.
[13] Ibid., p. 33.

to the debate on the second reading of the Indian Independence Bill, he categorically stressed this perspective:

It has been necessary to provide for legislatures for both India and Pakistan. These legislatures, besides having legislative powers, must also have constituent powers. They must also have a dual purpose of performing the ordinary functioning of a parliament and of making constitutions.[14]

It is possible therefore to argue that the Constituent Assembly came first, with the powers of the dominion legislature, 'for the purpose of making provision as to the constitution of the dominion' (section 8[1]). The power 'to make laws' for the dominion (section 6[1]) was vested in it later. The Constituent Assembly was certainly not a superfluity in the Independence Act. In the Constituent Assembly of India, further, actually there was no assumption of separate entities of the two parts of the Constituent Assembly. After 29 August 1947, when Munshi's resolution on the functions of the Assembly was adopted, 'the legislative functions' were actually discharged by the 'legislative department' of the Constituent Assembly, which was summoned and prorogued by the President of the Constituent Assembly, the overall head of the dominion legislature. Mountbatten acquiesced in it, as he surrendered the powers of summoning and proroguing the Assembly by the India Provisional Constitution (Second Amendment) Order.

An Autonomous Constitution

A criticism that is more relevant is that, whereas neither the India Independence Act nor the traditional British dominion practice made any distinction between 'constitutional' and 'ordinary legislative powers of the Assembly, the Indian Constituent Assembly created this distinction by submitting only the ordinary legislations for the Governor-General's assent.

The Congress intention, from the very beginning, was understandably, for framing a sovereign constitution. After 15 August 1947, the Assembly could possibly proclaim India as a sovereign democracy and then proceed to make a constitution. But it chose to 'assume power for the governance

[14] *The Statesman*, 12 July 1947.

That the British government wanted to transfer power to the Constituent Assembly and not to a provisional government may also be inferred from the Cabinet Mission's desire for a treaty with the Constituent Assembly (vide its statement, paragraph 22), though the 3 June 1947 statement was not specific on the point.

of India', without defining the nature of the act, and endorsed 'the recommendation', without mentioning the recommending authority, of Mountbatten's continued Governor-Generalship. In practice the executive Government of India, until 26 January 1950, was very much in the dominion pattern and constitution-making a sovereign act. On 17 October 1949, A.K. Ayyar, during a debate on the Preamble, told the Constituent Assembly:

I may also point out we were particularly anxious that the constitution which we are making or passing must not be traceable to section 7 or 8 of the Independence Act. We took the view that there is no necessity of Governor-General's assent being required for the new constitution.[15]

K.C. Wheare finds in this tendency a desire for constitutional 'autarchy' or 'autochthony'.[16] Referring to India he writes:

In the first place it would be urged that if the Constituent Assembly had passed the constitution and the Governor-General had assented to it, then undoubtedly the constitution would have had the force of law, and would have derived this force of law from the powers conferred by the Indian Independence Act of 1947. This certainly did not happen. Though the Constituent Assembly itself passed the constitution, the Governor-General did not assent to it. He was not asked to assent to it. In the view of the members of the Constituent Assembly, his assent was not required to complete the enacting process.[17]

Evidently, the British government had no objection to India making herself a republic, as is seen from the decision of the Commonwealth Prime Ministers' Conference of 1949. But the British government certainly expected India to maintain what may be called a form of commonwealth legality by submitting the constitution for British Parliament's approval. This Commonwealth legality had first been threatened by Ireland in 1922, when the Third Dail Eireann (a part of the members of the British Parliament) sat at Dublin to frame the Irish Constitution which derived its authority from 'god' and 'the people'. The British government was able to save the Commonwealth legality by recognizing the Dail Eireann as merely a part of Parliament at Westminster and passing the Constitution of the Irish Free State Act that conferred dominion status (informally, though, for the concept had not yet fully developed) on the Irish Free State. The Irish, however, finally disposed of the Commonwealth legality

[15] *CAD*, vol. X, p. 417.

[16] K.C. Wheare, *The Constitutional Structure of the Commonwealth*, pp. 8-9.

[17] Ibid., p. 96.

in 1937, when they framed a new constitution through the Dail and ratified it through a referendum. The Irish left the Commonwealth in 1948, but the 'break' in their constitutional history had taken place in 1937.[18]

This break indeed took place in India too, developing from 15 August 1947, when the Constituent Assembly 'assumed power', and becoming real only after Mountbatten left India and the President of the Constituent Assembly authenticated six 'constituent legislations'. A big step was the authentication of the Constitution on 26 November 1949.[19]

An Unreal Dichotomy

The last and the most important act of the drama was played on 26 January 1950, when the Governor-General gave the following proclamation in the Durbar Hall of the Government House at 10.30 a.m.:

> Whereas the people of India, having solemnly resolved to constitute India into a sovereign democratic republic, adopted, enacted and gave to themselves on the twenty-sixth day of November 1949, in their Constituent Assembly, the Constitution of India;
>
> And whereas it has been declared by the said Constitution that India, that is, Bharat, shall be a union of states comprising within the union the territories which were hitherto the governors' provinces, the Indian states and the chief commissioners' provinces;
>
> And whereas this, the twenty-sixth day of January 1950, has been fixed for the commencement of the said Constitution;
>
> Now, therefore, it is hereby proclaimed that on and from this, the twenty-sixth day of January 1950, India, that is, Bharat, shall be a sovereign democratic republic, and the union and its component units, the states, shall exercise all powers and functions of government and administration in accordance with the provisions of the said Constitution.[20]

The simple fact is that the dichotomy assumed by Jennings and Wheare did not exist. The formal assent of the Governor-General to the Constitution was indeed not taken, but the point is merely theoretical, for the Governor-General not only acquiesced in the new Constitution, he was also instrumental in enforcing it.[21] Certainly, the Indian Independent Act did not

[18] Ibid., p. 94.

[19] *The Gazette of India Extraordinary*, 26 November 1949.

[20] Ibid., 26 January 1950.

[21] The Governor-General did not only issue the proclamation, he used all the powers of the 1935 Act and the new Constitution, according to Article 392 (3), to issue the various mergers and other orders, including The Constitution (Removal of Difficulties) Order, No. 1, on 7 January 1950.

require the new Constitution, which superseded the Constitution of 1935—an act of the British Parliament—to be submitted for ratification to the same body, in spite of the Cabinet Mission's intentions. In no way can the 'break' in Commonwealth legality be regarded as revolutionary. If at all, the Constituent Assembly of India made what Dhirendra Nath Sen had called a 'revolution by consent'.[22]

[22] Dhirendra Nath Sen, *Revolution by Consent*?

PART II

CHAPTER 8

Mind and Procedure of the Constituent Assembly

Did the Constituent Assembly of India have a mind of its own?

Charles A. Beard, in analysing the legislative intentions of the fathers of the US Constitution took pains to examine the property background of every delegate of the Philadelphia Constitutional Convention as well as the general economic situation in 1787.[1] While some of Beard's conclusions have proved controversial, his methodology has proved to be of lasting value.[2] Property, as will be amply seen, played a significant role in the making of the Indian Constitution also. In fact, writing in the early fifties, A. Appadorai mentioned 'the influence of property upon government' as one of the subjects requiring priority in 'investigation by competent political scientists in India'.[3]

Yet, Beard himself, in the introduction to the 1935 edition of his book, admits: 'Seldom, if ever, is there total class-solidarity in historical conflicts.'[4] Warning against sweeping generalizations about the States-General of France (1789), Gaetano Salvemini also wrote in his work on the French revolution:

> The trouble begins when we come to regard the revolution as an historical force in itself. For instance, it is a fact that both constituent and legislative assemblies and the Convention were largely composed of lawyers, and that very few of the industrialists, tradesmen, bankers and other men of affairs who really formed the bourgeoisie were elected to it. Such citizens as these have their own business to attend to and find little time for politics; lawyers, on the other hand, besides being facile speakers—a great asset in public life—find in politics an excellent way of making a name for themselves and of increasing the scope and gains of their callings. For this reason the electors of the revolutionary period usually had a

[1] Charles A. Beard, *An Economic Interpretation of the Constitution of the United States.*

[2] T.I. Cook in *Contemporary Political Science: UNESCO Survey of Methods, Research and Teaching*, p. 79.

[3] Appadorai in ibid., p. 46.

[4] Beard, op. cit., p. 15.

choice of various candidates belonging to the legal profession, but were rarely free to choose between a lawyer and, for instance, an engineer.

This circumstance, though not unusual in modern representative assemblies, was of considerable importance during the French revolution; for it meant that the policy of these bodies, in emanating not from the bourgeoisie proper, but from its legal experts, was not always in conformity with the interests of the economically dominant class: being, in fact, an outcome of moral and intellectual habits of mind different from and even at times opposed to theirs. This explains certain ultrademocratic measures of the constituent and legislative assemblies that would never have been passed by a chamber of bankers and industrialists.[5]

It is on the application of the method, therefore, that the controversy rests. Besides, in the case of India, there is the almost insurmountable difficulty of inadequacy of data. An attempt to prepare a Who's Who of the Constituent Assembly members was unsuccessful.[6] Besides, no authentic account has been left of the economic background of individual members. Certain basic facts about the Assembly, however, are sufficiently revealing.

Composition of the Constituent Assembly

The Constituent Assembly was partly elected by the popularly elected provincial legislatures and partly filled by representatives of the states, about one-half of whom were the rulers' nominees and the rest elected through a greatly restricted franchise. Everywhere popular franchise was limited by property qualification.

The most important difference between the Indian Constituent Assembly and the Philadelphia Convention (1787) or the States-General of France (1789) is that the America as well as the French politics towards the end of the eighteenth century was articulate only in a general way, while in India a strong political factor had emerged by the time the Constituent Assembly was convened. That was the party system. It is in and through the political parties that the socio-economic forces in India had crystallized. A proper characterization of the Indian Constituent Assembly, therefore, can be made not by any mechanical inquiry of the individual property background of the members, but by an objective study

[5] Gaetano Salvemini, *The French Revolution*, p. 327.

[6] Even an enlightened member like M.R. Jayakar laughed at the idea of a Who's Who of the Constituent Assembly. Law Ministry File, CA/14/Cons.46, Miscellaneous Correspondences, Serial No. 1.

of the concerted growth of social, economic and political forces in this country.

Membership of the Constituent Assembly fell into four groups:

(1) The representative of the Congress;
(2) A few independent members elected with Congress tickets;
(3) Independents representing non-Congress provincial legislators (including the representatives of the small parties);
(4) The Muslim League who had chosen to stay in India.

As already noted, among the British Indian representatives, the Congress enjoyed an overwhelming majority. To them were added the elected representatives of the states, sponsored by the States People's Conference, a sister organization of the Congress. This fact gave the Constituent Assembly a harmony which was unique in nature.

Predominance of Congress

At the conclusion of the debate on the Draft Constitution, B.R. Ambedkar, himself a non-Congressite, openly recognized the role of the Congress party, which eminently dominated the Constituent Assembly:

> The task of the Constituent Assembly would have been a very difficult one if this Constituent Assembly had been merely a motley crowd, a tessellated pavement without cement, a black-stone here and a white-stone there in which each member or each group was a law unto itself. There would have been nothing but chaos. This possibility of chaos was reduced to nil by the existence of the Congress Party inside the Assembly which brought into its proceedings a sense of order and discipline. It is because of the discipline of the Congress Party that the Drafting Committee was able to pilot the Constitution in the Assembly with the sure knowledge as to the fate of each article and each amendment. The Congress Party is, therefore, entitled to all the credit, for the smooth sailing of the Draft Constitution in the Assembly.[7]

However, the Congress leadership was eager to get the cooperation of the other parties in the framing of the Constitution and working of the government. So it offered tickets to many non-Congressites. Several other parties had powerful lobbies in the Congress. Recruitment to the cabinet was partly made from outside the Congress periphery. Shanmukham Chetty, John Matthai, Syama Prasad Mookerjee and B.R. Ambedkar were such outsiders. Ambedkar joined the cabinet as the law minister in the

[7] *CAD*, vol. XI, p. 974.

midst of constitution-making and was made the Chairman of the Drafting Committee. He made substantial personal contribution to the framing of the Constitution. Other political opinions were respectfully heard, though the Constitution was framed mainly on the basis of the political ideals of the Congress.

Munshi claims that among the members of the Constituent Assembly there was no difference in the general outlook: 'There were no clear-cut opposition parties.' 'The composition of the Constituent Assembly as also the atmosphere in which the problems were discussed lent themselves to a broad anti-authoritarian outlook.'[8] It is, however, necessary to qualify the statement. As the trend of discussions amply shows, there was a wide desire to accommodate opposite viewpoints; there was, in any case, hardly any concession on fundamentals. There was practically no concession to the League and Akali demands of a loose federation or the socialist's demand for declaring India a 'socialist republic'. On some controversial issues the leadership had indeed to resort to 'whips'.[9]

Leadership of the Assembly

The Congress achieved substantial discipline largely through its militant past and partly because the bulk of its followers in the Constituent Assmebly chose just to follow the leadership in most cases of complication in the constitution-making task. Of the leadership there were two clear grades. Leaders like Nehru and Patel (the latter taking more minute interest in the job than the former), were at the apex of the whole pyramid. Granville Austin actually calls the Nehru-Patel-Azad-Prasad Leadership 'the oligarchy'. The term may appear controversial to many, but of the strength of this leadership there need not be any doubt. Next to them, the leadership grade was constituted by the cabinet ministers, important persons like K.M. Munshi, Pattabhi Sitaramayya, J.B. Kripalani, C. Rajagopalachari (until he became Governor-General) and a number of provincial prime ministers. On the fringe of this leadership was still another group of members like Thakurdas Bhargava, A.V. Thakkar, Sri Prakasa, B.M. Gupte and Brajeswar Prasad.

Outside the party's pale the Constituent Assembly contained a number

[8] Madan Gopal Gupta (ed.), *Some Aspects of the Indian Constitution*, pp. 72-3.

[9] K.V. Rao, in his *Parliamentary Democracy in India*, alleges that the use of whips on the Constituent Assembly members by the Congress Party was frequent, whereas Munshi writes that the use of whips was rare. Granville Austin's assessment lies midway between the two. See his *The Indian Constitution: Cornerstone of a Nation*, pp. 315-16.

of brilliant minds, some of them lawyers of exceptional ability. In this group, 'the oligarchy' consisted of Alladi Krishnaswami Ayyar, N. Gopalaswami Ayyangar and B.R. Ambedkar. People like K.M. Panikkar, S.P. Mookerjee and, in the early days, B.L. Mitter, constituted the second grade of this leadership. Standing midway between the two groups were those, whose association with the party was not long, but whose sheer brilliance made them respectfully heard. Such were the people like K. Santhanam and T.T. Krishnamachari. The latter, a strong critic of certain aspects of the Draft Constitution, was actually include into the Drafting Committee in late 1948.

Composition and Role of the Opposition

Opposition there certainly was, vocal but ineffective. The most important single reason of their ineffectiveness was indeed the lack of a common perspective. The opposition consisted of the Muslim Leaguers, the Akalis, the two or three Congress Socialists and the two Forward Blocists.[10]

The Constituent Assembly, of course, did not recognize party divisions and an extraordinary attitude of the Constituent Assembly was revealed by the election of Saadulla to the Drafting Committee though no Sikh was elected to it. 'Officially' the Congress Socialists and the Forward Bloc had no representation in the Constituent Assembly. In the first two sessions Somnath Lahiri was the only communist member. Some of the liberals were so closely connected with constitution-making that they could hardly be counted in the opposition. A formidable opposition, in the first two sessions was found in the person of M.R. Jayakar.

There were, of course, many 'critics' within the party. They ranged from a rabid Hindi-supporter to a secular socialist,[11] from a strong advocate of presidential system to a convinced parliamentarian, from a protagonist of a highly centralized state to a protagonist of loose federalism. The always-in-the-opposition persons were hardly heard. On several occasions, however, the leadership wanted to understand the critics or even accommodate them especially when questions of minor adjustment were involved. A few important names in this group were H.N. Kunzru, K.T. Shah and Shibbanlal Saksena.

[10] Besides Damodar Swarup Seth and Phulan Prasad Verma, Sarangadhar Das, representing the Orissa states group, possibly was a Congress Socialist.

H.V. Kamath and Viswambhar Dayal Tripathy belonged to the Forward Bloc.

[11] Twelve members of the latter group, including K.T. Shah, on 26 August 1949, decided to set up a Social Democratic Party to work in the Constituent Assembly (Legislative Wing) from 21 November 1949. *The Statesman*, Calcutta, 27 August 1949.

The fundamental opposition approach was twofold. It was mainly from the non-Congress opposition that the demand for greater provincial autonomy and statutory provision for minority rights was advanced. The Muslim League and the Akali party were in the vanguard of this move. It was mainly from the Congress opposition that the demand for a greater socialistic bias of the constitution was raised. On none of these demands is there any evidence of substantial concession. The second demand, however, crossed the first. There were ardent supporters of socialism in the Congress (equally among the secular and parochial elements) as well as in the League. On details, differences within the party, even involving leading persons, were occasionally exposed. But such differences were often solved through discussion and persuasion, and, sometimes by the use of 'whip'.

K.V. Rao's contention that the Constitution contains no trace of any contribution by 'others'[12] is certainly rash. In fact, for any general observer, it may be difficult to identify an exclusively Congress ideal about the Constitution. The Nehru Report was an 'all-party' document and had several marks of compromise. The share of the Congress in the Sapru Report was insignificant. The Congress, of its own, never formulated a model constitution for the country. On the other hand, 11 out of about 30 members of the Sapru Committee had membership of the Constituent Assembly for the full or parts of the period of its duration, and a few others were directly or indirectly associated with the work of the Assembly.[13] Tej Bahadur Sapru, himself, was a chief adviser to the Assembly leaders from his sick-bed in Allahabad. N.G. Ayyangar became a keyman of the whole job.

Ideologies

But the Congress had its ideas about the Constitution in common with many other sections of Indian opinion. The most fundamental of them were (1) a parliamentary government, (2) a politically centralized but

[12] K.V. Rao, *Parliamentary Democracy in India*, p. 21.

[13] The following members of the Constituent Assembly had been associated with the Sapru Committee:

(i) M.R. Jayakar, (ii) Homi Modi, (iii) P.K. Sen, (iv) N. Gopalaswami Ayyangar (in the General Committee), (v) John Matthai, (vi) S. Radhakrishnan, (vii) F.R. Anthony, (viii) Tekchand, (ix) Sachchidanand, (x) K. Santhanam (for some time, as Joint Secretary), and (xi) Harnam Singh.

Some other members of the Sapru Committee served in the Committees of the Assembly, e.g. N.R. Sarkar (Financial Experts Committee).

culturally diversified federal state, and (3) a dynamic social order, whose connotation varied from man to man. Because of its organizational peculiarity, again, the Congress could not have an agreed and precise definition of these ideas from its own point of view.

Within the Assembly two broad groups could be identified. The liberal idealistic leadership, mainly belonging to the party organization, was balanced by the weighty, conservative but constructive leadership which had had the experience of administration since 1937, consisting of provincial premiers (who were frequently consulted, though all of them were not members of the Constituent Assembly) and administrators. In the top leadership Nehru emotionally belonged to the former, Patel to the latter. The highly competent section of bureaucracy, composed of persons like B.N. Rau, S.N. Mukherjee and H.V.R. Iyenger who were associated with constitution-making, were close to the latter group.

The differences were less on purpose than on technique, which had indeed to be determined by each group's experience and outlook. this statement was also true about the wide national arena of politics, where the only incoherent forces of rather insignificant dimension were the Muslim League and the Communist Party. The Muslim League was present in the Assembly because of separate electorates; there was no communist after July 1947 in the Assembly.

There was another group, the lawyers, whose role was more important than identifiable. There were lawyers on both the wings. Nehru, Patel, Rajendra Prasad, Munshi were all lawyers. B.N. Rau was a master of law. At the same time, in between the 'political' and 'administrative' camps, a group of lawyers, like A.K. Ayyar, N.G. Ayyangar, B.R.. Ambedkar, B.L. Mitter (for some time), played vital roles in evolving formulas acceptable to both.

The approach is unavoidably leadership-oriented. For, if the constitutional picture of India was vague to the leadership, the cadre was still less aware of the dimensions of its task. Though the average intellectual level of the Assembly members was fairly high, the drafting of the Indian Constitution turned out to be one of the most difficult legal exercises of the time. The majority of Constituent Assembly members, as a result, chose to delegate the responsibility of detailed thinking to the leadership.

On 1 July 1946, B.N. Rau was appointed Constitutional Adviser. On 11 July 1946, Nehru, as the Congress president, appointed, according to the Working Committee's decision an expert committee to prepare the material and draft proposals for the Constituent Assembly. The committee consisted of Nehru, Asaf Ali, K.M. Munshi, K.T. Shah, K. Santhanam

(Assembly members), Humayun Kabir and D.R. Gadgil. It had a few sittings at the early stage (July and August 1946) and scrutinized the Objectives Resolution as framed by Nehru. Later, the initiative passed on to the Constitutional Adviser, B.N. Rau, who supplied the basic material to almost all the committees of the Constituent Assembly.

Foundations of the Constitution

In the reports of the various committees that were to serve as the foundation of the Draft Constitution of India after appropriate discussion and approval in the Assembly, the most outstanding influence that is perceptible is that of the Government of India Act, 1935, with its 321 sections and 10 schedules.

In the volume on 'Constitutional Precedents' prepared by Rau, however, there were extensive comparative studies of the foreign constitutions—though, here again, with an emphasis on the dominion constitutions. (The second series of 'The Constitutional Precedents' gives the salient features of the Statute of Westminster, the Constitutions of Canada, Australia, South Africa, the Eire, the Leeward Islands, the USA, the USSR, Switzerland, Danzig, Germany [1919], the Chinese Republic and Japan.) Yet, at least in some respects, the new Indian Constitution was going to be different from the Act of 1935. For instance, the Act of 1935 did not contain any bill of rights, whereas the Cabinet Mission scheme itself provided for one. The protection of minority and tribal interests, a cornerstone of the Cabinet Mission scheme, had been left, by the 1935 Act, under the special responsibilities of the Governor-General and the governors. India having decided to adopt a republican government, there was need to make new arrangements for such things as well as to redefine the positions of the chief executives at the centre and the units along with their discretionary powers. There was also the Congress commitment to linguistic re-organization of provinces.

A major issue before the fathers of the Indian Constitution was the establishment of social justice between the various religious and social groups to which the Indian leaders had already been committed. The most complicated situation existed within the Hindu religious institutions, the solution of which had long been overdue. Social problems within the Muslim community were also grave, but due to several political reasons the fathers of the Indian Constitution could not attack them with the vigour with which they did the Hindu social problems. In fact, the issue of minority rights, quite paradoxically, stood between the government and social reforms of the minority communities.

But the greatest problem before the Constituent Assembly in the post-partition era was economic in nature. An industrial revolution had already set in, producing a consequential class contradiction. Largely fed by the financial assistance of the propertied classes, the Congress had to meet the demands of private property, paying at the same time equal attention to the amelioration of the condition of the poor workers and peasants, which in this underdeveloped economy had already become unbearable.

On 9 March 1947, Rau prepared a note for Prasad and Nehru in which he considered the task of constitution-making after 20 February as 'formidable'. His proposal to circulate a questionnaire among the legislators was approved.[14] On 17 March 1947, he issued an elaborate questionnaire to all the members of the central and provincial legislatures seeking their views. Only a few replies were received. The same questionnaire was issued on 5 May 1947 to the members of the union and provincial constitution committees of the Assembly. The response was equally cool.[15] The members of the committees chose to take the lead from the rather 'independent' memoranda prepared by Rau.

THE COMMITTEES OF THE ASSEMBLY

The Constituent Assembly appointed a number of committees on procedural and substantive matters. Following is the list of the Committees of the Constituent Assembly:

A. *On Procedural Affairs*: (1) Rules of Procedure Committee, (2) Finance and Staff Committee, (3) Credentials Committee, (4) House Committee, (5) Press Gallery Committee, (6) Steering Committee, (7) Order of Business Committee, (8) Hindi Translation Committee, (9) Urdu Translation Committee, and (10) Committee to examine the effects of the Indian Independence Act.

B. *On Substantive Affairs*: (1) Committee for Negotiating with the States, (2) Advisory Committee (which in turn set up 5 important sub-committees on minority rights, fundamental rights, North-East Frontier Tribal and Excluded Areas [Assam], North-West Frontier Tribal and Excluded Areas, and Excluded and Partially Excluded Areas [outside Assam]), (3) Union Powers Committee, (4) Union Constitution Committee, (5) Provincial Constitution Committee, (6) Drafting Committee, (7) Expert Committee on Financial Provisions, (8) Committee on the Chief Commissioners'

[14] Rau's note on 9 March 1947, Law Ministry File, CA/18/Cons.47.

[15] Union and Provincial Constitution Committees' Files.

Provinces, (9) Special Committee appointed by the President to examine the Draft Constitution, (10) Ad-hoc Committee on National Flag, (11) Ad-hoc Committee on the Supreme Court, and (12) Commission on Linguistic Provinces.

C. *Subcommittees and Ad-hoc Committees*, set up by some of the above-mentioned committees of the House.

D. *Committee of the Whole House*, to discuss the salaries, etc., of the officials of the Constituent Assembly—on 22 and 24 January 1947. (Practically, the House adjourned on Saturday, 22 January 1947, in the committee stage. On 24 January, therefore, it reassembled as a committee, and then went into open session.) These meetings, like the meetings of the other committees were conducted in camera.

Most of these committees were, in fact, working as standing committees. The Drafting Committee functioned till the end of constitution-making. Some of the other committees used to meet even long after the submission of their reports. For instance, the Advisory Committee was dissolved only on 11 May 1949, after taking some vital decisions about reservation of seats in the legislature for communal minorities.

Of the major committees, the Committee for Negotiation with the States' Rulers (for securing the participation of the states in the Assembly) was appointed on 2 December 1947. The Advisory Committee on Fundamental Rights. Minorities and Tribal and Excluded Areas was set up by the Constituent Assembly on 24 January 1947. The Advisory Committee was presided over by Vallabhbhai Patel and was split up into five subcommittees with limited power of cooption from outside the Assembly. These subcommittees, on which quite a few outsiders worked, submitted their reports through the Advisory Committee. The subcommittee on the NWF Tribal Areas, indeed, became redundant after partition. On 25 January 1947, the Assembly elected the Union Powers Committee. The President of the Constituent Assembly was authorized, on 30 April 1947, to nominate two committees to report on a model union constitution and a model provincial constitution. The Constituent Assembly also directed that in certain matters the provisions contained in the Government of India Act, 1935, would be followed.

The Committee on Union Powers made its first report to the Constituent Assembly on 28 April 1947. The Committee on the Model Provincial Constitution headed by Patel and the Committee on the Model Union Constitution headed by Nehru reported on 15 and 21 July 1947 respectively. After the submission of all these reports the Constituent Assembly, on 29 August 1947, appointed a committee 'to scrutinise the draft of the text of the Constitution of India prepared by the Constitutional Adviser giving effect to the decisions taken already in the Assembly and including all matters which are ancillary thereto or which have to be provided in such "Constitution", and to submit to the Assembly for consideration the Draft Constitution as revised by the committee'.[16]

The fifth session of the Constituent Assembly was over on 30 August 1947. On the same day the president was authorized to appoint a committee to recommend constitutional changes in the centrally-administered areas. The Assembly next met on 27 January 1948, for a day, only to dispose of certain formal matters.

Drafting of the Constitution

The members of the Drafting Committee were:

(1) Alladi Krishnaswami Ayyar, an astute lawyer of liberal views from Madras who came with a Congress ticket and later made outstanding contribution to constitution-making.
(2) N. Gopalaswami Ayyangar, another brilliant legal brain from Madras, with a liberal outlook, a Congress ticket and a civilian background.
(3) B.R. Ambedkar, the leader of the Scheduled Castes Federation, also an outstanding lawyer, who shed several ideological differences with the Congress. On the eve of independence, he joined the government as the law minister, without leaving his party.
(4) K.M. Munshi, a Congress leader, occasionally working in the states' people's movement. Also a lawyer.
(5) Saiyad Mohammad Saadulla, a League supporter from Assam of rather liberal outlook and a profound legalist.
(6) B.L. Mitter, an ex-law member of the Government of India and the Dewan of Baroda, who made remarkable contribution to the integration of the states with India.
(7) D.P. Khaitan, an industrialist from West Bengal who had come with a Congress ticket.

The most remarkable feature of the composition of the Drafting Committee is that it consisted mainly of lawyers and not politicians. The only member of the committee who was a part and parcel of the Congress

[16] *CAD*, vol. V, p. 335.

organization was K.M. Munshi. As a matter of fact, by the time the Drafting Committee was set up, the broad ideas about the constitution had already largely crystallized. The political decisions had been taken; only giving them legal shape remained.

In the preliminary meeting of the Drafting Committee on 30 August 1947, Ambedkar was unanimously elected to the chair. After attending the first sitting of the Drafting Committee in August 1947, B.L. Mitter resigned from the Constituent Assembly on 13 October 1947 and was replaced in the Drafting Committee by N. Madhava Rau, another lawyer and official representative of the Eastern States Group (on 5 December 1947). (Later D.P. Khaitan died and was replaced by T.T. Krishnamachari on 5 February 1949.)

In the first meeting of the Drafting Committee on 30 August 1947, the Constitutional Adviser was asked to circulate the draft that he had prepared among the members of the Drafting Committee by 23 September. The scrutiny was to be completed by 24 October. However, Rau submitted the draft (consisting of 243 articles and 13 schedules) in early October and the Drafting Committee met on 27 October 1947, when Rau had left on his tour of the USA, Canada, the UK and Eire.[17] From abroad Rau, after taking the opinions of important jurists, President Truman and President Eamon de Valera, suggested certain amendments to his own draft.[18] He joined the Drafting Committee on 6 December 1947.

The meetings of the Drafting Committee were businesslike and continued for over 40 days from 27 October 1947. No special invitee, except the officials in attendance, was present. Shortly after B.L. Mitter's replacement, D.P. Khaitan died and was not replaced in this period. So the maximum figure of attendance in the Drafting Committee meetings was six and the average—four. At least six meetings were held with two members and four meetings with three members only.[19] Ambedkar, in his preface to the Draft, admitted that 'not all the members were present at all the meetings of the committee. But at every meeting at which any decision was taken the necessary quorum was present and the decisions were either unanimous or by a majority of those present.'[20] Ambedkar said that the

[17] An interesting sidelight is thrown by the report of Ambedkar in the first meeting of the Drafting Committee to consider Rau's draft that he had protested in writing to the Assembly chairman against the publication of Rau's draft.

[18] Shiva Rao, *Select Documents*, vol. II, pp. 217-34.

[19] Ibid., pp. 307-506; also see T.T. Krishnamachari's criticism of the Draft, *CAD*, vol. VII, pp. 231-2.

[20] Ambedkar's forwarding letter to the Assembly President, *Draft Constitution*, February 1948, p. iii.

Drafting Committee had generally followed the recommendations of the committees which had already submitted various reports. Reports of two committees (the Financial Experts Committees appointed by the president to report on the financial implications of the reports of the Committee on Model Union Constitution and the Committee on Centrally Administered Areas) which had not been discussed by the Assembly had not been fully adhered to.[21] Besides, the Drafting Committee made certain small but significant changes.

Reconsideration of the Draft

The Draft Constitution of India was published in February 1948 for circulation and public discussion. At this stage, hundreds of comments, criticisms and suggestions for amendment poured in not only from the Constituent Assembly members, but also from several individuals and public bodies. At the suggestion of the President of the Constituent Assembly, the Drafting Committee met on 23, 24 and 27 March 1948, and proposed some amendments. Subsequently, a Special Committee, consisting mostly of members of the Union and Provincial Constitution Committees and the Union Powers Committee under the presidentship of Nehru was formed by the President of the Assembly to go through the suggestion and comments along with the recommendations of the Drafting Committee. The most significant absentee was Patel. The Special Committee met on 10 and 11 April 1948, and made certain recommendations. Comments and suggestions were, however, still coming. Such comments, etc., included notes from the members of the Constituent Assembly, provincial governments, provincial legislatures, ministries of the Government of India and also from members of the public.

Finally, the Drafting Committee met from 18 to 20 October and 'examined all the comments and criticisms on the Draft Constitution so far received'. The Drafting Committee also examined some of the recommendations of the Special Committee, some of which they did not agree to. The Drafting Committee then decided to sponsor and back some amendments to the Draft Constitution. These new recommendations were published in a reprint of the Draft in late 1948. The most exhaustive list of amendments came from Jayaprakash Narayan.[22] Here, however, the reconsideration of the Draft did not end. The two volumes of *Notices of*

[21] Ibid., p. xi.

[22] See Ambedkar's Prefatory Note, to the President of the Constituent Assembly, with *The Draft Constitution of India* (October 1948)—Prepared by the Drafting Committee, Report Indicating Recommendations for Amendment by the Drafting Committee.

Amendments (*received up to 5 p.m. of 11 November 1949*) contained 3749 notices including those by the Drafting Committee (mostly under the names of Ambedkar, N. Madhava Rau and Mohammad Saadulla). Further proposals for amendments and amendments to amendment flowed both from the Drafting Committee and from the members of the Constituent Assembly.

The Draft Constitution in the Assembly

On 4 November 1948, when the Draft was moved in the Assembly, Hasrat Mohani moved for the postponement of consideration of the Draft Constitution 'till the election of a fresh and competent constituent assembly, on the basis of joint electorates and the formation of political rather than communal parties in India'.[23]

On 5 November, Damodar Swarup Seth, a Congress Socialist, moved that, whereas 'the present Constituent Assembly was not elected on the basis of adult franchise' and, whereas 'the final constitution of free India will be based on the will of the entire people of India', while the Constituent Assembly should continue to function as Parliament of the Indian Union, 'necessary arrangement should be made for convening a new constituent assembly to be elected on the basis of a universal adult franchise' and that the Draft Constitution prepared by the Drafting Committee be placed before the new Assembly 'for its consideration and adoption with such amendments as it may deem necessary'.[24]

Seth was emphatic that the Assembly created by the statement of the Cabinet Mission did not represent the whole country. 'At the most it can claim to represent that fifteen per cent of the population of India who had elected the members of the legislatures. The election too, by virtue of which the members of this House are here, was not a direct one, they are here by virtue of an indirect election.'[25] Seth got support only from another motion of a vocal backbencher, S.L. Saksena. Naturally, both the motions were defeated.

The seventh to tenth sessions were almost wholly devoted to the first two readings of the Draft. Towards the end of the tenth session, on 15 October 1949, Shrimati G. Durgabai moved for a revision of the Assembly's rules authorizing the president to refer the Constitution, after

[23] *CAD*, vol. VII, p. 44.
[24] Ibid., p. 211.
[25] Ibid., p. 212.

it was considered by the Assembly, to the Drafting Committee with instruction for renumbering of clauses, such revision of punctuation and such revision and completion of the marginal notes thereof as might be necessary, and to recommend such formal or consequential or other necessary amendments to the Constitution as might be required.[26]

The Revised Draft

Accordingly, when the 11th session of the Assembly began on 14 November 1949, Ambedkar moved for the consideration by the Assembly of the Draft Constitution as amended by the Drafting Committee. The new Draft comprised 395 articles and 8 schedules. Though the changes now introduced were claimed to be merely of formal character,[27] some of them were not just 'formal' or verbal, for, along with the renumbering of articles and like changes, the committee also made certain necessary alterations 'for making the meaning of some of the articles clearer or for filling up any lacuna in an article without making any substantial change' and 'for remedying the defects and omission' in the articles of the Draft Constitution.

Some of the more important changes related to citizenship (the present article 9, which was originally a proviso of article 5 only, now qualified articles 6 and 8 as well), rights to personal liberty and equality (article 15 of the Draft which was split up into two articles), the present article 34 (which was added for the purpose of enabling the legislature to validate and indemnify the acts of the persons in service during the operation of martial law), the present articles 77 and 166 (to each of which a clause was added authorizing the president and governors to make rules for the conduct of business and its allocation to ministers), quorum of legislatures (from 1/6 to 1/10), judiciary (addition of the present article 222, providing for transfer of judges of high courts by the president), states' powers (the new article 365, which provided that the states' inability to comply with executive directives of the centre would be considered as a failure), territorial reorganization of the states by the president's authority (through the addition of article 391).

Discussion on the amendments continued for three days during which a few changes of 'verbal' and 'consequential' nature were made. On

[26] *CAD*, vol, X, p. 289.

[27] Preface to *The Constitution of India as Revised by the Drafting Committee* (November 1949).

17 November 1949, the third reading of the Draft Constitution started amidst the members' joyful satisfaction. After nine days of discussion the Draft Constitution of India was passed. The House, thereafter, adjourned and met on 24 January 1950, for signing the Constitution. On the same day the Constituent Assembly elected its president as the President of India and since then worked as the provisional parliament of India till the first general election of 1952 in accordance with a decision of the Assembly on 10 October 1949 (in respect of Temporary and Transitional Provisions of the Constitution).[28]

In all, the Constituent Assembly sat openly for 167 days in 12 sessions. The first six of these sessions, as is apparent, were devoted to preparatory functions. The seventh to eleventh sessions covering 110 days were devoted to the discussion of the Draft and other necessary business. (Actually a net total of 114 days were devoted to the Draft Constitution).

[28] *CAD*, vol. X, pp. 79-80.

CHAPTER 9

Indian Outlook

In view of the peculiar composition of the Constituent Assembly, revealed by the foregoing discussion, it is necessary to examine political thinking in India around 1947. It is also necessary to examine the political and economic developments of the country in the three hectic but fateful years from the end of 1946 to the end of 1949 that saw the making of the Indian Constitution.

GANDHISM

Of all trends of thought influencing Indian mind at the time of constitution-making Gandhism was undoubtedly the most powerful, due especially to the mighty role it had played during the freedom struggle and the equally strong control of its followers on the Congress organization. Yet, the core of the Gandhian programme must be distinguished from the general Congress programme in as much as the latter was a product of different political and socio-economic ideologies, including Gandhism, operating on the broad Congress platform. Gandhiji himself took the initiative in keeping away conflicts between those ideologies during the freedom movement for which he wanted the broadest national front. As a result, these latent trends became active when freedom was within reach.

Gandhiji's philosophy of faith manifested itself, in the economic field, in the theory of trusteeship and firm rejection of class conflict. Yet Gandhiji, by all estimates, was the least of a dogmatist. Though in his writings there is no express reference to a welfare state, Gandhiji was always conscious of the need of a socio-economic content of the national movement.

It will be stretching one's imagination to find in Gandhiji's 1922 statement, about swaraj being a ratification by the British Parliament of the Indian public opinion, the seed of a constituent assembly,[1] for Gandhiji

[1] Sachchidananda Sinha, in his inaugural address to the Constituent Assembly, made this claim, *CAD*, vol. I, p. 5.

was never very enthusiastic about a constituent assembly as India's panacea. On the eve of the Constituent Assembly election Gandhiji, urged by several communications from intending participants, wrote in a note, entitled 'A Tragic Phenomenon':

I am free to confess that a constituent assembly is the logical outcome of a parliamentary activity. The labours of Deshbandhu Das and Pandit Motilal Nehru opened my eyes to the fact that the parliamentary programme had a place in the national activity for independence. I strove hard against it. It is certainly inconsistent with pure non-cooperation. But pure non-cooperation never held the field.[2]

Writing to Patel on 4 December 1946, Gandhiji made it known that he had 'very strong views' on the Constituent Assembly under the Cabinet Mission plan:

1. I am quite clear that if there is a boycott by the Muslim League of the constituent assembly, it should not meet under the Cabinet Mission's statement of 16th May. It clearly contemplated the cooperation of the major parties, viz., the Congress and the League. If the government convenes the constituent assembly in spite of the boycott, they can legitimately do so only under some other statement which they can draw up in consultation with the Congress. It should not be forgotten that however powerful the Congress has become, a constituent assembly, as contemplated today, can only meet by action of the British government.

2. Even in the Constituent Assembly meets in spite of the boycott but with the willing cooperation of the British government, it will be under the visible or invisible protection of the British forces, whether Indian or European. In my opinion we shall never reach a satisfactory constitution under these circumstances.[3]

Granville Austin makes the somewhat superficial comment that 'the Congress had never been Gandhian'.[4] In the militant life of the Congress, Gandhiji was definitely the vanguard. Gandhiji's role was, however, paradoxically subdued in the formulation of several policies of the Congress from time to time. After the struggle for independence was over, at least in the opinion of the institutional leadership of the Congress, the latter sat down for framing a constitution, quite insensitive to Gandhiji's personal feelings. When Shriman Narayan Agarwal complained to him that the new constitution did not even mention the gram panchayat, the central point of the Gandhian scheme, Gandhiji bitterly commented to a group of constructive workers of the Congress that 'the social orders of

[2] Quoted by D.G. Tendulkar in *Mahatma*, vol. VII, p. 187.

[3] *Letters to Sardar Vallabhbhai Patel* (of M.K. Gandhi), pp. 197-8.

[4] Granville Austin, *The Indian Constitution*, p. 39.

our dreams cannot come through the Congress of today. Nobody knows what shape the constitution will ultimately take. I say leave it to those who are labouring at it now.'[5]

CONGRESS

Though the Congress movement from the beginning aimed at constitutional reforms, its objectives, for a long time, were not set in clear terms. The Nehru plan (1928), Coupland observes, was hastily drafted and was aimed mainly at an interparty agreement. Many technicalities of a constitution were, therefore omitted.[6] The Nehru Committee emphasized that, 'without the fullest cultural autonomy . . . it will be difficult to create a harmonious nation'.[7] The federal plan, through peculiar twists of history, was widened in the succeeding years until the fateful partition of India changed the whole perspective of the Indian political problem.

The socio-economic content of the Congress programme was till 1930 hazy. The Karachi resolution of 1931 was somewhat precise social programme, for, besides demanding full political freedom from the British raj, the resolution promised to realize universal adult franchise for Indians, education and development for all, social and economic justice and equity for individuals and groups. In the election manifesto of the Congress, released in 1936, on the eve of the provincial elections, the objectives of the Karachi resolution were reasserted. At Faizpur, in 1936, Congress president, Jawaharlal Nehru characteristically laid down the 'real object' before the party as building up a powerful joint front of all anti-imperialist forces in the country. 'The Congress has been indeed in the past and is today such a united popular front, and inevitably the Congress must be the basis and pivot of limited action.'[8]

The eagerness and ability of the Congress to solve the nation's manifold problems were first put to test when it took up the provincial administrations after some hesitation. For two years before the war the achievements of the Congress were moderately satisfactory. Nevertheless, the Congress ministers were severely criticized for their rude handling of labour problems in several provinces. There was no revolutionary achievement in the field of land reforms either. In Madras and Orissa, some attempts were made with a limited success. 'The basis of permanent settlement

[5] Tendulkar, *Mahatma*, vol. VIII, p. 281.
[6] R. Coupland, *The Constitutional Problem in India*, part I, p. 94.
[7] All-Parties' Conference, *Report of the Committee*, p. 32.
[8] Quoted by Sitaramayya, *The History of the Indian National Congress*, vol. II, p. 34.

was not questioned in other Congress provinces, nor was there any interference with proprietary rights outside the settlement areas. But within the limits of the existing system the agrarian policy of the Congress went a long way. In the first place it dealt vigorously with tenancy rights and rents.'[9] Also, it made efforts at social reforms like reduction of indebtedness and abolition of untouchability, at the governmental level, and the formation of a Planning Committee at the party level.

The latest elaboration of the Congress policy prior to the convening of the Constituent Assembly was the manifesto for the provincial elections of the winter of 1945-6. In it the Congress envisaged a free, democratic and federal state with 'the fundamental rights and liberties of all its citizens guaranteed in the constitution', and a great deal of 'autonomy for its constituent units and its legislative organs elected under universal adult franchise'.

> Industry and agriculture, the social services and public utilities must be encouraged, modernised and rapidly extended. . . . For this purpose it will be necessary to plan and coordinate social advance in all its many fields, to prevent the concentration of wealth and power in the hands of individuals and groups, to prevent vested interests inimical to society from growing, and to have social control of the mineral resources, means of transport and the principal methods of production and distribution in land, industry and in other departments of national activity. . . . The state must, therefore own or control key and basic industries and services, mineral resources, railways, waterways, shipping and other means of public transport. Currency and exchange, banking and insurance must be regulated in the national interest.

The reform of the land system was 'urgently needed in India' and involved 'the removal of intermediaries between the peasant and the state', on payment of 'equitable compensation'. Promotion of educational opportunities and public health services were basic ingredients of this programme. Provisions for the improvement of the workers' condition were promised. The party also promised to take measures to remove rural indebtedness. In the international field the party looked forward to international cooperation and friendship.[10]

Liberalism

The moderates within the Congress formed themselves into the Liberal Party in late 1918 when the militants prevailed over the Congress to resist the Montford reforms. The Liberals were consistent advocates of working

[9] Coupland, *The Constitutional Problem in India*, part II, p. 138.
[10] *IAR*, 1945, vol. II, pp. 107-10.

under 1919 Act and dominated the Indian political scene to the extent the Congress abstained. On major impact of the Liberal Party was the encouragement of constitutionalism and parliamentary activity within the Congress.

After the failure of the Cripps talks the Liberals' effort for a constitutional solution led to the setting up of the conciliation committee—popularly known as the Sapru Committee, which passed fifteen resolutions on the future basis of the Indian Constitution in April 1945,[11] opposing the idea of partition and proposing, in its stead, a loose federation, with compulsory accession and no secession for the provinces. The committee envisaged the disappearance of paramountcy, but continued suzerainty of the Indian union, over the states and recommended the appointment of a minister-in-charge of functions in relation to the Indian states, with whom a body of three advisers from the Indian states would be associated. The Sapru Committee proposals proceeded on the basis of parity between the Hindus other than the scheduled castes on the one hand and the Muslims on the other in the lower house of the future central legislature and the executive, the overriding conditions being that the unity of India and joint electorates with reservation of seats for the Muslims were accepted.

The Sapru Committee, really speaking, attempted a synthesis of the Nehru Report and the Cripps proposals—though, due to the prevalent tension between the political parties, no serious heed was paid to it. After 1945 the party gradually disappeared and in 1949 was informally dissolved. A number of liberal leaders were, however, given Congress tickets for the Constituent Assembly elections.

COMMUNALISM

The Muslim League's political programme has already been fully discussed. Of the other trends, the Sikh communal aspiration, expressed mainly through the Akali party, was a major one. The recognition of the Sikhs as a major community in India by the British government placed it in a very significant, though localized, position in Indian politics. For obvious reasons the Sikh communal claim opposed the Muslim League's and at the time of the Cabinet Mission's arrival it looked as if the Congress and the Sikhs were putting up a joint front against the League claim on the Punjab.

To the Cabinet Mission, Master Tara Singh on behalf of the Akali party

[11] *Constitutional Proposals of the Sapru Committee*, December 1945.

submitted a memorandum which declared their support to a single constituent body and their firm opposition 'to any possible partition of India as envisaged in the draft declaration'. The memorandum also added that 'with the inauguration of provincial autonomy on the basis of the Communal Award, they have been reduced to a state of complete helplessness'.[12]

An all-India party possessing considerable influence in the country was the Hindu Mahasabha. The Mahasabha which was founded in 1915 as a Hindu cultural organization, was reorganized in 1938 into a political party by its president, Savarkar. In 1944, the Mahasabha published its own scheme of a centralized parliamentary government for India in the form of the 'Constitution of Hindusthan Free State', in which it demanded a federal government for India with autonomy for provinces and residual powers for the centre. The states would not be allowed to decline accession and the provinces would not be allowed to demand secession. 'The union government should have the power of superintendence and control in cases where the federating units go wrong in respect of national policy or interest and should be strong enough to exercise the power effectively.'[13]

Casteism

Of the two casteist parties—the Scheduled Castes Federation and the Justice Party—whereas the latter had held power in Madras for some time, before the Congress accepted office in 1937, the former had a greater political importance, particularly because of the legal acumen of its leader B.R. Ambedkar.

Ironically, Ambedkar, who happened to be one of the architects of the Indian Constitution in the Constituent Assembly, had all along looked at the Congress movement as a unitary programme dominated by upper-caste Hindus. In his presidential address to the Scheduled Castes Federation's conference at Bombay on 6-7 May 1945, Ambedkar opposed the idea of a constituent assembly:

> It is absolutely superfluous. So much of the constitution of India has already been written out in the Government of India Act, 1935, that it seems to be an act of supererogation to appoint a constituent assembly to do the thing over again. All that is necessary is to delete those sections of the Government of India Act, 1935, which are inconsistent with dominion status.[14]

[12] *IAR*, 1946, vol. I, p. 200.
[13] The Hindu Mahasabha, *Constitution of the Hindusthan Free State*.
[14] *IAR*, 1945, vol. I, p. 321.

The meeting of the Federation considered the

> government's recent statement of industrial policy and expressed the opinion that the policy by recognising private enterprise as a basic fact was calculated to do grave wrong to the toiling masses of this country. The Federation was firmly of opinion that state ownership of industry and . . . land was the only way which would prevent industrial policy resulting in making the rich richer and the poor poorer.[15]

At the sixteenth session of the Justice Party (7-8 May 1945), Shanmukham Chetty, in his presidential address, said that 'it had always been their policy that the quickest way of making political advance was to utilize every opportunity provided by the constitution in force for the time being, notwithstanding the limitations imposed by that constitution'. The conference passed a resolution demanding at least for the next ten years a composite government. The conference also demanded separate electorates for the non-Brahmins and Scheduled Castes.[16]

Communism

Ever since its birth in 1925 the Communist Party of India operated within the Congress, with the mission of supporting the anticolonial struggle of the Indian national bourgeoisie and criticizing what it considered the mistakes and reactionary policies of the latter.

The party demanded, in its memorandum to the Cabinet Mission, 'within six months, the total withdrawal of British troops from all Indian territory, including the states'.[17] The question of Indian unity was an internal question to be settled by the people themselves. It could not be made an excuse for the British refusal to transfer power. The immediate demand of the party was, therefore, the setting up of a provisional government to which all powers would be transferred forthwith. The provisional government would arrange the election of a constituent assembly within six months. It would be responsible to the assembly when the latter came into existence. Such a provisional government would negotiate a treaty with the British government on the payment of sterling balances and mutual trade relations, subject to ratification by the Constituent Assembly. The Constituent Assembly which the British had

[15] Ibid., p. 324.
[16] Ibid., pp. 316-21.
[17] *IAR*, 1946, vol. I, pp. 220-1.

envisaged, on the other hand, was undemocratic as it would be indirectly elected by a restricted electorate.

For the solution of the communal problem and the satisfaction of the cultural aspirations of the people of India it demanded the right to self-determination for them. A boundary commission would reallocate the provincial boundaries 'on the basis of natural ancient homelands of every people'. 'The people of each such unit should have the unfettered right of self-determination, i.e. the right to decide freely whether they join the Indian union or form a separate sovereign state or another Indian union'. The delegates elected from each national unit would decide whether to join one Indian union or not.

The Communist Party itself, however, stood for a 'free, voluntary, democratic Indian union of sovereign units'. It was firmly convinced that the best interests of the Indian masses would be served 'by their remaining together in one common union in a common brotherhood to defend the freedom and solve the problems of poverty which require the cooperation of all'.

The manifesto of the party for the election of 1946 went as far as declaring that all nationalities should be able to form their own sovereign states. The party had long been a champion of the movement of the states' people for the democratization of their administration.

Radicalism

'Socialist leadership arose within the Indian National Congress in response to what the socialists felt were three leadership "failures" associated with the second and third civil disobedience movements of 1930-34', writes Thomas A. Rusch.[18] The Congress Socialist Party's constitution declared that the objects of the party were 'the achievement of complete independence, in the sense of separation from the British empire and the establishment of a socialist society'.[19]

The first head-on clash between the Gandhiite leadership and the leftists within the Congress took place in 1939, when, with the support of the radicals, socialists and communists within the Congress, Subhas Chandra Bose defeated Gandhiji's personal nominee, Pattabhi Sitaramayya, and became the Congress president for the second time. In this clash Jawaharlal

[18] T.A. Rusch, 'Dynamics of Socialism in India', in R.L. Park and I. Tinker, *Leadership and Political Institutions in India*, p. 188.

[19] J.P. Narayan, *Towards Struggle*, p. 139.

Nehru, a leader of the radicals joined Gandhiji's side for, as he explained later in a letter to Bose (on 3 April 1939),

> . . . it meant under the circumstances a break with Gandhiji and I did not want this to take place. . . . It would mean also, I thought, a setback for the real left. The left was not strong enough to shoulder the burden by itself and when a real contest came in the Congress it would lose and there would be a reaction against it. I thought it probable that you would win the election as against Pattabhi, but I doubted very much whether you could carry the Congress with you in a clear contest with what is called Gandhism.[20]

Nehru's fear was very much real. There was no ideological cohesion among the so-called leftists in the Congress. When, after resigning from the Congress, Bose tried to mobilize them in the Forward Bloc, in the middle of 1939, in order to fight constitutionalism within the Congress, he failed. The Congress Socialist Party chose Gandhiji. Jayaprakash Narayan was categorical that, 'The Congress must lead the struggle. But it is crystal clear today, neither the Kisan Sabha nor the Trade Union Congress in their present stage of development can hope to fight imperialism with any degree of success. That task unquestionably belongs to the Congress.'[21]

The socialists and the Forward Bloc took an active role in the movement of 1942. After the war both became restless for independence. Both declined to submit any memorandum to the Cabinet Mission. Both opposed the Mission's plan and refused to join the assembly. But it was not until 10 June 1946 that the Forward Bloc openly accepted the ideology of class struggle for the achievement of socialism. In 1948, the party was split up into a 'Marxist' and a 'Subhasist' faction, with very little difference in their programmes.[22]

[20] Jawaharlal Nehru, *A Bunch of Old Letters*, p. 356.

[21] Narayan, *Towards Struggle*, p. 139. The position was reasserted as late as September 1946, when the Executive Committee of the Congress Socialist Party declared that the Congress must lead the freedom struggle.

[22] See Myron Weiner, *Party Politics in India*, pp. 125-6.

For a brief history of the growth of democratic socialism, see also S.K. Chaubey, 'Democratic Socialism: Early Growth of the Concept in India', in *Indian Journal of Political Science*, vol. XXVI, No. 4, October-December 1965, pp. 47-60.

CHAPTER 10

Cross-currents of Indian Politics

Economic Implications of Independence

Reporting 'several transfers of British business to Indian hands', on 17 May 1946 (i.e. shortly after the failure of the Cabinet Mission's Shimla talks), *The Eastern Economist*, a representative journal of the business community, commented that Britain had 'emerged out of the war victorious, but weaker'. The paper conceded, 'in all fairness, that Britain is trying vigorously and honestly to negotiate its way through the mass of strategic and economic difficulties that the war has piled on her'.

The Statesman of Calcutta reported on 17 June 1947 the 'transfer of British business interests to Indian hands involving about Rs. 25 crores' in Calcutta, though

> several big and commercial undertakings in Calcutta and elsewhere have remained completely unmoved by all these changes, and are known to have rejected offers of purchase from Indian interests which on a short-term reckoning were financially attractive. Evidently, their estimate is that, from a long-term point of view, no sound reason exists for supposing that British business will not continue to flourish very satisfactorily in India.

The paper also noted the gratification of 'the Clive Street business circles' at Nehru's assurance to British business. *The Economist* (London, 4 June 1947) hoped that 'the essential strategic and economic ties between Britain and India will remain even if it is under different political forms'.

The transfer of power in India was smooth. The direct Indo-British economic conflict was over. No threat to foreign interests was seriously contemplated. As a result, it was not considered necessary to draw any special treaty for the protection of British interests in India as a concomitant of the Indian Independence Act, which was, nevertheless, preceded by the Indo-British Financial Agreement, drawn on 14 August 1947. It took a much larger time and effort, however, to straighten the internal economic and political issues.

Economic Scene

As early as 1929, Vera Anstey, the eminent British economist, considered the possibility of India as 'an economic unit in the making':

The difficulties confronting economic unification are the vast size of the country and the political elements contained therein. On the other hand, India forms a clearly geographical unit, a not inconsiderable extent of economic unification has already been achieved, and there are a number of strong unifying forces at work.[1]

Since at least the first world war the strongest social force that favoured the unification of the country was the need for economic centralization—the inevitable result of industrial development, which notwithstanding all odds was progressing steadily.

At the end of the Second World War, Indian industry was far more organized than at any time before. Consequently, tremendous pressure was being exerted by it on the government for moulding the national economic policy in its interests. The biggest and most controversial issues on which private Indian business felt it necessary to speak out and assert the right to property were economic control and nationalization. The attitudes of Indian businessmen to these questions, however, were sometimes contradictory.

Indian businessmen, for instance, were well aware that the system of controls that had been introduced during the war could not be done away with. On the other hand, it could be utilized to serve the purpose of a newly emerging economic order—that was state capitalism. So *The Eastern Economist* emphasized that 'the system of economic controls which the government has slowly built up must continue for some time at least after the war to smoothen the transition to peace economy'. On the assumption, therefore, that the future economy of our country would be largely state-directed, it endorsed 'a progressive strengthening of the present system of controls, in scope and character, so that not only may it strengthen the smooth transition to peace economy, but may also become the instrument of long-term economic planning in our country'.[2]

In early 1947, the Commodity Prices Board, consisting of the noted economists A.D. Gorwala and D.R. Gadgil, was appointed. It submitted its report in the same year recommending 'not abolition but the improvement of the system of controls'.[3] On the other hand, the Foodgrains Policy

[1] Vera Anstey, *The Economic Development of India*, p. 485.

[2] *The Eastern Economist*, 14 January 1944.

[3] C.D. Deshmukh, *Economic Developments in India.*

Committee, appointed in September 1947, and consisting of mostly industrial personalities, in its interim report, adopted by a majority and submitted in December the same year, recommended the reduction of the government commitments 'under the present system of food controls'.[4] The demand for decontrol was supported by Gandhiji on moral ground, as the control had encouraged black-market and other malpractices. Control was abolished. As a result, prices rose steeply and control had to be reimposed within a few months.

Behind this controversy, the greatest reason was the suspicion about the growing demand for nationalization, which made *The Eastern Economist* declare on 14 June 1946: 'We reject unreservedly the Soviet ideal of complete and immediate socialisation of the whole range of the economy.' Nehru, therefore, had to use the occasion of his address to the 20th annual session of the Federation of Indian Chambers of Commerce to remove some of the apprehensions of Indian businessmen about the economic policies to be pursued by the government. 'It is entirely wrong', he said, 'if you imagine that this government is out to injure industry. That would be folly on our part. We want to provide facilities for industry and facilities for production—technical, scientific and power resources and all that.'[5] He reiterated his assurance to private enterprise, on 4 April 1947, in an address to the All-India Manufacturers' Organization.[6]

Economic Planning

Essentially connected with the questions of control and nationalization was the question of planning. The real controversy on Indian planning had started with the publication of what is commonly known as the Bombay Plan—a product of the deliberations of a group of big industrialists led by G.D. Birla—which rejected the 'Soviet-type socialism'. The Bombay Plan was in essence a capitalist plan with the state control unavoidable in the middle of the twentieth century.

The Economic Programme Committee of the National Planning Committee struck a compromise between state socialism and private enterprise. It promised equal opportunities to all classes of people and special opportunities for the backward. Private enterprise was not to be abolished, but at the same time basic industries were to be expanded under public sector. While land would be exploited on the basis of cooperative

[4] Ibid., p. 46.
[5] *IAR*, 1947, vol. I, p. 191.
[6] Ibid., pp. 201-3.

farming, zamindari was to be abolished. Small-scale industries would be promoted through cooperatives, especially in the rural areas. It was on the basis of these recommendations that the Industrial Policy Resolution of 1948 was drafted. The controversy did not however end there.

For sheer economic reasons Indian industry needed a change in the agricultural system resulting in the development of capitalism in agriculture. And from this point of view they condemned the zamindari system of India. *The Eastern Economist*, in its issue of 28 June 1946, making a strong case against the continuation of zamindari, emphatically declared that 'the landlord has no economic justification for his existence'.

Years of Strain

The general economic condition of the country in the post-war years was critical. C.D. Deshmukh calls 1946 'the year of missed opportunities'. 'There was a misreading of the immediate post-war trend in the economic situation', he writes.[7] In an atmosphere of political uncertainty, 'governmental economic planning became a little cold; and private enterprise based on expectations could not go ahead, even if it wanted to, to the accomplishment of ambitious designs. Civil strife added to our trouble.' The year was characterized by serious and persistent labour unrest. 'The business outlook therefore, in 1946, despite all the talk of planning, expansions, agricultural and industrial revolution, was contractionist.'[8]

The first post-war Indian budget was inflationary. To counteract the resultant inflationary tendency of the national economy, the government introduced a contractionist policy in the next year, which culminated in the Liaqat Ali budget. Whereas the 1946 budget was considered by the business circle as 'bullish, a rehabilitation budget', the February 1947 budget was considered 'drastic'. 'The budget for 1947-8', says C.D. Deshmukh, 'presented by Mr Liaqat Ali, had many elements of corrective policies and invocations, but as a whole it proved too much of a shock, particularly to the business and industrial community. It was in severe contrast with the previous budget and, while its points were recognized, their motive was questioned.'[9]

The year of independence for India was thus a year of difficulties, aggravated by partition and communal troubles. Some amount of confidence was restored when Shanmukham Chetty announced in

[7] Deshmukh, *Economic Developments in India*, p. 32.
[8] *The Eastern Economist*, Annual Number, 3 January 1947.
[9] Deshmukh, *Economic Developments in India*, p. 48.

November a new budget.[10] In 1948 there was some improvement in the situation. In the same year the Reserve Bank of India was nationalized. At the end of 1949 some amount of stability was achieved in the economic situation, partly due to the political stability achieved through the completion of constitution-making and the integration of the Indian states.

Political Scene

Immediately after the elections to the provincial legislative assemblies in early 1946, Asoka Mehta, a noted Congress Socialist, analysed in *Janata*, the party organ, the 'election pattern—their lessons'. He found in the election results the end of the old and moderate political parties, like the Liberals and the responsivists. He also found the end of the communal parties except in those places where they had been propped up by separate electorates. The vital challenge to the Congress would come not from the communalists, but from the communists, Mehta said.[11]

Around Independence, the Congress policy was in a state of flux. Ever since the elections to the Constituent Assembly the Congress sought to bring in its periphery the other political groups.[12] In the interim government several 'outsiders' were given important portfolios, the section with which no rapprochement was sought being the leftist parties. It did not take very long, however, for differences to grow in the coalition government and Sarat Bose, Shanmukham Chetty and John Matthai gradually parted company with the Congress government due to serious differences.

The internal situation of the Congress was no less confusing. Commenting on the proceedings of the last pre-independence Congress conference, *The Statesman*'s special representative in the UP wrote in the issue of 23 November 1946 that, contrary to average expectations, the Congress session at Meerut 'was not quite uneventful'. In the same meeting Vallabhbhai Patel, speaking on the communal situation in the country, gave the controversial call to the Hindus to 'organize in self-defence against the hooligans', as 'sword must be met by sword'. 'Of greater importance to the internal organization of the Congress', wrote the correspondent, 'was the unconcealed ideological opposition on leading issues from the younger element represented by the Congress Socialists. Their approach

[10] See *The Eastern Economist*, January 1948.

[11] Asoka Mehta, *The Political Mind of India*, pp. 88-9.

[12] On 9 August 1946, sat a public meeting at Wardha, Nehru called for a 'united front' for the two critical years ahead and foresaw freedom within one year. *The Statesman*, 11 August 1946.

to problems, varying from the attitudes to states' politics to the more remote question of evolving a constitutional pattern for India, has always been known to be different from the main rightwing within the Congress, but it was for the first time that theses divergent ideologies came up for discussion in the poem.'[13]

Ever since J.B. Kripalani's election as Congress president at Meerut, relations between the governmental and organizational wings of the party deteriorated. In November 1947, when the AICC met in New Delhi, Kripalani resigned, openly blaming the government leaders for not cooperating with the organizational leadership. He was succeeded by Rajendra Prasad and only then complete harmony was established between the government and the party. The next year Pattabhi Sitaramayya took over as Congress president.

Crisis of Communalism

The Muslim League, on the other hand, found itself after partition in a rather odd position. As a political party within the Constituent Assembly it was in a hopeless minority without any protection of the communal veto. Besides, its own internal coherence was disappearing. There was an extreme communal group within it and another rather liberal wing. A still smaller section led by Hasrat Mohani believed in socialist ideology.

The shock of Gandhiji's murder created a widespread commotion in India against all types of communal politics. There were moves in the central legislature for banning political activities of all communal organizations. In February-March 1948, the League leaders had several meetings and finally the majority of them decided to disband the League in the Constituent Assembly and provincial legislatures. The Madras Muslim League disagreed while a few Leaguers like Saadulla extended cooperation to the Congress. On two points, however, they appear to have advanced a common front—resistance to over-centralization of the Indian federation and opposition to interference with the personal laws of the Muslims.[14]

In March 1948, also, the Akali Dal decided to disband its legislative wing, the Panthik Party, and join the Congress. An extremist group led by Tara Singh, however, maintained their identity in the East Punjab legislature.[15]

[13] Ibid., 23 November 1946.

[14] *The Statesman*, February-March 1948 and *The Times of India Directory and Who's Who*, 1949, 1950.

[15] Ibid.

Labour Movement

During the war, though politically isolated, the Communist Party maintained its firm grip over the leadership of the trade-union movement, notwithstanding a minor split caused by the secession of the Royist faction from the AITUC. On coming to power, the Congress first tried to deal with the labour questions through the Hindustan Mazdoor Sevak Sangh and made efforts to capture the AITUC. Being unsuccessful, in May 1947, the top leaders of the National Congress met in a high-level conference at New Delhi, at the initiative of Patel, and decided to have a separate labour organization. As a result, the Indian National Trade Union Congress was born.[16]

Charles A. Myers commenting on the Congress labour policy around independence, writes:

> Despite the popular mandate with which the Congress assumed office, Congress labour policies came in for serious criticism by the non-Congress labour leaders. Some of this reflected basic difference of opinion with the Congress policy of compulsory arbitration. Congress sponsorship of the INTUC was especially disliked. Whatever the justification, the Indian labour movement entered upon a new phase of political unionism with the formation of two more central organizations.[17]

In June 1947, the Central Committee of the Communist Party of India formulated that though the forces of freedom movement had compelled the imperialists to open negotiation with Indian leaders, they were manoeuvring to forge a new alliance with the princes, big landlords and big businessmen of India in order to control the Indian state and economy. Nevertheless, the party decided that the agreement, embodied in the Mountbatten proposal, offered 'new opportunities for national advance' and that 'the two popular governments and constituent assemblies are the strategic weapons in the hands of national leadership'. But in December 1947, the Central Committee of the Communist Party of India rejected the second part of its June thesis and called the acceptance of Mountbatten plan as an abject surrender on the basis of an the 'imperialist-feudal-bourgeois combine'. The resultant political movement of the party was put down with rigorous oppressive measures by the government. The Communist Party was banned in certain parts of the country.

[16] R.C. Saksena, *Labour Problems and Social Welfare*, p. 92.

[17] C.A. Myers, *Industrial Relations in India*, p. 115. The two central trade-union organizations referred to by Myers were the Hind Mazdoor Sabha sponsored by the socialists in December 1948 and the United Trade Union Congress sponsored by K.T. Shah and Mrinal Kanti Bose, who, due to differences with the communists, broke away from the AITUC.

NEW FRONTIERS OF LEFTISM

The Congress Socialists Party decided not to accept the nominations to the Constituent Assembly. Damodar Swarup Seth (UP) and Phulan Prasad Varma (Bihar), however, accepted Congress nomination as the decision of the party was said not to have reached them in time. The were allowed to continue as members of the Constituent Assembly.[18]

On 28 February 1947, at a special conference, the Congress Socialist Party decided to drop the word 'Congress' from its name. Its president, Ram Manohar Lohia, charged the Congress leaders of compromising with vested interests. In March 1947, the party opened its membership to non-Congressites.

Ever since the transfer of power Gandhiji was also becoming more and more eager about a positive socio-economic programme of the Congress and gave patronage to the socialists. He actually proposed Jayaprakash Narayan and Narendra Deva for Congress presidentship after Kripalani's resignation with the support of Nehru and to the dislike of rightwing leaders like Patel. After Gandhiji's assassination the socialists charged Patel of neglecting Gandhiji's security. Nehru defended Patel and the Congress right avenged it by piloting a resolution prohibiting political groupism within the Congress. The socialists were now convinced of the reactionary trend in the Congress, and at the sixth annual conference in March 1948 the party decided to quite the Congress and resign all seats they had secured in the provincial and central legislatures. Its leader, Jayaprakash Narayan, declared that the Draft Constitution of India which had just been framed was 'clumsy' and 'not inspiring'. Thereafter the socialists could not stay in the Congress. They preferred to work in the opposition. They demanded the dissolution of the Constituent Assembly and its reconstitution on the basis of adult franchise. If the Assembly was not dissolved, the socialists would think of other methods.

It should, however, be pointed out here that the socialists drew this conclusion about Indian political situation out of their independent study and had no sympathy for the communist ideas of that time. At the Nasik convention in March 1948, the party modified its stand. On 28 June 1948, Achyuta Patwardhan said in an election meeting in UP that in time of national crisis the socialists would join with the Congress rather than the

[18] This information was received from Ganga Saran Sinha, an old socialist leader, through personal communication.

communists. Very soon, in the trade-union movement the socialists parted company with the communists.[19]

The socialists gained nothing by leaving the Congress. Only in the UP legislature where they had some strength, Narendra Deva, with ten colleagues, resigned. The socialists in the INTUC, led by Hariharnath Shastri, chose to stay with the Congress. In the byelections that followed the socialists were defeated. Even Narendra Deva lost in the elections. The socialists then counted their steps back. On 27 October 1948, the national executive of the party directed its representatives in the Constituent Assembly to put forward the views of the party that the final adoption of the constitution should be left to a constituent assembly that would be elected by universal adult franchise. As the party was aware that the view would not possibly be accepted, their alternative demand was to make the constitution liable to change, in the next ten years, by a simple majority decision of Parliament.[20]

In January 1947, at the Ara Conference, the Forward Bloc also discussed its policy towards the Constituent Assembly. The conference referred the issue to the Forward Bloc council which decided in March 1947 to withdraw from the Constituent Assembly, the immediate dissolution of which was called for in view of its lack of universality. H.V. Kamath, then a member of its Working Committee, differed from the decision and remained within the Congress party in the Constituent Assembly. The other Forward Bloc member of the Constituent Assembly, Vishwambhar Dayal Tripathy (from UP), appealed to the leadership for reconsideration of the decision and held his seat in the Constituent Assembly. In July 1948, the all-India Council of the party decided to quit the Congress and instructed Tripathy to resign the Constituent Assembly seat. Tripathy opted for the Assembly.[21]

[19] *The Statesman*, March-June 1948. Also Thomas A. Rusch's article, op. cit., and Myron Weiner, op. cit., pp. 33, 57.

[20] *The Statesman*, 29 October 1948.

[21] Information supplied by the State Council office of the Forward Bloc, West Bengal. Kamath confirmed it, though denied that Forward Bloc took any disciplinary action against him. Rather, he said it was the Congress Party which took disciplinary action against him in 1949.

CHAPTER 11

End of the Indian Problem (I)

Constituent Assembly and Native States

Invitation to the States

While the Chamber of Princes was in general agreement with the Cabinet Mission's plan and declaration about the lapse of paramountcy, they wanted to have certain matters clarified. The standing committee of the Chamber of Princes set up a Negotiating Committee on 10 June 1946 to open negotiation with the Negotiating Committee of the Constituent Assembly of British India. On the eve of transfer of power in India, the rulers of the states became alert to the impending challenge to their rights and position, so long maintained with British support. The immediate objective of the rulers was, therefore, to bargain with the new Government of India from a position of strength. On the other hand, when the British were packing from the Indian mainland, defence of states' rights would be a liability which they had no reason to bear against the possibility of antagonizing Indian opinion. At the most, therefore, what the British could do was to terminate the existing relations with the states and make them free to bargain with the new Government of India on their own terms.

The General Council of the All-India States People's Conference on the other hand, expressed strong resentment at being ignored in the talks of the Cabinet Mission. In its conference from 8 to 10 June 1946, its demands for a fully responsible government in the states and representation of the states' people to the Constituent Assembly on behalf of the states were reasserted. The meeting heard Jawaharlal Nehru declare: 'While we have accepted the continuance of the ruler as a constitutional head, it must be made perfectly clear that the only ultimate rights we recognize are the rights of the people'.[1]

The same meeting, however, heard a much softer tone from Vallabhbhai Patel. He advised the states' subjects to get involved in isolated direct

[1] *IAR*, 1946, vol. I, p. 213.

actions in the states at the moment, but to be patient and carry on the agitation peacefully for responsible government on the basis of a creative approach to the princes as a whole and not to fritter away their energy on isolated battles.[2]

The trend of thought Patel represented was thus in favour of talks at government level and arriving at a settlement with the princes through concession and persuasion. There was, of course, an advantage of such a policy. Under constant threats of popular upsurge, when there would be no British force to crush it, the princes were very likely to respond to persuasion, and a 'smooth' accession of the states might not be difficult.

At the Meerut session of the Congress, the loudest demand for immediate starting of democratic movement in the states was expressed. Pattabhi Sitaramayya, president, All-India States People's Conference, moved the resolution on Indian states declaring that any confederation of states (which the states were then seeking to establish among themselves) without the consent of their people would not be tolerated. Whereas Vallabhbhai Patel pleaded for patience among the states' people, a number of amendments were moved soliciting the extension of Congress support to the popular movement in the states. There were even charges against the official leadership of failure to advise the states' people on their movement. Jawaharlal Nehru himself had to deny the charge.[3]

On 21 December 1946, upon a resolution moved by K.M. Munshi, the Constituent Assembly elected a Negotiating Committee with six members 'to confer with the Negotiating Committee set up by the Chamber of Princes and with other representatives of Indian states for the purpose of (a) determining the distribution of seats in the Assembly not exceeding 93 in number which, in the Cabinet Mission's statement on 16 May 1946, are reserved for the Indian states, and (b) deciding the method by which the representatives of the states should be returned to this Assembly'.[4]

Some rather odd demands were raised at that stage. P.R. Thakur, a scheduled caste Congressite, wanted a member of the scheduled castes, and Jaipal Singh, an independent adivasi leader, wanted an adivasi in the committee to ensure fair representation of their communities in the states.

Moving the Objectives Resolution, Nehru said in the Assembly that, 'in a sense, this resolution does not interfere with the inner working of those units. They will be autonomous and, as I have said, if those units

[2] Ibid., p. 215.
[3] *The Statesman*, 25 November 1946.
[4] *CAD*, vol. I, p. 155.

choose to have some kind of constitutional monarchy at their head, they will be welcome to do so.'[5]

PROTRACTED NEGOTIATION

Yet the first and the second sessions of the Constituent Assembly were not attended by the states' representatives. On 29 January 1947, the Chamber of Princes at New Delhi demanded that:

> The entry of the states into the union of India, in accordance with the accepted plan, shall be on no other basis than that of negotiation and the final decision shall rest with each state. The proposed union shall comprise, so far as the states are concerned, the territories of only such states as may decide to join the union, it being understood that their participation in the constitutional discussions will imply no commitments in regard to their ultimate decision, which can only be taken after consideration of the complete picture of the Constitution.[6]

The constitution of each state, its territorial integrity and the succession of its reigning dynasty in accordance with the custom and usage of the state could not be interfered with by the union or any unit thereof. The Constituent Assembly could only settle the union constitution in accordance with the Cabinet Mission's plan, and was not authorized to deal with questions bearing on the internal administration or constitution of states or groups of states.

The negotiating committees of the Constituent Assembly and of the states met on 8-9 February 1947 in order to discuss the distribution of seats in the Constituent Assembly to the princely states.[7] The princes chose to open the basic question of the protection of their rights without which they could not join the Constituent Assembly. Patel categorically told them, 'No responsible person, no Congressman, has said, "We do not want you".' The chancellor of the Chamber of Princes, however, explained the princes' suspicion:

> The resolution passed by the Constituent Assembly ex-parte has been perhaps responsible for taking this course. This is suspicion number one. There have been instances . . . of statements by irresponsible persons, which have given cause for these doubts and suspicions.

Nehru's reply to these doubts makes interesting reading. He said that questions about monarchy and territories could not arise until the princes

[5] Ibid., vol. II, p. 300.
[6] *The Statesman*, 30 January 1947.
[7] B. Shiva Rao, *Select Documents*, vol. I, pp. 643-721.

decided to join the Indian union. For the moment, however, their participation in the Constituent Assembly had to be discussed. Participation in the Constituent Assembly was different from participation in the union. It was nobody's fault that the princes' representatives were not present when the Objectives Resolution was passed. But the whole object of that resolution would have been defeated if it was not passed at an early stage.

We wanted to have some kind of blueprint of what we were looking for. We have to deal not only with individuals, we have to deal with vast masses of people in India. We have to deal with a situation, if I may say so. If we did not try our utmost, the whole of India would be a cauldron within six months. It would have been a cauldron within the last six months—and I don't know whether it will not be a cauldron in the next six months due to the economic situation.... It is matter of vast forces being at work. We are trying to control them and direct them into particular channels.... As it is, public opinion is more advanced in the Constituent Assembly; it is a revolutionary type of opinion. So we have to put some ideal before them and we took the greatest care to put that both in terms of the Cabinet Mission's statement and in such a way as not to alienate the rights of any community, state or province, and in broadest shape imaginable.

The princes were in a paradoxical position which was well known to them. Taking strength from the Cabinet Mission the princes assumed a legal position which would give them sovereignty the moment paramountcy lapsed. They would thus be strong enough to carry on a bargain with the union of India on equal terms. Yet, though they were agreeable to the idea of joining a federation on their own terms, surrendering only those powers which had been legally possessed by the paramount power, they at the same time realized the irresistible strength of the popular movements in their states demanding democratic reorganization of administration and complete merger with the newly emerging Indian nation. Amidst this painful dilemma, therefore, many a prince decided to wait and see how things developed. After the arrival of Mountbatten, however, the relatively enlightened section of the princes found the need of an immediate settlement. In a memorandum submitted to the Chamber of Princes, the Maharaja of Cochin warned that if the states did not help in the formation of a stable, strong and central authority, the result would be weakening of the stable elements in British India working towards a settlement and consequent increase in the power and prestige of the leftwing. 'If the latter came to power the position of the states can well be imagined.'[8]

[8] *The Free Press Journal*, 3 April 1947.

PRINCES' PARTICIPATION IN THE ASSEMBLY

On the eve of the General Conference of States' Rulers in the first week of April 1947, the Maharaja of Bikaner openly condemned the 'sitting on the fence' theory of some of the rulers and declared his intention to join the Constituent Assembly. A group of princes, led by Bikaner, having thus strongly decided in favour of joining the Constituent Assembly, the Chamber of Princes had second thoughts on the question. The general conference of rulers reiterated the willingness of the states to join the Constituent Assembly and cooperate in the constitution-making, provided that the general understandings between the two negotiating committees were ratified by the Constituent Assembly. Nehru, on behalf of the Negotiating Committee of the Constituent Assembly, told the princes that a formal ratification of the joint decisions by the Assembly was not necessary. Yet a strong section of the princes decided to join the next session of the Assembly, as decided by the general conference of rulers. On the other hand, at the All-India States People's Conference at Gwalior (18-20 April 1947), Nehru regretted that the reforms that the princes were initiating were inadequate. He warned that all those, who would not join the Constituent Assembly thereafter, would; be regarded as hostile states. 'Our aim at present is to liberate as much of India as we can . . . and then to deal with the question of independence for the rest. I know we have to make a lot of concessions. But sometimes one has to pay a high price in the interest of the country's larger interest.'[9]

Nehru advised the Praja Mandals to demand constituent assemblies for their states. In reply to the criticism of the rather mild resolution of the conference, Nehru hinted that, though the Constituent Assembly of India had to meet the rulers halfway, it was a powerful weapon through which further advances were possible.

On the opening day of the third session of the Assembly, on 28 April 1947, 18 representatives of the states took their seats. B.L. Mitter, the astute Dewan of Baroda, said, 'We are here by right of being Indians and not by sufferance. We claim that we are in a position to make a substantial contribution to the common task.'[10]

A little later Nehru presented the report of the Negotiating Committee. He said that he had given it as his personal opinion that 'while we were deciding in favour of a republic for the whole of India, that did not bar

[9] *IAR*, 1947, vol. I, p. .213. Also, see Menon, *The Story of the Integration of the Indian States*, pp. 72-74.

[10] *CAD*, vol. III, p. 313.

any state from continuing the monarchical form of government so far as that state was concerned, provided of course, that there was the same measure of freedom and responsible government in the states'. However, he had told them that 'in this matter my decision is of little account. What counts is what this Assembly desires in this matter'. The Assembly had earlier made it clear that it did not wish to interfere in the internal arrangement of the states. It was for the people of the states to decide what they wanted. 'The question, in fact, does not arise in this Assembly. Here we are dealing with union matters, subjects of fundamental rights and the like.'[11]

Nehru reported the committee's success in reaching an accord with the States' Negotiating Committee on the distribution of the 93 seats roughly on the basis of the strength of population. On the method of choosing the representatives the committees had agreed that at least 50 per cent of them would be elected by the elected legislatures or, where such legislatures did not exist, 'other electoral colleges'. Some small states had to be grouped together for the purpose. The formula was ratified by the general conference of rulers.[12]

The problem of the states' participation being solved, the Rules of Procedure Committee of the Assembly recommended that

> the members of the Assembly representing the Indian states were entitled to take part in the proceedings of the Assembly on all days set apart for the business of constitution-making. They further had the right, on days set apart for the functioning of the Assembly as the dominion legislature, to participate in business relating to subjects in respect of which the states have acceded to the dominion. Though it was competent for the Constituent Assembly to deny or limit their participation in business relating to subjects in respect of which the states had not acceded, the Assembly should not bar or restrict their participation in such business also.[13]

The recommendations were accepted.

Participation of a handful of states in the proceedings of the Constituent Assembly, however, did not imply their merger with the Indian union or their obligation to accept the Indian Constitution. On the basis of the Cabinet Mission's plan a state department was set up with V.P. Menon as its secretary on 5 July 1947. Patel, the presiding minister of the department, assured the princes, in his inaugural speech, that 'we are no enemies of

[11] Ibid., p. 352.
[12] Ibid., pp. 363-74.
[13] Ibid., vol. V, p. 316.

the princely order'.[14] On 25 July, Mountbatten, in an address to the Chamber of Princes, endorsed Patel's appeal for accession.

Long and arduous negotiations between the state department and the states followed.[15] These negotiations certainly involved tremendous pressure tactics in order to counteract the fissiparous tendencies of several princely states. Two major points that emerged out of such negotiations were: the signature of three categories of instruments of accession (covering defence, external affairs and communication) and a Standstill Agreement with each state (which would make possible the continuation of all treaties and obligations between the crown and the states).

Place of the Indian States in the Constitution

The Union Constitution Committee's report, which was placed in the Assembly on 25 July 1947, recommended that 'the states should be on a par with the provinces as regards the federal legislative list subject to the consideration of any special matter which may be raised when the lists have been fully prepared'.[16] The executive authority of the President of India would extend over the matters mentioned in the list and covered by any special agreement made with a state. The executive authority of the ruler of a federated state would, however, continue to be exercisable in that state with respect to the federal authority. The first provision about the executive authority proved controversial. The prime ministers of a number of states gave notices of amendments following which N. Gopalaswami Ayyangar moved an amendment seeking that the federal intervention would be made 'in cases where it is considered necessary'. The prime ministers accepted the amendment. Yet, A. Ramaswami Mudaliar, the Dewan of Mysore, reiterated 'the essential principle that it shall be the rule that states shall have their own executive authority and that in special cases exception can be made'.[17]

On the other hand, quite a few speakers expressed their strong feeling about the continuation of the privileges of the rulers. Alladi Krishnaswami Ayyar explained the new stipulation as follows: so long as the states' administration was all right, the federation would not interfere.

But the federation is the sole judge and the only judge of the efficiency of the

[14] *The Statesman*, 6 July 1947.

[15] Quite a few popular representatives from the states complained in the Assembly that in the negotiations with the states their popular representatives were being ignored. See for instance the speech of Jainarain Vyas on 23 July 1947.

[16] *CAD*, vol. IV, p. 750.

[17] Ibid., p. 896.

administration throughout the union and every state agency and every provincial agency and every other agency must be the agency of the federation to the extent. The object of this amendment is very simple. If the state machinery is functioning properly, then you need not interfere. . . . But the ultimate power must rest with the federation, that is the principle to which we are committed. But that does not mean that the federation or the federal executive will go on experimenting.[18]

B.L. Mitter summed up: 'This is a simple clause embodying two principles; first is supremacy of the federal authority and second the continuation of the status quo.'[19]

By another amendment moved by Ayyar it was added that the government of the federation might, 'by agreement with any acceding Indian state but subject to the provisions of the constitution in regard to the relationship between the Indian federation and an acceding Indian state, undertake any legislative, executive or judicial functions in that state'.[20]

The Provincial Constitution Committee had earlier recommended that 'subject to the provisions of this constitution and of any special agreement, the executive authority of each province shall extend to the matters with respect to which the provincial legislature has power to make laws' (clause 8). In an explanatory note it was pointed out that the 'special agreement' meant an agreement between a province and an Indian state. Santhanam, at the time of discussion on 16 July 1947, raised the point that such 'agreement' could not be outside the union constitution's authority. The President of the Assembly, therefore, appointed a committee to examine clause 8 of the report. The recommendation of the committee, as placed by B.L. Mitter on 18 July, was that a province might undertake any legislative, executive or judicial functions vested in any state with the previous sanction of the federal government and by an agreement with the state, provided that such agreement related to subjects in the provincial of concurrent legislative list.[21] The clause, therefore, was redrafted and passed.

15 August—A Landmark

The transfer of power on 15 August 1947 made the princes realize their position. Five hundred and forty-seven states had joined the Indian union, though a number of them were yet unrepresented in the Assembly.

[18] Ibid., p. 897.
[19] Ibid., p. 901.
[20] Ibid., p. 906.
[21] Ibid., p. 666.

Hyderabad, Junagarh and Kashmir were still outside the orbit. Mountbatten, however, in his speech in the Constituent Assembly, observed that 'the only state of first importance that has not yet acceded is the premier state, Hyderabad'.[22] His silence about Junagarh and Kashmir is interesting.

The Draft Constitution mentioned the states of India in Part III of the first schedule—in two divisions. In division 'A' were the names of the 19 states that had till then acceded to India. In division 'B' those states that would accede in future would be mentioned. The Drafting Committee recognized that it was 'not possible to enumerate each of the states' because the various mergers would lead to changes in the size and existence of the states. There would be no power of parliament in respect of posts and telegraphs, telephones, wireless or broadcasting and corporations owned or controlled by a state (article 224 of the Draft). Parliament's power to legislate for the state would be subject to the terms of agreements between the union government and the states (article 225).

For the time being the Government of India, by agreement with any princely state, but subject to the provisions of the Constitution in regard to the relationship between the union and such state, could undertake the executive, legislative and judicial functions vested in the state (article 236-1). It would also be competent for the government of a state in Part I, with the previous sanction of the president, to undertaken by an agreement the legislative, executive and judicial functions of the Indian state (article 237-1). The executive, legislative and judicial powers of the union and state governments in such cases would extend over the princely states within the spheres of such agreements. They were supplemented by article 142(2) of the Draft Constitution.

Through an agreement between the union government and the government of a princely state, the union government could take power of collection and distribution of levy, tax or duty on the state. Such an agreement would continue for a period of not more than ten years. The president could terminate or modify any such agreement after five years and after consideration of the report of a finance commission to be appointed by him (article 258). The union government would have authority over 'the strength, organization and control of the armed forces raised and employed in states'. In an accompanying note the chairman of the Drafting Committee expressed his strong feeling against this provision permitting the states to maintain their independent armies which, however, was in conformity with the earlier decision of the Assembly.

[22] Ibid., vol. V, p. 17.

Where the ruler of a state would cede full powers to the Indian union, the territory would be administered as a Part II state (formerly the centrally administered territories) according to draft article 212 (2) previously formulated.

New Phase of Integration

After 15 August, a new process of integration was initiated by the states ministry with the object of democratizing the governments of the states and linking them up with the Indian administration either by merger with neighbouring provinces or by 'unionisation' in groups. A few states were brought under the administration of chief commissioners. Most of the princes, on pain of popular revolts and even, in some cases, of 'communist menace', readily handed over power. The first of the states thus integrated with India were the Orissa states which had been put together and merged with Orissa, and the Chhattisgarh states which in the same way had been merged with the province of Central Provinces and Berar. These mergers were complete by 1 January 1948. On 27 January 1948, therefore, when the Constituent Assembly met, Yudhisthira Mishra, an elected representative of the Orissa states, challenged the right of the members nominated by rulers of these states to sit in the Assembly after the rulers themselves had handed over all their powers and privileges. The president, however, ruled that the members cold continue.[23]

V.T. Krishnamachari, B.H. Zaidi, Sardar Singhji of Khetri and Jaidev Singh, all official nominees of the states, in a memorandum to the Drafting Committee, suggested that,

> the Indian states should adhere to the constitution framed by the Constituent Assembly by the execution of an instrument of accession the detailed particulars of which should be set forth in the constitution itself. We would also suggest that negotiations should be initiated without further delay for the settlement of the terms and conditions of the agreements referred to in articles 225 and 258 of the Draft constitution.[24]

The Drafting Committee's rejoinder proposed to keep Part III of the first schedule initially blank, 'because we cannot assume that the Indian states will accede to the new union before they know the shape of the new constitution. But after the Draft Constitution, together with all amendments, has been taken into consideration by the Constituent

[23] Ibid., vol. V, p. 24.

[24] Siva Rao, *Select Documents*, vol. IV, p. 211.

Assembly, a reasonable period may be allowed for negotiation with the Indian states as to which of them would be prepared to accede.' When the names of the acceding Indian states would have been ascertained they would be inserted in the appropriate part of the first schedule to the Constitution finally passed. If any Indian state would choose to accede subject to terms use could be made of article 225 of the draft.[25]

Events, however, moved faster than the Constituent Assembly so that accession and integration were both mostly completed before the Constituent Assembly finished its work. During the seventh session of the Assembly, on 4 November 1948, G. Durgabai moved a few amendments to the rules of the Constituent Assembly relating to the reallocation of seats of the Constituent Assembly to the representatives of the states as agreed in a meeting of the Government of India and the rulers and premiers. As reasons of the proposed changes, Durgabai cited the basic changes that had taken place in the constitutional scheme.[26] Altogether 10 states had joined Pakistan, reducing the states' quota in the Constituent Assembly of India from 93 to 89.

According to the new scheme of allocation the states were classified into two parts. In Part I were put 17 states (including Hyderabad and Kashmir) which would have 49 representatives in the Assembly at least half of whom would be elected. In Part II were put all other states, which would have 40 seats, any vacancies in which would be filled by election. (An exception to these rules was made by the Assembly on 4 May 1949 when the ruler of Kashmir was permitted to nominate all 4 representatives to the Assembly, in consultation with his premier, in view of the special political situation in Kashmir.) On of these members, however, not all did turn up till the last day of the Assembly's session.

In August 1947 the Governor-General had issued the Extra-Provincial Jurisdiction Ordinance which was turned into an act in December 1947. The hesitation of Hyderabad to join India led to police action by India. Its 16 representatives remained absent from the proceedings of the Constituent Assembly all along. The participation of all states by Hyderabad brought the total strength of the Constituent Assembly to 308, the states' representatives numbering 73.

[25] Ibid., p. 260. The Drafting Committee, however, proposed that the President might direct that any state or group of states at any time would be governed for all purposes as if the state or the group of states formed part of a state specified in part I of the first schedule (former provinces) and he might give all incidental and consequential directions for the purpose (proviso to draft art. 212/2).

[26] *CAD*, vol. VII, p. 3.

The integration of the states in the new phase necessitated the amendment of the Government of India Act, 1935, in the form of the new sections 290 A and 290 B. During the proposal of this amendment on 5 January 1949, Patel reported a large advance in the integration of the states.[27]

The fascinating story of the integration of the Indian states is beyond the scope of this work. It would be sufficient to state here that this integration was almost wholly attained outside the Assembly through negotiations with the rulers of the states and their official representatives. The Constituent Assembly indeed provided a forum for such negotiations; technically, however, all agreements were based on the consent of the Government of India on the one hand and the rulers on the other. Patel gave a short account of it in the Assembly on 12 October 1949.

> When the states entered the Constituent Assembly of India, it was thought that the constitution of the states would not form part of the constitution of India. It was also understood that unlike the provinces the accession of the states to the Indian union would not be automatic but would be by means of some powers of ratification of the constitution. In the context of those commitments and the conditions then obtaining certain provisions were incorporated in the Draft Constitution which placed the states in certain important respects on a footing different from that of the provinces.

As a result of the policy of integration and democratisation of states pursued by the Government of India since December 1947, the process of what might be described as 'unionisation' of states has been greatly accentuated. . . .

These important developments enabled us to review the position of the states under the new constitution and to remove from it all vestiges of anomalies and disparities which found their way into the new constitution as a legacy from the past.[28]

Constitutions for the States

When the covenants establishing the various 'unions of states' were entered into, it was contemplated that the constitutions of the various unions would be formed by their constituent assemblies within the framework of the

[27] Ibid., pp. 1270-1. The amendment established regular administrative relation between the provinces and certain acceding states on their neighbourhood, being an improvement on the Extra-Provincial Jurisdiction Act.

[28] Ibid., vol. X, pp. 161-3.

covenants and the Constitution of India. Those provisions were made in the covenants on the basis of the theory that the assumption, by the Constituent Assembly of India, of the constitution-making authority in respect of the states would constitute an infringement of the autonomy of the states. As, however, the states came closer to the centre, it was no longer considered necessary to stick to the idea of separate constitutions being framed for the different constituent units of the union of India. With the concurrence of various unions and states, therefore, it was decided that the constitution of the states should form an integral part of the Constitution of India.

The states ministry, at first, suggested a model constitution for all states and unions of states which their respective constituent assemblies might adopt and, by a formal resolution, request the Constituent Assembly of India to incorporate in the Constitution of India. Thereafter the state or the union would formally accede to the union of India as set up by the new constitution. This procedure had, however, to be abandoned because, except in Mysore, Saurashtra and Travancore-Cochin, the Constituent Assembly had nowhere been formed. And the time was short. Meanwhile on 10 April 1948, the Special Committee recommended the omission of all references to rulers, in draft article 212(2).[29]

The question was, therefore, discussed threadbare in a meeting on 19 May 1949, between the Government of India's representatives and the rulers and their ministers. A revolutionary decision was taken there to the effect that the Constitution of India would apply in the states with necessary modifications. By one great stroke, therefore, republicanism of the Indian Constitution wiped out the anachronism of monarchy in the native states.

The Constituent Assemblies of Mysore, Saurashtra and Travancore-Cochin accepted the Indian Constitution though they proposed a few modifications which were largely accepted by the Constituent Assembly. In the other states, as there was no constituent assembly, the Rajpramukhs (designation of the rulers) issued proclamations accepting the Constitution. It was promised by the Government of India, however, that when legislatures in such states would come into existence they could propose further amendments of the Constitution. In view of Kashmir's special political position she would accept the Constitution but the people's ratification had to be secured later. (This was not done owing to further political developments.)

[29] See Shiva Rao's *Select Documents*, vol. IV, p. 409. The Drafting Committee coined the term 'Rajpramukh'.

The establishment of the new relation of the states with the Government of India necessitated a set of important changes in the Draft Constitution. On 12 October 1949, therefore, Ambedkar moved for the insertion of a new chapter (Part VI-A) in the Draft Constitution. Article 211-A laid down that the provisions of Part VI of the Constitution would apply in relation to the states for the time being specified in Part III (covering most of the states and unions) of the first schedule as they applied in relation to the states for the time being specified in Part I of that schedule (the former British Indian provinces) subject to certain modifications. Articles 224, 225 and 237 of the Draft were abolished. Certain other articles were amended.

The Last Phase

It should be made clear that the integration was neither formalized nor complete till 26 January 1950, when the Constitution came into force. The problem of Hyderabad was a case in point. Hyderabad did not send any representative to the Constituent Assembly. After a military rule of over one year in Hyderabad, Patel was able to tell the Constituent Assembly on 12 October 1949, that the Nizam had signified acceptance of the Constitution of India. The revised first schedule proposed by Ambedkar on 13 October 1949 showed Hyderabad at the head of the Part B states. Even on 25 January 1950, the Hyderabad (Exchange of Enclaves) Order was passed, by the Governor-General, on the basis of an 'agreement' between the governments of India and Hyderabad.[30]

On 15 October 1949, during the debate on the revised first schedule, Shibbanlal Saksena sought clarification as to why the territories of Jammu and Kashmir were defined as those existing at the commencement of the Constitution and not before 15 August 1947. Was not the Constitution reconciling itself to the fact of partial occupation of the territories? Rajendra Prasad confessed that it was 'a purely political question and we cannot decide it by a resolution of this house'.[31]

On 17 October 1949, N.G. Ayyangar moved article 306A—which now forms article 370 of the Constitution offering a special status to Kashmir. Kashmir was, at that moment, under a ceasefire and partly occupied. In view of 'the special conditions of Kashmir', it was not yet 'ripe for this

[30] The Government of India decided to effect the Exchange of Enclaves before 26 January 1950, through the 1935 Act.

[31] *CAD*, vol. X, p. 319. Prasad also said: 'Whatever we have got now we have got, and if we get more, we shall have more'. Ibid.

kind of integration', Ayyangar said. He also reminded the members of the pledge given to the people of Kashmir that in the matter of a constitutional arrangement they would have a chance to express their views:

At present, the legislature which is known as the Praja Sabha in the state is dead. Neither that legislature nor a constituent assembly can be convoked or can function until complete peace comes to prevail in that state. We have, therefore, to deal with the government of the state which, as represented in the council of ministers, reflects the opinion of the largest political party in the state. Till a constituent assembly comes into being, only an interim arrangement is possible and not an arrangement which could at once be brought into line with the arrangement that exists in the case of the other states.[32]

On 25 November 1949, Yuvaraj Karan Singh, regent of Jammu and Kashmir, proclaimed the acceptance of the Indian Constitution 'as far as applicable to Jammu and Kashmir'.[33] On 26 November 1949, Patel announced in the Constituent Assembly that all the states and unions of states had accepted the Constitution of India. The President of the Assembly on the same day duly took note of the fact that

the constitution as it stands practically makes no difference so far as the administration and distribution of powers among the various organs of the state are concerned between what were the provinces and what were the Indian states before. They are now more or less on the same footing and, as time passes, whatever little distinction still exists is bound to disappear.[34]

Even then, the 'Khasi Hill states on the north-east of India were not affected by the process of integration until the inauguration of the Constitution'.[35] As Saadulla, member of the Drafting Committee from Assam, pointed out during the third reading of the Draft Constitution, the Khasi states had only entered into an instrument of accession and an annexed agreement about the legislative competence of the Assam legislature.[36] There was no formal acceptance of the Constitution by the Khasi states. It was Schedule I of the new Constitution which declared the Khasi states and the Assam tribal areas (hitherto controlled according to the Extra-Provincial Jurisdiction Act) as parts of Assam.

[32] Ibid., pp. 423-5.
[33] *Gazette of India Extraordinary*, 25 January 1950.
[34] *CAD*, vol. XI, pp. 987-8.
[35] *White Paper on Indian States*, p. 45.
[36] *CAD*, vol. XI, p. 735.

CHAPTER 12

End of the Indian Problem (II)

Minority Rights

THE COMMITTEE STAGE

The Minority Rights Subcommittee was set up on 27 February 1947 by the Advisory Committee, according to the Cabinet Mission's plan. It had a preliminary meeting on the same day and the following day but had to sit further in April (17-19) and July (21-7) to formulate its report. In the first two sessions the Muslim League was absent.

The task of the subcommittee was going to be difficult. In its preliminary meeting, Rajagopalachari deprecated the general desire to take up the question of 'political' minorities. He was in favour of concentrating on 'the minority rights socalled', while G.B. Pant and several minority leaders wanted discussion on both, as the Cripps broadcast, after the Cabinet Mission's announcement, had made the task of the subcommittee clear.[1] The next day the subcommittee approved of Munshi's questionnaire for the members, which asked:

(1) What should be the nature and scope of the safeguards for a minority in the new constitution? (2) What should be the political safeguards of a minority (a) in the centre and (b) in the provinces? (3) What should be the economic safeguards of a minority (a) in the centre and (b) in the provinces? (4) What should be the religious, educational and cultural safeguards for a minority? (5) What machinery should be set up to ensure that the safeguards are effective? (6) How is it proposed that the safeguards should be eliminated, in what time, under what circumstances?[2]

MINORITY RIGHTS SO-CALLED

The subcommittee actually did not take up the political questions till July 1947, when the League participated in the work of the Constituent Assembly. In April it began to examine the report of the Fundamental

[1] B. Shiva Rao, *Select Documents*, vol. II, p. 388.

[2] Ibid., p. 391.

Rights Subcommittee from the minorities' point of view[3] and sought the following additions: (1) Reservation of public offices for the classes that were not adequately represented in the services, qualifying equality of opportunity; (2) freedom to 'practise' and 'propagate' as well as to profess religion; (3) education through mother-tongue and script; (4) protection of the language, script and culture of minority groups; (5) free admission of all the minorities in the state-aided schools and other educational institutions; (6) equal state-aid to the institutions of minorities; (7) abolition of discrimination in places of public use; and (8) restriction of the right of residence and possession of land in tribal areas. Most of these demands were conceded, though a few proved controversial.[4]

The Subcommittee on Fundamental Rights considered the suggestions and produced the interim report on fundamental rights.

Religious Freedom

Religious rights became a central point of minority rights. On 26 March 1947, the Subcommittee on Fundamental Rights adopted a modified version of Munshi's draft article on the freedom of conscience and the right to freely profess and practise religion. Such rights would not include economic, financial and political activities associated with the religious activities. The subcommittee adopted Ayyar's clause about communities being free to set up their religious institutions. The two women members, Amrit Kaur and Hansa Mehta were, however, opposed to this form of religious right which would block the long-needed reforms of practices like devdasi and child-marriage. The objections led to the removal of the right to 'practise' religion.[5]

In the Minorities Subcommittee, whereas M. Ruthnaswami advocated the right of propagation as certain religions, like Christianity and Islam, were essentially 'proselytising religions', P.R. Thakur demanded the right to practise religion 'such as the playing of music before mosques'.[6] The Minority Subcommittee added the right to 'practise' as well as to 'propagate' religion.

Both in the Advisory Committee and in the Constituent Assembly

[3] The proceedings of the subcommittees are found in Shiva Rao's *Select Documents*. vol. II.

[4] Ibid., pp. 208-9.

[5] Ibid., pp. 122, 165. Powerful support was also accorded to Kaur and Mehta by A.K. Ayyar.

[6] Ibid., p. 201.

heated controversies on this freedom persisted.[7] The Christian members were particularly concerned about the freedom of propagation, whereas allegations of undue influences being used in the 'propagation' of religion (conversion) were freely hurled by some Hindu members. However, the Advisory Committee accepted the suggestion of the Minorities Committee, which was also incorporated in the Draft Constitution.

When Tajamul Husain, during discussion of the Draft Constitution, moved amendments through which he sought to restrict religious freedom to practising it 'privately' and to put a ban on persons having any visible mark of religious identity, a number of Muslims opposed it. In view of the heat already generated on the question, the House turned down the amendment.[8]

Munshi's draft about conversion involved some controversy. According to the draft, conversion of a minor (below 18) without the parents permission would not be recognized under the law. Conversion through coercion or undue influence or the offering of material inducement was prohibited and made punishable by the law of the union. The Fundamental Rights Subcommittee revised them. The Advisory Committee finally amended the second provision to the effect that conversion through coercion, etc., would not be 'recognized' by law and dropped the provision about the conversion of a minor. In the Constituent Assembly Munshi revived the controversy through an amendment which sought to add two disqualifications for conversion to the original one—'fraud' and 'minorhood'.[9] Asked to explain the new proposal, Munshi gave an evasive answer. Finally, the article was dropped by the Assembly, on its return from a re-examination by the Advisory Committee, on 30 August 1947.[10]

The House readily accepted Munshi's amendment that, notwithstanding the religious freedom, the state would be able to legislate for the purpose of 'throwing open Hindu religious institutions of a public character to any class or section of Hindus', as well as for social welfare or reforms, though L. Krishnaswami Bharati wanted a definition of 'religious institutions of public character'.[11] Accepting Munshi's amendment, Patel congratulated the House on its acceptance of 'this very controversial matter which has taken several days in the committees and gone through several

[7] *CAD*, vol. VII, pp. 817-40.
[8] Ibid., vol. III, p. 480.
[9] Ibid., vol. V, p. 396.
[10] Ibid., vol. III, p. 476.
[11] Ibid., p. 471.

committees'.[12] So was adopted the clause on the management of religious institutions with a slight modification.

The question of religious instruction in educational institutions underwent several drafting operations. Adopting Rau's draft the Advisory Committee recommended that religious instruction would not be compulsory in 'any school maintained or receiving aid out of public funds (clause 16). The clause was first referred back, on 1 May 1947,[13] to the Advisory Committee which returned it in the same form on 30 August 1947. The clause was further referred to an ad hoc committee[14] whose recommendation was incorporated in the Draft Constitution,[15] and passed on 7 December 1948.

The recommendation was broken into three parts in the Draft Constitution: (1) No religious instruction would be given by the state in the educational institutions 'wholly maintained out of state funds'; (2) religious instruction was made optional in an institution receiving aid from or recognized by the state; (3) a community or denomination could yet give such instruction 'outside the working hours'. The controversy persisted until the article was passed, after an amendment to clause I, deleting 'by the state', and S.L. Saksena's amendment deleting clause 3 altogether, on 7 December 1948.[16]

The Fundamental Rights Subcommittee also accepted the proposal of Rau to incorporate the right of religious denominations to manage their affairs, and to own, acquire and dispose of property, in the teeth of opposition of Masani and Shah.[17] Munshi's proposal for freedom from taxation for religious purposes was also accepted. On 7 December 1948, however, the rights of religious denominations were subjected to 'public order, morality or health'.[18]

In line with Ambedkar's suggestion, the Fundamental Rights Subcommittee, on 26 March 1947, proposed that the state would not recognize any religion as state religion. K.T. Shah wanted a categorical declaration of the state being secular.[19] On 14 April 1947, the proposal

[12] Ibid., p. 477.
[13] Ibid., p. 480.
[14] Ibid., vol. V, p. 393.
[15] *The Draft Constitution of India*, February 1948, article 22.
[16] *CAD*, vol. VII, pp. 886-7.
[17] B. Shiva Rao, *Select Documents*, vol. II, p. 123.
[18] *CAD*, vol. VII, p. 859.
[19] B. Shiva Rao, *Select Documents*, vol. II, p. 123.

was altogether dropped presumably because of certain objections raised by Munshi and Panikkar.[20]

CULTURAL AND EDUCATIONAL RIGHTS

It was according to the demand of the Minority Rights Subcommittee that the Advisory Committee forwarded clause 18 of its report, embodying the cultural rights of the minorities. When Mahavir Tyagi opposed any commitment to a particular policy about the minorities, until the question of partition was settled and the attitudes of the other state towards its minorities was known, Ambedkar categorically said that minority policy of India was not a relative one. Yet, subclause (2) of the clause, relating to the freedom of admission of all communities in 'state educational institutions' and banning of compulsory religious instructions, was referred back to the Advisory Committee.[21] The clause came back in the same form and was passed on 30 August 1947.[22] It formed article 23 in the Draft Constitution, which was passed on 8 December 1948 with Bhargava's amendment inserting a clause that no citizen would be denied admission into a state-aided institution on grounds only of religion, race, caste, language or any of them, for the original clause II.[23]

As expected, a great amount of heat over the question was generated by some of the Leaguers in the Assembly. Their fundamental demand, on articles 20 and 23 was to express the rights in a positive, rather than in a negative, language. Thus, Z.H. Lari proposed an amendment to article 23 to provide that the minorities would be 'protected' in respect of their language, etc., and would not merely 'conserve' them, as provided in the Draft Constitution. Lari actually charged the Drafting Committee of having altered the spirit of the Advisory Committee's recommendations, through the change of language—a charge, which Ambedkar took pains to deny.[24]

The problem of minorities had several and confusing dimensions. Because of long Gandhiite commitments of the Congress members there was a general eagerness for constitutionalizing prohibition. It was for Karimuddin (a Muslim Leaguer), however, to move in the Assembly for incorporation of prohibition in the social principles part (on 22 November 1948). On Ambedkar's request the article was held over. On the next day

[20] Ibid., pp. 165, 169.
[21] *CAD*, vol. III, pp. 497-503.
[22] Ibid., vol. V, p. 402.
[23] Ibid., p. 897.
[24] Ibid., pp. 893, 922-4.

two amendments were moved to article 38 of the Draft seeking the incorporation of prohibition. It was for Jaipal Singh to make a strong attack on the moves as an encroachment on the religious rights of adivasis.[25] Climaxing the debate Bhopinder Singh Mann (Sikh) moved for prohibition of tobacco[26]—a taboo in his society. Ambedkar accepted the first prohibition and not the second. So the first move was successful, the second defeated.

On the same day, when the House took up Thakurdas Bhargava's motion about protection of useful cows[27] there was a passionate attack from the Muslim Leaguers who definitely thought that their religious rights were disregarded. The Congress members vainly tried to cite economic reasons for the banning of cow slaughter. Finally, of course, it was passed and formed article 38-A of the Draft Constitution (social policy).

One major issue on which the Muslim League members of the Constituent Assembly seemed to have taken a doubtful stand was the protection of the Muslim personal law. Whereas Masani, Mehta and Kaur in the Fundamental Rights Subcommittee demanded the guarantee of a uniform social code within ten years,[28] it was accepted only as a social policy, and the Minority Rights Subcommittee wanted it to be voluntarily acceptable to the minorities.[29] During discussion on the Directive Principles in the Draft Constitution, on 23 November 1948, a number of amendments were moved by the Leaguers requiring a guarantee that the personal laws of the minorities would not be affected. Munshi replied that such amendments could not prevent the state from legislating for social reforms (according to article 19 of the Draft). He was joined by A.K. Ayyar and Ambedkar in making a fervent advocacy of a uniform civil code. The amendments were negatived.[30]

The demand for the protection of the personal law of the Muslims was sought to be revived by Mohammed Ismail twice, in course of discussion of the draft articles on the right of freedom and the religious rights.[31] On both occasions it was rejected as the House had already accepted, as a Directive Principle of State Policy, the development of a uniform civil code.

[25] Ibid., p. 560.
[26] Ibid., p. 563.
[27] Ibid., p. 568.
[28] B. Shiva Rao, *Select Documents*, vol. II, p. 162.
[29] Ibid., p. 206.
[30] *CAD*, vol. VII, p. 552.
[31] Ibid., pp. 721, 821.

Political Minorities and Statutory Reservation

In B.N. Rau's questionnaire, suggestions about the statutory provisions for the protection of minority interests had been invited. Of the six Provincial Constitution Committee members who replied,[32] Amrit Kaur (an Indian Christian and a Congressite) pleaded for proportional representation to the legislature and executive, four members were for statutory reservation in the legislature (including two for conventional representation in the executive) and one against reservation. In the Union Constitution Committee reservation for minorities in the legislature was desired by Panikkar, Mookerjee and the Ayyangar-Ayyar formula.[33] The Union and Provincial Constitution Committees, however, decided to take the lead from the Advisory Committee on this point. Much of steam-rollering was done in the Constituent Assembly to remove the last vestiges of 'the problem of minorities'.

When, on 27 August 1947, Patel moved the report of the Minority Rights Subcommittee in the Constituent Assembly, he said that he was

> happy to say that this report has been the result of a general consensus of opinion between the minorities themselves and the majority. Therefore, although it is not possible to satisfy all, you will see that this report has been the result of agreement on many points, and wherever there has been disagreement, the recommendations have been carried by a very large majority, so that except perhaps on one point the report has been practically an agreed report.[34]

The committee, it was reported, had considered three main points: (1) Representation in legislatures (joint *versus* separate electorates and weightage); (2) representation in the cabinet; and (3) representation in the services.

(1) It was decided by an overwhelming majority (28 votes to three) that separate electorates should be abolished and substituted by reservation of seats in the legislature. Even then the Anglo-Indians would not claim any reservation and be satisfied with the provision for adequate nomination by the governors of the provinces where they were inadequately represented. Parsis had no claim for special treatment. Decisions on the plains tribes of Assam were withheld till the publication of the report of the committee on tribal areas in Assam. For the Indian Christians reservation of seats in provincial legislatures

[32] Provincial Constitution Committee's File.
[33] Union Constitution Committee's File.
[34] *CAD*, vol. V, p. 213.

without weightage was recommended.[35] In view of the uncertainty over the boundary of the Punjab, decision about the Sikhs was held over. Of greater strength were the Muslims and the scheduled castes, for whom reservation of seats for 10 years initially was recommended.

(2) The committee favoured the growth of a convention rather than any statutory provision for allotment of positions in the cabinet to the minorities in common with the Act of 1935.

(3) Reservation of certain posts in the services for certain communities (the backward classes and the Anglo-Indians) was recommended, though service, it was thought, would generally go on the basis of merit.

During discussion of the report, on 27 August, B. Pocker Sahib Bahadur, a League member from Madras, moved an amendment demanding separate electorates for the Muslims.[36] He was supported by Choudhury Khaliquzzaman; though the other Muslims remained silent, it showed that the League's demand for separate electorates was not yet dropped. The amendment was lost. The report was accepted the next day.

In Part XIV of the Draft Constitution special provisions for protection of minority rights and interests were made. The following major steps were suggested:

(1) Reservation of seats in the House of the People for (a) the Muslims and the scheduled castes, (b) the scheduled tribes, and (c) the Indian Christian community in Madras and Bombay (article 292).

(2) Reservation of seats in the state legislative assemblies for (a) Muslims, (b) the Indian Christian community of Madras and Bombay and (c) the autonomous districts of Assam (article 294).

(3) Nomination of adequate number of Anglo-Indians in the legislatures of the centre and the states if they were inadequately represented (articles 293 and 295).[37]

(4) Claims of all minority communities would be taken into consideration, consistent with the maintenance of efficiency of the administration, in the making of appointment to services and posts in connection with the affairs of the union or of states (viz. railways, customs, postal

[35] The Indian Christian movement was chiefly under the aegis of the Congress. The important leaders of the Indian Christians, Dr. H.C. Mukherjee and Amrit Kaur, were Congressites of long standing.

[36] Ibid., p. 229.

[37] The Anglo-Indian campaign for special protection was described in Frank Anthony's presidential speech at the All-India Anglo-Indian Conference, 1956.

and telegraph services). They would also get some special educational grants (article 296).

(5) For the first two years the Anglo-Indians would enjoy all old privileges about appointment in certain services (article 297). They would continue to get certain special grants for the first three financial years (article 298).

(6) Special officers on minority affairs would be appointed by the central government (article 299).

THE MINORITY RIGHTS: SECOND PHASE

The cause of separate electorates and statutory reservation in the executive was lost with the announcement of the 3 June plan. There was actually a revulsion against it after the murder of Gandhiji. Though the Drafting Committee had incorporated in the Draft Constitution the recommendation of the Advisory Committee, after publication of the draft a large number of amendments poured in demanding the abolition of reservation. The Drafting Committee considered them as questions of policy and therefore did not move any amendment on their behalf.

The general discussion of the Draft Constitution revealed a varied approach of the minorities and a changed strategy of the Muslim League. Hasrat Mohani's emotional speech called for the abolition of separate treatment of the minorities and creation of non-communal political parties.[38] All but two speakers of the Muslim League wanted abolition of separate electorates. Of these two, whereas Pocker Sahib reiterated the demand for separate electorates,[39] Mohammed Ismail insisted on separate electorates as well as reservation of seats.[40] But the majority of the Leaguers were certainly confused. A number of them persuaded themselves to give up both these claims. The case for separate electorates was evidently lost. Reservation of seats for the minorities would mean, in many cases, members of the minority community being elected by the majority community.[41] Hence they would really represent the majority community. The partition had left a substantial number of Indian Muslims scattered all over the country, creating an electoral disadvantage for them. So they wanted 'proportional representation for the legislative elections. Part of this strategy was their demand for a Swiss-type executive, elected through proportional representation. Both the moves were defeated.

[38] *CAD*, vol. VII, p. 46.
[39] Ibid., p. 364.
[40] Ibid., p. 332.
[41] Ibid., p. 287.

Of the other minorities, the Sikhs were the biggest group and more or less concentrated. They generally welcomed the minority provisions.[42] So did the Anglo-Indians and the Indian Christians.

On 25 May 1949, Patel submitted the report of a very important meeting of the Advisory Committee held on 11 May 1949, including the report of a special subcommittee.[43] The latter had been appointed with Patel (as chairman), Nehru, Rajendra Prasad, Ambedkar and Munshi on 24 February 1948 to examine 'certain minority problems affecting East Punjab and West Bengal'. The subcommittee could not recommend either communal electorates or weightage in the legislature for the Sikhs as they had no shortcoming as a minority. They also did not recommend any arrangement for West Bengal different from that for other provinces. It was also reported that, when the Advisory Committee had been considering the report of the subcommittee on 30 December 1948, some members had felt that 'conditions having vastly changed since the Advisory Committee had made their recommendations in 1947', there should be no reservation of seats for the Muslims, Christians, Sikhs or any other religious minorities.[44] A number of resolutions to that effect were given notice of by H.C. Mukherjee (the Indian Christian leader of the Congress), Tajamul Husain (a Shia Muslim of Bihar, who declared in the Assembly that he never had close connection with the Muslim League), P.R. Thakur, Lakshmikanta Moitra and, jointly, Govind Das and Thakurdas Bhargava (all Hindu Congressmen), seeking to recommend to the Constituent Assembly the abolition of reservation of seats for minorities.[45]

Patel, however, wanted each minority to give opinion about itself and the meeting of the Advisory Committee adjourned till May 1949. The leaders of the Muslim and the Sikh communities failed to meet during this period. The Sikh members of the East Punjab Legislative Assembly met on 10 May 1949 in Delhi. So when the Advisory Committee met again on 11 May 1949, it had before it the resolution of Mukherjee and an amendment to it by V.I. Muniswami Pillai seeking the maintenance of reservation for scheduled castes. Mukherjee's resolution found 'the wholehearted support of an overwhelming majority of the members of the Advisory Committee'.[46] Actually, one member out of four Muslim

[42] See Hukam Singh's Speech, in ibid., p. 552.

[43] Ibid., vol. VIII, pp. 269-72.

[44] Ibid., p. 313.

[45] Proceedings of the meeting in the Law Ministry File, CA/22/RR 49.

[46] See Saadulla's speech, *CAD*, vol. VIII, p. 304.

members of the Advisory Committee present in the same meeting supported it. Another Muslim, Jafar Imam, a Leaguer, opposed it, while the two Congress Muslim members, Abul Kalam Azad and Hafizur Rahman, were silent. Tajamul Husain was absent.[47]

There is no 'proof' that the majority of the Muslim members of the House were in favour of the resolution that was moved by Patel on the same day and carried overwhelmingly by the Assembly:

(1) that notwithstanding any decision already taken by the Constituent Assembly in this behalf, the provisions of part XIV of the Constitution of India be so amended as to give effect to the recommendations of the Advisory Committee contained in the second report, and
(2) The following classes in East Punjab, namely Muzhabis, Ramdases, Kabir Panthis and Sikligars be included in the list of representation in the legislatures given to the scheduled castes.[48]

Tajamul Husain said that out of the 33 Muslim members of the Assembly 10 had migrated to Pakistan. Four Leaguers from Madras were for separate electorates, four Leaguers (two from Bihar and two from Assam including Saadulla) were for reservation and one Z.H. Lari, was for cumulative voting, leaving one member whose opinion was unknown.[49] He claimed in his team 13 members (there is no proof of the validity of the claim, anyway). He even claimed that, taking Lari, he was in the 8-7 majority on the day of discussion, when 15 Muslim members were present in the Assembly. To consider Lari, who was opposed to both separate electorates and reservation, as a member of Tajamul Husain's bandwagon may appear unreasonable to many; for, as already seen, many Leaguers considered proportional representation a better safeguard than reservation. In any event, the sace for proportional representation had long been lost. Lari's effort to reopen the case after the loss of reservation was futile.[50] There was, at the same time, a strong feeling among many Muslim leaders that separate electorates or reservation will turn a Muslim into an alien in the eye of the majority community in India.

On 23 and 24 August, articles 292 and 294 of the draft were so amended that reservation of seats only for the scheduled castes, scheduled tribes and autonomous districts of Assam (in the House of the People and the

[47] See Tajamul Husain's speech, ibid., p. 337. Congressite Muslims, led by Azad, were formerly advocates of reservation. Tajamul Husain had always opposed all kinds of safeguards. See also Munshi, *Pilgrimage to Freedom*, pp. 207-8.

[48] *CAD*, vol. VIII, p. 272

[49] Ibid., pp. 355-6.

[50] Ibid., pp. 282-5.

legislative assemblies) was maintained. By another amendment the system of reservation was limited to a period of ten years. Certain minor changes were made in respect of the Anglo-Indians. Mention of the scheduled tribes in the Constitution was, however, considered unnecessary. On 17 September 1949, the eighth schedule of the Draft Constitution listing the scheduled tribes was deleted.[51]

On 14 October 1949, when article 296 (reservation of services for minorities) was being discussed, Ambedkar moved an amendment seeking the abolition of reservation in services except for the scheduled castes and tribes (who were backward people). The Muslim and Sikh members strongly objected to the alteration of an already decided policy. The Sikhs directly blamed the Congress for breaking promises. Hukam Singh, who had supported abolition of reservation in the legislatures, now opposed the move:

> The Sikhs are told, when they remind the Congress of their past pledges in 1929, 1946 and again in 1947, that circumstances have changed. The Sikhs were recognized as one of the three main communities in the Cabinet Mission plan of which the Constituent Assembly is the creature. The only changed circumstance is that the Muslims have got Pakistan. Does it stand to reason that, because the Muslim have secured Pakistan, therefore the Sikhs have ceased to be minority?[52]

Patel, however, denied that the Congress wanted to impose any decision on any community against its will.[53] The amendment was adopted. It is useless to hold any individual or even the Congress party responsible for this radical change. Ralph H. Retzlaff writes: '(1) Had the initial timetable which called for the completion of the drafting of the constitution by the fall of 1947 been adhered to and (2) had the minorities, especially the Muslims, adopted a conciliatory attitude, it is clear that the constitution would have included political safeguards of the minorities'.[54]

[51] The list of regional languages took its place in the final draft.
[52] *CAD*, vol. X, p. 235.
[53] Ibid., pp. 246-50.
[54] Ralph H. Retzlaff, in R.N. Spann, *Constitutionalism in Asia*, p. 66.

CHAPTER 13

Framing of the Constitution (I)

The Social Structure

The framing of a set of fundamental rights was implied in the Objectives Resolution, that had been adopted by the Assembly, as well as the Cabinet Mission's scheme. Moreover, most of the members were determined to have 'uniform fundamental rights',[1] providing at the same time safeguards for minorities and backward classes and areas.

During the third session of the Assembly, the chairman of the Advisory Committee, Patel, on 29 April 1947, requested the Assembly to grant him extension of time for submission of the final report on fundamental rights. The request being conceded, Patel submitted what he called 'a preliminary or an interim report' on fundamental rights.[2]

Clause 2 of the subcommittee's report said that the existing laws and ordinances inconsistent with the given fundamental rights would be abrogated to the extent of such inconsistency. The state would also not pass in future any law prejudicial to the fundamental rights. Clause 22 elaborated the constitutional remedies to be secured from the courts. The Supreme Court was given the power to enforce such rights. Such powers included the power to issue directions in the nature of the writs of *habeas corpus*, *mandamus*, prohibition, *quo warranto* and *certiorari*. The right to secure remedies would not be suspended unless 'when, in the case of rebellion or invasion or other grave emergency, the public safety may require it'. The union legislature by law could restrict these rights in the case of the armed personnel. Broadly, the committee classified the justiciable rights under seven heads: (1) citizenship, (2) equality (including abolition of untouchability), (3) freedom (including the right to life), (4) religion, (5) culture and education, (6) miscellaneous (including the right to property), (7) constitutional remedies.

[1] K.M. Munshi, *Pilgrimage to Freedom*, p. 293. The integrationist approach to fundamental rights was predominant among Congress members right from the beginning.

[2] *CAD*, vol. III, p. 399, Report in pp. 437-44.

Every person born in the union or naturalized according to its laws would be a citizen of India. Irrespective of race, religion, caste or sex, citizens would have equality *vis-à-vis* the state, and access to places of public importance, though separate provision might be made for women and children. There would be equality of opportunity in public services. Untouchability was to be abolished and heritable titles would not be conferred by the state. Subject to public order and morality or, in case of grave emergency, to restrictions imposed in the interest of the security of the country, freedom of speech and expression, peaceful assembly, associations or unions, movement and residence was to be granted. No person was to be deprived of his life or liberty without due process of law, in the eye of which all citizens were equal. Subject to regulation by the law of the union, trade, commerce and intercourse among the citizens or units would be free, though units could impose reasonable restrictions in public interest. Traffic in human beings, forced labour and employment of children below the age of 14 in factories, mines and other hazardous works were to stop. Full religious freedom as well as the right to maintain their own religious institutions was granted to all communities, subject to public order, morality or health and other constitutional restrictions, e.g. against conversion through coercion or undue influence. Cultural and educational rights of all communities were duly granted. Among miscellaneous rights, right to property was not to be taken away except by law, for public purposes and against payment of compensation.

Committee Stage

Earlier, the Fundamental Rights Subcommittee had three sessions.[3] The preliminary took place on 27 February 1947. The second session was from 24 to 31 March 1947, to formulate the main principles. Certain comments and criticisms of the subcommittee members then followed in view of which the draft was revised on 14 and 16 April 1947. The subcommittee had before it four memoranda submitted by B.N. Rau, K.M. Munshi, K.T. Shah and Harnam Singh. When the subcommittee met, Ambedkar submitted an elaborate document on state and minorities (27 March 1947) embodying the fundamental rights particularly with reference to the scheduled castes. Kripalani was elected chairman of the committee. After the Fundamental Rights Subcommittee made its report, the Minority Rights Subcommittee examined them. Finally, the whole

[3] Proceedings of meetings of the Subcommittee on Fundamental Rights from B. Shiva Rao, *Select Documents*, vol. II.

Advisory Committee took decisions on the basis of the Report of the Fundamental Rights Subcommittee and the comments of the Minority Rights Subcommittee thereon.

Form of the Rights

In the framing of the fundamental rights the two opposing theories that clashed head-on were those of B.N. Rau and K.M. Munshi. An enlightened administrator, Rau had a way of looking at the problem which was different from that of K.M. Munshi, a lawyer freedom fighter, long committed to the Congress programme.

In his preliminary note on the fundamental rights prepared for the guidance of the Constituent Assembly members on 2 September 1946, Rau had warned that to enunciate the fundamental rights in general terms and leave it to the courts of law to enforce them will have the following consequences:

(1) The legislature not being in a position to know what view the courts will take of a particular enactment, the process of legislation will become difficult.
(2) There will be a vast mass of litigation about the validity of laws and the same law that was held valid at one time may be held invalid at another and vice versa: the law will therefore become uncertain.
(3) The courts, manned by an irremovable judiciary not so sensitive to public needs in the social or economic sphere as the representatives of the periodically-elected legislative body, will, in effect, have a veto on legislation exercisable at any time and at the instance of any litigant.[4]

However, he admitted that such rights under the care of the judiciary would give a feeling of security to the racial and religious minorities. Yet he preferred the system of those later democracies of Europe which had their declaration of rights but had not given the courts the power to declare an offending state-law unconstitutional.

The other insistent suggestion of Rau was to formulate certain social policies, following the Constitution of Ireland, which the government would be obliged to implement. These policies would be different from 'the fundamental rights strictly socalled', which the government would desist from violating. It should be pointed out that the distinction Rau

[4] B.N. Rau, *Constitutional Precedents*, 3rd series, p. 18.

made was a distinction between what he called 'positive rights' and 'negative rights', being particularly impressed by Lauterpacht's *An International Bill of Rights of Man*, and not between non-justiciable and justiciable rights, as the Fundamental Rights Subcommittee construed it. As a matter of fact, B.N. Rau's 'negative rights' were all worded in a negative language. (The whole text of Rau's draft articles on fundamental rights has not been available even to the Shiva Rao Committee. But quotations from his draft give the impression that Rau, a man bred in the climate of British law, was against making rights justiciable.)

Munshi's draft bill of right was 'intended to be a legal instrument creating definite and legally enforceable rights and corresponding duties between the union, units and citizens of India'. Munshi opposed the British precedent about fundamental rights. 'The Nehru Report, the Karachi Resolution on Fundamental Rights and the Sapru Report show that the Indian political outlook has always insisted on fundamental rights being included in the constitution', he wrote. The essential guarantees of fundamental rights were, to him, the following:

(a) Enforceability must be the essence of any instrument defining fundamental rights and duties.
(b) A person or a state under an obligation cannot claim the right to determine whether he could comply with the obligation and if so to what extent.
(c) The observance of the fundamental rights and duties must be determined by a procedure and a machinery common to the union as a whole.
(d) Limitations to such law whenever necessary must only be imposed by the law of the union.[5]

Judicial Guarantee to Rights

Munshi's conclusion was, therefore, that fundamental rights should be guaranteed by judicial review. Those rights, which were not enforceable in a court, again, were declarations of general nature and had no use in the body of a constitution. Munshi's views got initial support of most of the members of the subcommittee. Whereas Ayyar's note and initial speeches at the meeting of 27 February 1947 strongly favoured Munshi's outlook, only Harnam Singh favoured the evolution of an extrajudicial machinery to enforce the rights. The subcommittee accepted Munshi's

[5] B. Shiva Rao, *Select Documents*, vol. II, p. 71.

draft as the working paper.[6] Though Munshi wanted the rights to be clearly and unconditionally laid down, his draft contained an elaborate preface, where he laid down some 'general' conditions: The preface said:

(1) Unless otherwise provided by the Constitution, these rights would be enjoyable by all citizens.
(2) 'Rights' included 'power, privilege and immunity' and 'duty' included liabilities and obligations.
(3) All existing laws and usages in force within the territory of India inconsistent with the rights would 'to the extent of inconsistency' be abrogated, these rights would not be abridged or taken away by any legislation of the centre and the units.
(4) No restrictions would be imposed, except in the manner provided in the chapter and unless they were of general nature and in the interests of public order, morality, health, general welfare, correlative duty in respect of others and national defence.

All but the third condition were dropped by the Fundamental Rights Subcommittee. But then riders were put on almost all the individual rights one by one.

It was K.M. Panikkar, a latecomer in the Advisory Committee, who raised the objection in the committee's meeting of 24 April that automatic abrogation of all existing laws inconsistent with the rights would be undesirable. While Patel, chairman of the committee, was inclined towards Panikkar's views, Munshi strongly defended his position that abrogation of certain laws would be necessary. Munshi's view was sustained, though the general feeling was that the effect of such abrogation should be fully examined.

Munshi's draft of the rights contained elaborate provision for constitutional remedies through the Supreme Court. The Supreme Court was given wide powers of issuing writs of *habeas corpus*, *mandamus*, prohibition and *certiorari*. Ayyar was opposed to the grant of all the writs (except *habeas corpus*) to the Supreme Court under original jurisdiction. In the last series of meeting (15 April) of the Fundamental Rights Subcommittee Panikkar doubted the ability of the Supreme Court to enforce all rights through writs. He wanted two groups of rights—one small group to be enforceable by the Supreme Court, the other enforceable by the high courts. The clause was retained, the Supreme Court being given another writ—*quo warranto*. Ayyar raised these objections again

[6] Ibid., 24 March 1947, p. 73.

in the Advisory Committee (on 21 April). A subcommittee with Ayyar, Ambedkar and Munshi finally worked out a compromise through which scope for the unit courts to issue these writs made open.

SUBSTANCE OF THE RIGHTS

In spite of the difference over the 'form' of the rights, their substance was certainly not in dispute. It actually turned out that some of the rights, which the Munshi draft stood for, were not legally enforceable, at least in the opinion of the subcommittee. Right to education and the workers' rights were instances of such items. Finally, therefore, the subcommittee accepted the formula of dividing rights into 'justiciable' and 'non-justiciable' parts.

A consequence of this controversy over the form of rights was the question whether the 'justiciable' rights would be put in a clear positive language (of which Munshi was the advocate) or in a negative language (for which Rau stood). Munshi's stand again created some difficulties. For example on 24 March 1947 when the right to equality was being discussed, Munshi wanted in the draft a positive statement about the right followed by a statement in a negative form to the effect that there shall be no discrimination on grounds of religion, race, sex, etc. 'Sir Alladi was opposed to this form of drafting on the ground that it would give rise to serious difficulties. He thought that it would be enough to declare that there shall be no discrimination on such and such ground'.[7] Munshi got the support of the majority. It was, at first, decided to retain Munshi's statement that all citizens were equal before the law. Munshi's positive statement about equality was later transferred to the non-justiciable part despite protests (15 April 1947). Certain parts of the rights to education and the provision relating to the preservation of monuments were transferred to the non-justiciable part. The subcommittee also dropped the first three clauses of the Munshi draft on the right to property, making a positive statement. The whole result was a mixture of the formulas of Munshi and Rau on the draft rights.

During the third session of the Assembly the Report of the Fundamental Rights Subcommittee was discussed and accepted. Apprehensions were at the very beginning expressed about the consistency in the distinction between 'justiciable' and 'non-justiciable' rights, the most forceful speakers being H.N. Kunzru, the liberal leader and Somnath Lahiri the

[7] Ibid., p. 117.

only communist member in the Assembly, who said that 'these are fundamental rights from a police constable's point of view . . . here we find that none of the existing provisions of the powers of the executive have been done away with'.[8] The latter also endorsed Kunzru's suggestion that the other part of report should come out before any full-scale discussion, as he was afraid that the social and economic rights would be ignored. Earlier P.R. Thakur, a Congressite, had complained about the absence of social and economic rights.[9]

Replying to the debate Patel said that the report was well considered and had gone through three committees. There was one school of thought which wanted to include all rights in one part. Another school wanted only the minimum number of fundamental rights to be mentioned. Finally, a golden mean had been found in dividing the rights in two parts.[10]

Right to Freedom

The draft right to freedom could be divided into three parts: (1) freedom proper, (2) protection of personal liberty and property according to 'due process of law', and (3) right to universal adult franchise. Each of these freedoms raised some controversy at the committee stage[11] (and later). It was in the second meeting of the Fundamental Rights Subcommittee, on 25 March 1947, that a proviso was attached to each of the freedoms. In succeeding stages the rights and their provisos were redrafted several times. On 14 April 1947, the subcommittee, in its third meeting, added a precondition to these freedoms, following Ayyar's grave warning about the disturbances all over the country (in a note dated 4 April 1947) and Munshi's strong support to his view. So the freedoms, with their provisos, were made subject to 'public order, morality or the existence of grave emergency'.

Freedom *versus* Security

A salient example of the new trend was the consideration of the 'freedom of speech' by the Advisory Committee. While Ayyar proposed restriction on speeches that could 'promote class-hatred', Panikkar sought to add 'religious' hatred to this disqualification. It fell on the non-Congress

[8] *CAD*, vol. III, p. 385.
[9] Ibid., p. 403.
[10] Ibid., p. 409.
[11] B. Shiva Rao, *Select Documents*, vol. II, pp. 119-20.

cabinet minister, S.P. Mookerjee to oppose Ayyar's move:[6] Even simple expression of opinion against a party in power may be construed as class or communal hatred and punished accordingly; but if the majority party or the party in power does the same thing, they will not be brought to book.' Munshi argued, 'The right of free expression is now recognized all over the world, and it has been felt that speeches and writings tending towards class or communal hatred, if they do not go to the extent of causing violence or crime, may be permitted. The reason why "class or communal hatred' was omitted was that it was felt this might permit the units to make all kinds of drastic laws. . . ."

Munshi won through a division.[12] But Ayyar opposed the rights of secrecy of correspondence (on the basis of the Indian Evidence Act which had permitted secrecy in only a few cases) and the secrecy of the household against unreasonable searches (on the basis of the Criminal Penal Code) and won against Rajagopalachari, with the support of Munshi.[13] Munshi's original draft granted freedom to bear arms according to law. The subcommittee omitted it. Mookerjee's effort to revive it at the Advisory Committee was defeated.[14]

During the debate over the report, Patel[15] proposed the right to freedom (clause 8) without all but one of the provisos originally accompanying the items (e.g. with 'freedom of speech and expression', law to be made against seditious, obscene, blasphemous, slanderous, libellous or defamatory publication or utterance; with freedom of assembly, law to be made against violent or dangerous meetings, etc.). The one proviso, in a modified form, that was retained, provided for the state's power to impose restriction on residence or holding of property in the interest of minority groups and tribes without any qualification of 'reasonableness' at the demand of the tribal members and with the blessing of Nehru.[16]

In the Congress Assembly Party meeting on 29 April 1947,[17] the modifications had been made in accord with the general feelings of the house, and were welcomed by a large number of members who had earlier given notice of amendments. On clause 9, which had provided for personal

[12] Ibid., pp. 231-3.

[13] Ibid., p. 239. In the Assembly Karimuddin tried to revive the rights, but failed. *CAD*, vol. VII, p. 794 (3 December 1948).

[14] B. Shiva Rao, *Select Documents*, pp. 236-8. Kamath tried to revive it in the Assembly on 1 December 1948 but failed. *CAD*, vol. VII, p. 718.

[15] 30 April 1947.

[16] *CAD*, vol. III, pp. 445-57.

[17] *The Hindustan Times*, Delhi, 30 April 1947.

liberty and 'equal treatment of law', Munshi's amendment for substituting the latter by 'equality before the law' was adopted[18] without discussion During discussion on the freedom of trade between units, an amendment was incorporated providing that the restrictions, to be imposed by units, were to be non-discriminatory about units.[19]

The Drafting Committee reorganized the clause quite ruthlessly. As a general qualification of the rights—'other provisions of the article' were introduced. The old provisions of the Advisory Committee's report virtually came back with all the clauses in article 13 of the draft. Further, the draft article 297 provided that nothing in article 13 would prevent the state from making a law during an emergency. Some Assembly members vehemently objected to the new provisions but could gain only a few minor points.

Their gains included the following: (1) Mihirlal Chattopadhyay's amendments for removal of the introductory stigma 'subject to the other provisions in this article,[20] (2) Munshi's substitution of 'sedition' in clause 2 by 'any matter . . . which undermines the security of or tends to overthrow the state,[21] and (3) Thakurdas Bhargava's incorporation of 'reasonable' before 'restriction' in clauses 2 to 6.[22]

An interesting feature of the discussion of 'freedoms' was the serious objection raised by several members against the word 'reasonable' qualifying restrictions. J.J.M. Nichols-Roy, vindicated by Jaipal Singh, said that 'The word "reasonale" will create a great deal of contention and confusion.' Munshi supported him[23] and the Assembly upheld them. Yet, when the draft constitution came in for discussion, on article 13, Thakurdas Bhargava moved an amendment (No. 49) to the same amendment whose main purpose was to put the word 'reasonable' before 'restrictions' in clauses 2 to 6. By oversight or, more possibly, in the bargain with the Drafting Committee, Bhargava did not press for the word in clause 2 (restriction on speech and expression). This point was not pressed for voting either. But the Drafting Committee agreed to accept the word 'reasonable' in clauses 3 to 6. Bhargava, in putting forth this case, stressed the need of even a limited judicial protection of freedom.

[18] *CAD*, vol. III, p. 468.
[19] Ibid., vol. VII, p. 475.
[20] Ibid., p. 713.
[21] Ibid., p. 730.
[22] Ibid., pp. 735-6.
[23] Ibid., vol. III, pp. 461-4.

PERSONAL LIBERTY

In the Fundamental Rights Subcommittee Munshi and Rau had a confrontation on the principle of 'the due process of law'.[24] Though Munshi got 'the due process of law' adopted by a 5-2 majority, Rau carried on his relentless fight. It was at the Advisory Committee meeting on 21 April 1947, that Ayyar was found hesitant about the due process clause. 'Personally I am for retention of the clause', he said, though he saw points in B.N. Rau's objections also. G.B. Pant, a newcomer to the committee and a strong advocate of land-reform, found in the clause the danger to zamindari abolition plan. 'We are leaving the fate of the country in the hands of the lawyers', argued Pant, 'who will be raised to the bench and they will have to interpret this law.' Such interpretations would be also various. 'We must have fool-proof language, if I may say so'.[25]

It was here that Patel endorsed a suggestion of Panikkar that personal liberty and property be separated. Rajagopalachari gave an alternative formula: 'No person shall be deprived of his life or liberty without due process of law, nor shall any person be denied the equal treatment of the laws within the territories of the union provided that this shall not prevent the enactment of laws in the interests of public order and security.' The proposal was accepted. Pant did not agree but preferred silence.[26] The Advisory Committee also dropped the restriction on prolonged and unreasonable detention without trial, presumably on ground of superficiality in view of the retention of the due process clause.

That the bureaucracy was opposed not to absolute right to property as such, but the absolute judicial supervision of rights is proved by the fact that Rau's grievance against the 'due process' clause was not yet removed. In the draft constitution prepared by Rau that clause was retained. But Rau's visit to the USA and talk with Frankfurter, the retired chief justice of the Supreme Court of the USA, caused the revival of the controversy. From Washington Rau proposed the removal of the clause. Yet the Drafting Committee on 31 October 1947 and 19 January 1948 decided to retain it, though it added the epithet of 'personal' before 'liberty' to make the meaning of the clause more specific. It was some time between 14 February and 20 February 1948 that the 'due process' was finally decided to be dropped for a 'more specific' phrase, 'procedure established by law' in the Japanese and the Irish way.[27]

[24] B. Shiva Rao, *Select Documents*, vol. II, p. 122.
[25] Ibid., p. 245.
[26] Ibid., pp. 245-7.
[27] Footnote to article 15 of the Draft Constitution of India, February 1948.

The change was not at once welcomed. No less a member than Sitaramayya proposed an amendment for the substitution of 'in accordance with law' for 'according to the procedure established by law'. In turning down the new suggestion, however, the Drafting Committee now referred to the early US practice, where 'due process of law' meant 'due procedure prescribed or established by law' and did not involve any substantive question. 'This is the form in which the clause occurs in the Japanese constitution.'[28] Obviously, the Drafting Committee had made up its mind. Yet, on 6 December 1948, the article was moved after it had been held up on 3 December on the request of the Drafting Committee. Baig moved for substitution of 'in accordance with law' for 'the procedure established by law', whereas an amendment of Upendranath Barman, Damodar Swarup Seth and S.F. Krishnamoorthy Rao, and another Thakurdas Bhargava, for the return of 'the due process of law' got powerful support from Munshi. Ayyar confessed, 'I am still open to conviction',[29] though he supported the Drafting Committee's proposal.

The discussion was not completed on 6 December and was again held on the next day, on the Drafting Committee's (T.T. Krishnamachari's) request. On 13 December when the article was brought before the Assembly, Ambedkar made a brief speech in which he only confessed that he was 'somewhat in a difficult position' with regard to article 15 and Bhargava's amendment. One position over the question was to make the judiciary sit in judgement over the legislature.

> Is that a desirable principle? The second position is that the legislature ought to be trusted not to make bad laws. . . . There are dangers on both sides. For myself, I can not altogether omit the possibility of a legislature packed by partymen making laws which may abrogate or violate what we regard as certain fundamental principles. At the same time, I do not see how five or six gentlemen sitting in the Federal or Supreme Court . . . be trusted to determine which law is good and which law is bad.[30]

He left the question to the House, which upheld the Drafting Committee proposal. The draft article 15 was passed, though members continued to feel aggrieved. In August 1949, the Drafting Committee proposed to move an amendment in the form of article 15A with a view to 'affording protection to persons against certain arrests and detention'.[31] The article

[28] B. Shiva Rao, *Select Documents*, vol. IV, p. 39.

[29] *CAD*, vol. VII, p. 854.

[30] Ibid., pp. 999-1001.

[31] Letter of S.N. Mukherjee to H.V.R. Iyengar, then Secretary to the Home Department, dated 16 August 1949, Law Ministry File, CA/19(13)/Cons.49.

sought to provide that every arrested person, as soon as possible, would be informed of the ground of arrest; that no person would be detained without the authority of a magistrate; that this would not apply in the case of a preventive detenu who could be detained for three months and that after three months the ground of every preventive detention would be examined by an advisory board consisting of a person of the rank of a high court judge, who could recommend further detention. The home ministry immediately put up strong objection to the executive's power of preventive detention of persons being subjected to the authority of an 'advisory board'. 'It is reasonable to say', Iyenger wrote, 'that the legislature should settle the conditions under which the executive shall exercise this extraordinary power.'[32]

The Drafting Committee bowed to the home ministry's pressure and proposed in the Assembly a revised article 15A, which provided that parliament by law could prescribe the circumstances under which certain types of preventive detention could be for a period longer than three months. There is little justification, therefore, in Austin's assertion that article 15A was proposed 'despite the home ministry's objections'.[33] The compromise is quite apparent, so is the prevalence of the legislature on the judiciary.

While introducing the amendment (article 15A) on 15 September 1949, Ambedkar said, 'I think it has to be recognized that, in the present circumstances of the country it may be necessary for the executive to detain a person who is tampering either with public order . . . or with the defence services of the country'.[34]

The 'circumstances' were not explained, though the implication related to the communist and communalist disturbances. The debate on the amendment was short and there was only one reference to 'the communists'[35] by K. Kamaraj.

Franchise

In the Fundamental Rights Subcommittee, in spite of Rajagopalachari's contention that the provision of universal adult franchise in the fundamental rights part would amount to an encroachment on the constitutional structure of the country, which was being thrashed out by other committees, the

[32] Iyengar to Mukherjee, 19-20 August 1949, Ibid.
[33] G. Austin, *The Indian Constitution*, p. 110.
[34] *CAD*, vol. IX, p. 1498.
[35] Ibid., p. 1544.

principle was 'unanimously' accepted. Elections were to be universal, free and secret and controlled by an independent commission. The Minority Rights Subcommittee in April 1947 endorsed them. In the Advisory Committee further doubts were raised about the attitude of the states towards this decision.[36] Ambedkar categorically said: 'While we are anxious that the Indian states should come in, we shall certainly stick to certain principles and not yield simply to gather the whole lot of them in our constitution.'[37] Finally, the Advisory Committee recommended to the Assembly the grant of voting rights to all citizens at the age of 21, the conduct of voting by secret ballot and the superintendence and control of elections to be left under an election commission. The paragraph was also adopted, but as desired by the Advisory Committee, was transferred to 'some other part' of the constitution.

Provisions for elections formed Part XIII of the draft constitution, but the right of franchise was not mentioned in it. On 16 June 1949, the Constituent Assembly adopted the principle of universal adult franchise in the form of an amendment (article 298B). By an earlier amendment (298A) voting right was granted irrespective of religion, race, caste, sex or any of them.[38]

The machinery of elections was evolved in an interesting way. It was the Minority Rights Subcommittee which had insisted upon a neutral and autonomous election commission to conduct free elections. The Advisory Committee endorsed the formula and the draft constitution of February 1948 provided, in article 189, for a union election commission, whose personnel would be appointed by the president, and an election commission for each state, whose personnel would be appointed by the governor, to superintend control and direct the elections. But on 15 June 1949, Ambedkar moved an amendment in the Assembly envisaging 'a radical change' in the proposed system. The new plan was to have an integrated election commission, with members appointed by the president and wanted, in the language of Ambedkar, 'to centralize' the election machinery in the hands of a single commission to be assisted by regional commissioners, not working under the provincial government' but under the central government. The change was found necessary 'because today we find that in some of the provinces of India, the population is a mixture'. It had been brought to the notice of the Drafting Committee as well as of

[36] B. Shiva Rao, *Select Documents*, vol. II, p. 251.
[37] *CAD*, vol. II, pp. 438-9.
[38] Ibid., vol. IX, pp. 931-2.

the central government that in some provinces 'the executive government is instructing or managing things in such a manner that those people who do not belong to them either racially or linguistically are being excluded from being brought under the electoral rolls'.[39]

Property

Discussion in the Assembly of the right to property of the people evoked special interest.

> Clause 19 of the Advisory Committee's report recommended that No property, movable or immovable, of any person or corporation, including any interest in any commercial or industrial undertaking, shall be taken or acquired for public use unless the law provides for the payment of just compensation for the property taken or acquired and specifies the principles on which and the manner in which the compensation is to be determined.

As already noted, the drafting of the right to property suffered from the contradiction of the 'positivist' and 'negativist' approaches. Munshi's draft had proposed that right to property was guaranteed and could be restricted only for 'public reasons'.[40] Property (which, to Munshi, would mean only immovable property) could not be expropriated except by law and 'in return for just and adequate consideration according to principles previously determined by it'.

The long discussion of the Fundamental Rights Subcommittee had turned on (1) whether movable property was also to be added, (2) whether the expression 'just compensation; was to be substituted for 'compensation', and (3) whether the legislature was to be given the power to fix the compensation. The discussion was actually on the question of 'how section 299 of the 1935 Act was to be adapted'. This was virtually the only reference to a 'right' of the subjects in the Government of India Act, 1935, and the subcommittee again fell back on it. The final upshot of the discussion was a modified clause (clause 27) on the right to property.

> No property movable or immovable of any person or corporation, including any interest in any commercial or industrial undertaking, shall be taken or acquired for public use unless the law provides for the payment, according to principles previously determined, of just compensation for the property acquired.[41]

[39] Ibid., vol. VIII, pp. 904-6.
[40] Article X of Munshi's draft. B. Shiva Rao, *Select Documents*, vol. II, p. 78.
[41] B. Shiva Rao, *Select Documents*, vol. II, p. 128.

The provision, however, ran into rough weather in the Advisory Committee. Pant, the UP chief minister, who had joined the Advisory Committee late, wanted to know if 'public use' could cover tenancy legislation. Ayyar's reply was affirmative—as, he pointed out, the draft had closely followed section 299 of the 1935 Act. However, B.R. Ambedkar submitted, 'The reason why the previous sanction of the Governor-General is stipulated in subsection 3 is because the term "public use" or "public purpose" as used in section 299 (of the 1935 Act) is a very wide one and not only includes limited governmental purposes but also social progress.' Therefore, some limitation to this broad fundamental right was needed to validate programmes like tenancy legislation.

Two proposals cropped up. Rajagopalachari wanted the substitution of 'governmental' purposes for 'public' purposes; Panikkar wanted the omission of the word 'just'. Pant endorsed Rajagopalachari, though their amendment was defeated in voting. 'Just' was, however, dropped. A common feeling of the members of the Advisory Committee was the undesirability of court intervention in this affair.[42]

The total impression that one gets out of a study of the Advisory Committee's treatment of the subject is that, though they wanted judicial guarantee for the fundamental rights, they were not ready to surrender the supremacy of the legislature to the judiciary, at least on the question of tenancy reforms.

During discussion of the Advisory Committee's Report on Fundamental Rights in the Constituent Assembly, on 2 May 1947 Raja Jagannath Bakhsh Singh (UP, general) moved an amendment, stipulating the epithet of 'just', before the word compensation. K.T. Shah, radical Congressman, on the other hand, had given notice for adding a proviso to it to the effect that 'natural wealth, like rivers or flowing water, coastal waters, mines and minerals or forests' would not be recognized as private property.[43] This resolution was not moved. When, in the short but interesting debate that followed, some zamindar members expressed their apprehensions about the government's intention to abolish zamindari, Patel who had moved the clause, warned:

> Land will be required for many public purposes, not only land but so many other things may have to be required. But the state will acquire them after paying compensation and not expropriate them. That is the real meaning of the clause. But the zamindars or some of their representatives thought that their interests

[42] Ibid., pp. 272-5, 291.

[43] *CAD*, vol. III, pp. 505-6.

must be safeguarded by moving an amendment or by making a speech here. But they are not going to safeguard their interests in this way. They must recognize the times and move with the times. This clause here will not become law till tomorrow or the day after, it will take at least a year more, and before that, most of the zamindaris will be liquidated. Even under the present acts or laws in the different provinces, legislation is being brought in to liquidate zamindars either by paying just compensation or adequate compensation or whatever the legislatures there think fit. Therefore, it is wrong to think that this clause is intended really for them. It is not so. The process of acquisition is already there and the legislatures are already taking steps to liquidate the zamindaris.[44]

The question of the right to property again rose on 10 September 1949, when the draft constitution's article 24 came in for discussion. The article of that draft provided that no person would be deprived of his property save by authority of law. No property could be acquired or taken possession of for a public purpose except by a law fixing the amount of compensation. By a very important amendment, moved by Nehru, it was provided that no such law authorizing the acquisition or possession of property would have effect 'unless such law having been reserved for the consideration of the President has received his assent'. Another part of the amendment provided that if any bill pending before the legislature of state at the commencement of the Constitution after being passed by the legislature received the president's assent, the law would not be questioned as being unconstitutional.[45]

The effect of the amendment proposed by Nehru was to impose a control or supervision over the right to property (following, perhaps, the 1935 Act rather than the US example). The aim of the second proposal was to save the different land-reform measures already afoot in provinces from being obstructed. Nehru's speech while moving the proposal was significant. Nehru was clear that there was 'no question of any expropriation without compensation', that it would be fair and equitable. But the equity would apply not only to the individual but also to the community. Congress being long committed to the abolition of zamindari, no legal subtlety, no judiciary would be allowed to come in its way. Expert legal advice on the clause was also that, on its proper construction, the clause left no room for the intervention of the judiciary, except when 'there has been a gross fraud on the constitution'. 'And if it comes in the way, ultimately the whole constitution is a creature of Parliament.'[46]

[44] Ibid., p. 518. In UP, Bihar and Madras land reform legislation was already afoot.
[45] Ibid., vol. IX, pp. 1191-2.
[46] Ibid., pp. 1191-5.

Amendments were actually moved on this form of the right to property, and six of them of rather minor significance were accepted. On 12 September the article was passed. By still another proposal any law of a state, enacted not more than one year before the commencement of the Constitution, might within three months from such commencement be submitted by the governor of the state to the president by public notification and thereupon, if the president by public notification so certified, it would not be called in question in any court on the ground that it contravened the provisions of the same article or of the Government of India Act, 1935.

Fundamental Rights and Integration

Some of the fundamental rights in India, as in the USA, in fact, contributed to the development of India's political integration that was being worked out in the Constituent Assembly. One may recall here for a study in contrast that the incorporation of the fundamental rights, through the first ten amendments of the US Constitution, was aimed at removing some of the suspicions for the federal integration of the American states, though actually they increased the powers of the federation.

The provisions about citizenship had to be worked out till the last part of the Assembly's session. It should be pointed out that, at no stage of the proceedings of the Advisory Committee, was there any demand for double citizenship.

According to Munshi's draft the Advisory Committee recommended, though after some members had expressed doubt about its necessity,

> that full faith and credit would be given throughout the territory of the union to public acts, records and judicial proceedings of the union and every unit thereof and the manner in which and the conditions under which such acts, records and judicial proceedings would be proved and the effect thereof determined would be prescribed by the law of the union.

The Constituent Assembly accepted it without debate. In the draft constitution it appeared under the head of Administrative Relations between Union and States (article 238).

Another fundamental right which helped the process of integration was the freedom of trade. Munshi's draft sought to grant freedom of trade between units to all persons. The Fundamental Rights Subcommittee made it subject to union laws and restricted only to citizens. In the last series of meetings of the subcommittee, Ayyar wanted to make it explicit that the units had the right to impose taxes and duties on it and restrict it in times of emergency. In the Advisory Committee's meeting Rajagopalachari also wanted the units to have power to collect revenues on interstate trade. The demand was conceded, but Panikkar warned against arbitrary laws of the units. Ayyar, on behalf of the Union Constitution Committee, said, 'We wanted to permit the units to enjoy the indulgence they have been enjoying. But we should guard against converting the country into competing units.[47] The draft constitution in article 16 provided for this freedom, and the stipulations were provided in articles 243-5 in the part dealing with the union-state relation.

While article 16 came up for discussion in the Constituent Assembly, a young Congressman from Madras, C. Subramaniam, raised the point that interstate trade and commerce being a 'union subject' and article 16 being subjected to laws of parliament and the states (under article 244), the content of the right was missing, and the article was useless.[48] Ambedkar replied that the scope of article 244 was limited. About the role of parliament *vis-à-vis* article 16, Ambedkar said that the Drafting Committee had the opposition from the Indian states in integrating the interstate trade under the authority of parliament.

> If it was possible for us to include trade and commerce in list I . . . we would not have found it necessary to bring trade and commerce under article 16. But as the door was blocked, on account of the basic considerations which operated at the beginning of the Constituent Assembly, we had to find some place, for the purpose of uniformity in the matter of the trade and commerce throughout India, under some head. After exercising a considerable amount of ingenuity, the only method we found of giving effect to the desire of a large majority of our people, that trade and commerce should be free throughout India, was to bring it under fundamental rights.[49]

On 8 September 1949, Ambedkar moved as amendment a new part (X-A) in order to 'assemble all these different articles, scattered in the different parts of the Draft Constitution, into one single part and to set them out seriatim'.[50]

Directive Principles

After the Fundamental Rights Subcommittee completed its discussions and formulations, Rau drafted its report to the Advisory Committee. At the very beginning of the meeting of the Advisory Committee an interesting

[47] B. Shiva Rao, *Select Documents*, vol. II, 159, 254.
[48] *CAD*, vol. VII, pp. 798-800.
[49] Ibid., pp. 802-3.
[50] Ibid., vol. X, pp. 112-13.

confrontation took place between Munshi and Rau. By a stroke of drafting ingenuity, Rau had provided, in the introductory clause in the chapter on the rights, that any existing or future law inconsistent with the rights guaranteed 'in this constitution' would be invalid. Munshi pointed out the difference between the rights in 'this part' as originally decided by the Fundamental Rights Subcommittee and rights in 'this constitution' as drafted by Rau. Obviously, Rau's draft was an attempt to provide judicial guarantee to the rights guaranteed in the other parts as well. The Advisory Committee would make no mistake about it and changed Rau's version.[51]

During his tour abroad Rau sent in certain amendment proposals on his own draft constitution (October 1947), two of which related to the clauses that provided for invalidation of the existing and future laws of the state on grounds of inconsistencies with the rights in the justiciable part.[52] The effect of the amendment proposal was that no law made by the state in discharge of its duty under the principles of social policy would be invalid on ground of its inconsistency with the justiciable rights. This proposal also was not accepted by the Drafting Committee.

The most important point about the directive principles of social policy is that, they had never discussed in the Constituent Assembly before the draft constitution was presented. If their origins are to be found in the rather academic benevolence of B.N. Rau, their adoption may be considered as a golden compromise between the desire of Congress to achieve 'a social revolution' and the pressure of the vested interests.

On 18 November 1948, the directive principles of state policy came in for discussion. Karimuddin's amendment to delete the word 'directive' and Kamath's amendment to substitute it by the word 'fundamental' were rejected after a brief reply from Ambedkar assuring that the state would try to implement the principles.[53] K.T. Shah's amendment on the next day for 'obliging' the state to implement them was rejected without even a reply. The members discussed the principles for four days during which K.T. Shah offered a somewhat radical alternative to article 31 (core of the part) which was unceremoniously rejected without debate. Much heat was generated, on the other hand, on lesser issues like prohibition, cow-slaughter and personal laws.

[51] B. Shiva Rao, *Select Documents*, vol. II, pp. 215-16.

[52] Rau's letter dated 11 November 1947, Law Ministry File, CA/116/Cons.47.

[53] *CAD*, vol. VII, p. 476.

Assessment of the Rights

Granville Austin finds in the fundamental rights and directive principles 'the core of the commitment to social revolution' of India.[54] It is difficult to accept the view without reservation. The concepts of equality and freedom are indeed revolutionary and have great social content. But it is doubtful whether the fundamental rights in the Indian Constitution proceeded much further than that. Secularism has long been accepted to be a condition of political stability, and India certainly can claim great credit on account of this achievement.[55] So is property a symbol of a stable polity. But these are concepts which Europe achieved by 1848, one hundred years earlier than the making of the Indian Constitution. Social revolution in 1948 should evidently have a different content from the social revolution in 1848.

The abolition of untouchability was common in the Munshi and Ambedkar drafts. Presumably, on Ambedkar's insistence, restriction of caste, etc., on the use of wells and places of pubic use was removed. But when Masani moved that 'No impediments to marriages between citizens shall be based merely upon differences of religion', the resolution was defeated 5-4. Ambedkar's resolution to remove difference between 'legitimate' and 'illegitimate' children was defeated 6-3. Mrs Hansa Mehta's resolution banning child-marriage was also deferred to the policy part and finally dropped.[56]

Munshi's 'rights of workers' were shifted into social policy, K.T. Shah wanted the right to employment. It was not granted. He asked if the right to equality of citizens meant that there would be no discrimination against any class or community. The question was considered outside the scope of the subcommittee. Rau's draft of the 'social policies' was however, accepted without much controversy, and with the addition of a few carried-over items of rights. The only substantially radical proposal accepted as a 'fundamental right' was that of K.T. Shah, to prohibit the grant of titles by the state.

That the right to property had to be ensured by the Constituent Assembly was an imperative of the political and economic forces in this country. The only attack on it came in the form of government supremacy in fixing the amount of compensation for zamindari abolition. The zamindars, as

[54] Austin, *The Indian Constitution*, p. 50.

[55] Indeed V.P. Luthera thinks that India is a 'directionist', and not a secular state. See his *The Concept of a Secular State and India*.

[56] B. Shiva Rao, *Select Documents*, vol. II, pp. 128-9.

already seen, were no favourite of the new rules of India. And the practical problems of payment of compensation were pointed out by the Congress premiers themselves (like Pant). But a fundamental challenge to property as such was never clearly thrown except through insertion of the directive principles of state policy embodying the ideals of an equalitarian welfare state. The leadership's commitment to property on the other hand has been revealed on more than one occasion.

Answering the criticism of the draft constitution by radical Congress-ites, socialists and even some Leaguers (like Mohani), that the constitution had no socio-economic outlook, Alladi Krishnaswami Ayyar gave the following defence:

> The constitution, while it does not commit the country to any particular form of economic structure or social adjustment, gives ample scope for future legislatures and the future parliament to evolve any economic order and to undertake any economic legislation they choose in public interests. In this connection the various articles which are the directive principles of social policy are not without significance and importance.[57]

In a similar spirit Ambedkar replied to K.T. Shah's amendment on draft article 1 for calling India a 'secular federal socialist state', with the comment that the constitution was 'merely a mechanism for the purpose of regulating the works of the various organs of the state'. What the policy of the state should be, how the society should be organized in its social and economic side were matters which must be decided by the people themselves according to time and circumstances.[58]

The main outlook of the constitution, therefore, is political in spite of the directive principles. Two other major features of the fundamental rights under the Constitution are:

(1) At least some of the basic rights of the Constitution are closely linked with the state and government structures of the country. Citizenship is indeed closely linked with the state and government of a country. But the facts that the right to franchise found no place in Part III of the Constitution, freedom of trade practically became a constitutional instrument of integrating the Indian polity and the right to property had to be safeguarded by the requirement of the President's approval to every state legislation encroaching upon property are distinct pointers to the trend of a modern state towards centralism. The

[57] *CAD*, vol. VII, p. 336.

[58] Ibid., pp. 402-3.

incorporation of a uniform set of fundamental rights into the Indian Constitution itself is a part of this process.

The deliberate rejection of 'due process of law' in favour of 'the procedure established by law' speaks eloquently about the Constituent Assembly's intention not to make the judiciary a superlegislature. Yet in India, as in the USA, the judiciary has not only assumed the power of judicial review but also challenged parliaments' power to amend the fundamental rights. The power was asserted first in the case of *Golaknath* v. *the State of Punjab*, and was taken a step further in the case of *Keshavananda Bharati* v. *the State of Kerala*.[59]

(2) If the fundamental rights in the Indian Constitution contributed to the development of a massive political superstructure in India, its place in determining the intra-governmental power relation is no less significant. The most elaborately written Constitution as it is, the

[59] S.C. Writ Petition No. 135 of 1970. The issue had been in Supreme Court in the cases of *Shankari Prasad* v. *Union of India* (1952 SCR 89), *Sajjan Singh* v. *State of Rajasthan* (1965 SCR 933) and *Golaknath* v. *State of Punjab* (AIR 1967 SC 1667), with the contention that article 13 (ii) rules out a 'law' effecting amendment of the fundamental rights. In the case of Shankari Prasad the court held that 'law' in article 13 was one made in exercise of the legislative power of parliament and not constitutional law made in exercise of its constituent power. In the Sajjan Singh case, though the two judges in the minority (including Justice Hidayatullah) agreed with the majority (three), not to revise the court's earlier opinion, Hidayatullah expressed the subjective opinion that, 'the Constitution gives so many assurances in part III that it would be difficult to think they were playthings of a special majority'. In the Golaknath case, Chief Justice Subba Rao, delivering the judgement on behalf of five of the ten judges, held that amendment is 'law' within the meaning not only of article 13 (ii), but also of article 245 (dealing with union-state relations). He approvingly quoted Nehru at the time of introduction of the interim report on fundamental rights in the Constituent Assembly, calling the rights 'fundamental', but obviously ignored the other comments. In a separate judgement, Hidayatullah endorsed him and observed that erosion of the right to property would lead to the erosion of all fundamental rights.

By the Twenty-fifth Amendment (1971) article 31 (was incorporated for saving the laws giving effect to the Directive Principles of State Policy, putting such laws beyond the scope of judicial review. In the Keshavananda Bharati case (1973) the Supreme Court held this exclusion invalid. During the emergency, therefore, the Forty-second Amendment (1976) inserted two clauses seeking to take article 368 away from the scope of judicial review. In *Minerva Mills* v. *Union of India* (AIR 1980 SC 1789) the Supreme Court turned down this part of the amendment as it militated against the principle of judicial review which was a part of the basic structure of the Constitution which the Supreme Court had, in *Keshavananda Bharati* v. *State of Kerala* (AIR 1973 SC 1461, F.B.), declared unamendable. The fact that the court did not object to the insertion of 'secular, socialist' in the Preamble may, possibly, be explained by two assumptions, (1) The Court did not take them seriously; (2) Several judgments have asserted that neither 'socialism' nor 'secularism' in India should be interpreted in their 'western' senses.

Indian Constitution allotted rather limited space for the functioning of the judiciary as guardian of the Constitution. Parliament, ultimately, is the master of the rights, which were never intended to be unalterable. This was established when the Supreme Court acquiesced in the 44th amendment which pushed the right to property out of Part III of the Constitution of India into Part XII as article 300A.

CHAPTER 14

Framing of the Constitution (II)

The State Structure

Consequence of Partition

Ambedkar in 1940 wrote:

> The essence of Pakistan is the opposition to the establishment of one central government having supremacy over the whole of India. This gives rise to the second important point. That point is that the issue of Pakistan shall have to be decided upon before the plans of a new constitution are drawn and its foundations are laid. If there is to be one central government for India, the design of the constitutional structure would be different from what it would be if there is to be one central government for Hindusthan and another for Pakistan.[1]

Until 3 June 1947, however, partition of India was by no means a *fait accompli*. The states' participation in the new India in some way was also visualized and considered as a matter of time. The future political plan for India was built around the scheme of a rather loose federation. At the Meerut session of the Congress in November 1946, its president, Kripalani, outlined the proposed constitution as follows:

> It will be a democratic constitution and will be federal in character. We may not, however, forget that, in the administrative as in the economic field, centralisation more than is absolutely necessary is inimical to liberty. It is good, therefore, that the provinces in free India shall have the maximum autonomy consistent with external and internal security.[2]

The Committee on Union Subjects, elected on 25 January 1947, submitted its report to the Constituent Assembly on 28 April 1947. Elaborate provisons of defence, foreign affairs and communication's were laid down as union subjects permissible under the Cabinet Mission's plan. The sources of revenue were also mentioned therein. The committee further

[1] B.R. Ambedkar, *Pakistan or Partition of India*, p. vii.

[2] *The Statesman*, 23 November 1946.

mentioned a fairly big list of 'implied or inherent powers' of the union. In addition to those subjects, which in the view of the committee came under the scope of the union government, the committee hoped that a few subjects (e.g. insurance, company laws, banking and planning) would also be included in the union list by agreement.

Such an arrangement will ensure uniformity throughout the territory of the union in matter bearing on trade and commerce as has in fact been recognized in many federal constitutions. We have included planning in the above list for the reason that although authority may rest in respect of different subjects with the units, it is obviously in their interest to have a coordinating machinery to assist them.[3]

During the submission of the report, however, N. Gopalaswami Ayyangar requested the House not to take it as final mainly in view of the fact that the Muslim League had not yet participated in constitution-making and its future actions were not known. There was thus no motion for the consideration of the report. His request was unanimously granted. For nobody was definite about how the political geography of India would shape. The Assembly president had, at the beginning of the third session on the same day, given expression to this sense of uncertainty:

Whatever the nature of the constitution that may have to be drafted, whether for one undivided India or only for parts of it, we shall see to it that it gives satisfaction to all coming under its jurisdiction. . . . It may be that the union may not comprise all the provinces. If that unfortunately comes to pass, we shall have to be content with a constitution for a part of it. This may mean not only a division of India but a division of some provinces. . . . Let us not be daunted by the immensity of the task or diverted from our purpose by developments which may take place but go ahead with faith in ourselves and the country which has sent us here.[4]

Partition of India, according to the plan of 3 June 1947, changed the whole perspective of the constitutional problem of India. The 'communal settlement' as contained in the Cabinet Mission's plan became redundant. The demand for 'safeguards' and 'autonomy' for the Muslims in India no longer carried the old sense. The problem of the Sikhs or other less important minorities had never attained the dimension of the Muslim problem in as much as the former had never put forward a demand for separate states and had demanded only 'safeguards'.

The compulsion of what had always been regarded as the core of the Indian problem being absent, a trend towards centralization became

[3] *CAD*, vol. III, pp. 375-8.
[4] Ibid., p. 345.

irresistible. Yet, the new Indian situation did not at all rule out the necessity of a federation. The composite character of the Indian social organization was too real to be ignored. Besides, the provincial aspirations aroused by the previous reforms were heading towards their logical culmination. A federal structure of state with considerable autonomy for the provinces and regions was, therefore, a historical imperative though the union was certainly going to be much stronger than what had been anticipated by the Cabinet Mission.

A federal structure was also necessitated by the problem of the princely states. It took a pretty long time to determine the relation between princely India and the Indian mainland after the transfer of power. Yet it was apparent from the very beginning that at least for some time the states would maintain their identity and even authority within the union of India.

The Committees

The two most important committees responsible for the formulation of the state structure of India were the Union Constitution Committee and the Union Powers Committee, both chaired by Nehru and overlappingly manned by most of the stalwarts. Three days after Mountbatten's declaration on 6 June 1947, the Union Constitution Committee decided that (a) the constitution would be federal with a strong centre, (b) there would be three exhaustive lists of powers, the residuary powers lying with the union in the pattern of the 1935 Act, (c) the states would be on par with the provinces in respect of the federal legislative list, subject to the consideration of any special matter which might be raised when the lists would be fully prepared, and (d) the executive authority of the federation would be coextensive with the legislative authority.[5]

The report of the committee was submitted by Jawaharlal Nehru on 21 July 1947. He pointed out that the report was in full conformity with the Objectives Resolution. He said that the distribution of legislative powers between the federation and the units would be decided upon according to the recommendation of the Union Powers Committee.[6] Yet the Union Constitution Committee recommended that there should be three exhaustive lists of subjects—one for the centre, one for the units and one concurrent, with the residuary powers for the centre. The report also laid down the principles of administrative and financial relations

[5] Union Constitution Committee's File.

[6] *CAD*, vol. IV, pp. 734-5.

between the centre and the units. All chief commissioners' provinces would remain directly administered areas as before. The report also said that whereas the federal government could entrust the governments of the units with functions in relation to any federal matter, it could direct them with respect to that matter.

As territories of the union were mentioned (i) the governors' provinces, (ii) the chief commissioners' provinces, (iii) the Indian states that would accede [for whom there would be two types of administrative arrangement: (a) single states and (b) groups of states]. In a supplementary report the committee recommended that parliament should have power to alter the name of a unit.

The Union Powers Committee's second report, of 20 August 1947, noted that, 'Some parts of the country are seceding to form a separate state and the plan put forward in the statement of 16th May on the basis of which the committee was working is, in many essentials, no longer operative. In particular we are not now bound by the limitations on the scope of union powers.'

The committee, therefore, concluded unanimously, 'that it would be injurious to the interests of the country to provide for a weak central authority which would be incapable of ensuring peace, of coordinating vital matters of common concern and of speaking effectively for the whole country in the international sphere'. At the same time, the committee stressed that 'there are many matters in which authority must be solely with the units and that to frame a constitution on the basis of a unitary state would be a retrograde step both politically and administratively'. Hence, it concluded, in agreement with the Union Constitution Committee, 'that the soundest framework for our constitution is a federation with a strong centre'.[7]

The contrast between the spirits of the two reports was hardly to be missed. Hasrat Mohani moved an amendment for postponing consideration of the report until the revised and final report on the union constitution as well as the modified Objectives Resolution was considered.[8] His arguments were mainly two: (i) He wanted India to be declared a Union of Socialist Republics; (ii) He opposed the differential treatment of the provinces and the states. Mohani's amendment was rejected.

[7] About the choice of the federal form of state M.C. Setalvad writes: 'Though it does not appear that the Constituent Assembly at any stage applied its mind to the choice between a unitary government and a federal structure, it would seem that under the circumstances the country was placed, it had no alternative'. *The Indian Constitution, 1950-1965*, p. 2.

[8] *CAD*, vol. V, p. 53.

When the report of the Union Powers Committee was taken up for consideration K. Santhanam, besides the Muslim Leaguers, was the most forceful speaker to point out that the report had a strong unitary bias. He summed up the new position thus:

We have got almost a unitary centre which is trying to hand over certain powers to the provinces and the whole plan of the Union Powers Committee is based on that procedure. They have tried to take the Government of India Act as their basis and considered what items can be transferred from the provincial list to the concurrent list and provincial list to the federal list.[9]

While admitting that the recommendations of the Union Powers Committee urged a strong centre, Alladi Krishnaswami Ayyar repudiated Santhanam's charge in the following words:

While a good number of items in the central list can be brought under the heads of defence, foreign affairs and communications, the three main heads envisaged by the Cabinet Mission scheme, the other items such as bills of exchange, banking, corporation law, interunit trade bear upon the general welfare of the country. . . . We have been crying about a strong centre. If you look at the provincial list, very few (subjects) if at all the provincial list have been taken up and transferred to the federal list.[10]

Ramaswami Mudaliar was severely critical of the provisions for financial allocation.[11] In spite of being the Dewan of Mysore, he spoke 'from the viewpoint of the provinces' as well as the Indian states, D.P. Khaitan, the industrialist Congressite from Bengal, on the other hand, supported the revenue-distribution proposals which had been considered extensively centre-oriented by Santhanam. He pointed out that

all the taxes that are put in the central list are only such as can be conveniently administered by the centre, as are necessary for the sake of uniformity in the different provinces and as are absolutely essential for the purposes of the development of agriculture, industry, etc. We have got to build a large mileage of railways, we have got to have a large mileage of roads, we have got to develop a mercantile marine, we have got to develop so many things, which can only be done by the centre.[12]

B.L. Mitter, as a member of the committee, explained that, 'The committee went into the matter of distribution of powers on a definite

[9] Ibid., p. 56.
[10] Ibid., p. 75.
[11] Ibid., pp. 84-9.
[12] Ibid., p. 99.

principle. It is this, matters of national concern should be vested in the centre and matters of provincial concern should be vested in the provinces. We found that the Act of 1935 was a good guide because in making the list in the 1935 Act the same principle was kept in view.'[13]

In his reply to the debate N. Gopalaswami said, 'I think I am right in saying that there is hardly a single item in the present provincial list in the Government of India Act which this much-criticized committee, the Union Powers Committee, has transferred to the federal list.'[14]

Discussion on the second report of the Union Powers Committee was not completed in the fifth session of the Assembly. The draft constitution almost wholly adopted the recommendations in the form of the seventh schedule, which was discussed item by item from 29 August to 3 September 1949 and adopted with slight modification.[15]

Alladi Krishnaswami Ayyar submitted a separate note to the Constituent Assembly in which he suggested that instead of giving the three lists of union, state and concurrent powers and placing the residual powers in the centre, following section 100 of the 1935 Act, the draft constitution should mention first the state subjects, then the concurrent subjects, and then the union subjects.[16] The proposal was not accepted, however.

It was also provided in the draft constitution, following the 1935 Act, that if one or more states delegated the power of legislation on a state subject to parliament, parliament would be competent to legislate on the subject (draft article 229). A major development in the Drafting Committee took place when, in November 1947, B.N. Rau, from abroad, suggested granting the union the power to legislate concurrently with the states on a state subject in case of a special resolution by the council of states.[17] The Drafting Committee, therefore, provided that in case of a resolution by two-thirds of the total membership of the council of states to the effect that parliament should pass laws on a state subject, in the expediency of the national interest, parliament should be able to do so. Besides, '. . . in view of the present abnormal circumstances which require central control over essential supplies, the committee has provided that, for a term of

[13] Ibid., p. 101. B.L. Mitter, Dewan of Baroda, worked hard for the integration of states with India, won displeasure of his ruler and had to quit.

[14] Ibid., vol. V, p. 103.

[15] Ibid., vol. IX, p. 719-958.

[16] Separate notes submitted to the Constituent Assembly by Sir Alladi Krishnaswami Ayyar, member, Drafting Committee, Appendix to *Draft Constitution of India*, February 1948.

[17] B.N. Rau's letter from Washington, dated 11 November 1947, Law Ministry File, CA/116/Cons.47. See also Ambedkar's Preface to the *Draft Constitution* of February 1948.

five years from the commencement of the constitution, trade and commerce in, and the production, supply and distribution of certain essential commodities as also the relief and rehabilitation of displaced persons, shall be on the same footing as concurrent list subjects.'[18]

Financial Integration

The Expert Committee on Financial Provisions, appointed by the President of the Constituent Assembly submitted its report in December 1947.[19] The committee, consisting of two civilians and a businessman from Bengal, made important recommendations on the distribution of revenues. Recognizing the fact that the Indian federation was a product of devolution of authority the committee said:

> The basic functions of a federal government are defence, foreign affairs and the service of the bulk of the national debt, and they are all expensive functions. . . . The head 'communications' would ordinarily at least pay for itself. The federal government may also have to assume leadership in the co-ordination and development of research and higher technical education. Normally, however, apart from war or large-scale internal disorder, the expenditure of the centre should be comparatively stable. The needs of the provinces are, in contrast, almost unlimited, particularly in relation to welfare services and general development. The provinces, therefore, must have as many independent sources of revenue as possible. On the other hand, it is not practicable to augment their sources of revenues to any considerable extent by adding more subjects to the provincial legislative list without simultaneously upsetting the equilibrium of the centre. We cannot, therefore, avoid divided heads.

The net effect of the committee's recommendations would be that 'the centre would have to transfer to the provinces a sum of the order of Rs. 30 crore annually'. The committee recommended that the provinces should not be able to collect foreign loan except on the permission of the federal government. No major change in the list of federal taxes was recommended. Among other things, the committee recommended 'stock exchanges and future markets' to be included in the union legislative list. The recommendations of the Expert Committee were called by T.T. Krishnamachari (then a critic of the draft constitution) 'half-hearted'. Yet, Krishnamachari felt that, 'either the Drafting Committee was not

[18] Ambedkar's prefatory note with the *Draft Constitution*, February 1948.

[19] *Report of the Expert Committee on the Financial Provisions of the Union Constitution*, submitted on 5 December 1947. Members of the committee were (1) Nalini Ranjan Sarkar, (2) V.S. Sundaram and (3) M.V. Rangachari.

competent to examine even the half-hearted recommendations made by the Expert Committee, or they felt that it would be better to tread on safer ground and adopt the status quo which idea, I think, more or less dictated the decisions made by the Expert Committee itself'.[20]

The Drafting Committee did not adopt the recommendations of the Expert Committee on Financial Provisions regarding the distribution of revenue between the centre and the units, 'in view of the unstable conditions prevailing at the present moment',[21] and recommended that the existing system of distribution should continue for the next five years, and should be altered after a fresh examination by a Finance Commission. There was evidently no desire to relax the grip of the centre on the national financial structure.

The 'Special Problems' of India

The future of the centrally administered areas and excluded and partially excluded (including tribal) areas constituted the last problem in connection with the state structure. The Advisory Committee, it has already been noted, had set up subcommittees on the North-West Frontier and the North-East Frontier (Assam) Tribal and Excluded Areas and the Excluded and Partially Excluded Areas outside those regions. Partition made the NWF Committee redundant. On 30 July 1947, the Constituent Assembly authorized the president to appoint a committee to recommend administrative changes in the five centrally administered areas of Panth-Piploda, Andaman and Nicobar Islands, Coorg, Ajmer-Merwara and Delhi.

The Committee on Centrally Administered Areas submitted its report on 21 October 1947. The committee recommended the merger of Panth-Piploda and Ajmer-Merwara (in view of the smallness of the former's size). Andaman and Nicobar were to be administered directly by the centre and called a chief commissioner's province. Delhi, Ajmer-Merwara and Coorg would be called lieutenant-governors' provinces and would 'normally be administered by a council of ministers responsible to the legislature as in other provinces', with the president as an arbitrator between the lieutenant-governor and the ministers in case of differences between them. According to the rules and orders issued by the president they were to be administered by the lieutenant-governors or chief commissioners with the assistance of local legislatures or councils of

[20] *CAD*, vol. VII, p. 223.

[21] *Draft Constitution of India*, p. 115n.

ministers or councils of advisers or both.[22] The Andaman and Nicobar Island (Part IV states) were to be more directly administered by the president through chief commissioners. Merger of certain princely states and taking over of their administration by the Government of India led to the increase in the number of the units of the Indian union. As noted earlier, the final draft of the Constitution placed them in Parts II and III. The administrative patterns were more or less unaltered.

The Subcommittees on the Tribal, Excluded and Partially Excluded Areas (i) of Assam, and (ii) outside Assam submitted their reports on 18 August and 4 November 1947 respectively. The two reports were considered by the Advisory Committee on 24 February 1948 and adopted.[23] The setting up of several autonomous districts with various hill areas in Assam and numerous safeguards for the tribal people outside Assam were recommended. The Drafting Committee placed the special provisions for the administration of the tribal areas outside Assam and the tribal-inhabited areas in Assam in the fifth and sixth schedules respectively. Their special representation in legislature and services was retained through various provisions of the constitution.

The draft constitution provided for a tribes advisory council in states containing scheduled tribes and scheduled areas. The council would advise the state government on all matters pertaining to the administration of the scheduled areas and the welfare of the scheduled tribes in the state. It would also advise the governor as to which legislation of the centre or the state would or would not apply to a scheduled area.

On 5 September 1949, Ambedkar moved for the substitution of the original fifth schedule by a new one.[24] The main purpose of the amendment was to circumscribe the powers and role of tribes advisory council in the states containing the scheduled areas and scheduled tribes that had been proposed by the draft constitution. Under the new proposals the president would decide whether to set up such a council for the scheduled tribes in a state not living in a scheduled area. The amendment also sought to empower the state governor rather than the tribes advisory council to restrict the application of a parliamentary or state assembly's legislation to a scheduled area. The new amendment also authorized parliament to

[22] According to an amendment moved by Ambedkar on 2 August 1949 on draft article 213, the power to make provision for a 'council of advisers and/or a local body, elected or nominated or partly elected and partly nominated, was given to parliament instead of the President'. *CAD*, vol. IX, pp. 74-5, 100-1.

[23] B. Shiva Rao, *Select Documents*, vol. III, pp. 780-2.

[24] *CAD*, vol. IX, pp. 965-6.

amend the fifth schedule in future. On 17 September 1949, the original eighth schedule, mentioning the scheduled tribes, was deleted.

The sixth schedule was taken up on 5 September 1949. The discussion went on till 7 September, para by para. Ambedkar moved an amendment providing for flexibility in the territorial jurisdictions of the autonomous districts.[25] The debate generated considerable heat on the question of relationship between the plains and the hills of Assam.

A Union of States

The draft constitution called India a 'union of states' to consist of four kinds of states (mentioned in the first schedule):

Part I — The former governors' provinces.
Part II — The three chief commissioners' provinces of Delhi, Ajmer-Merwara (including Panth-Piploda) and Coorg.
Part III— *Division A*: 18 native states that had already acceded to India.
Division B: All other native states that would join India in future.
Part IV— The Andaman and Nicobar Islands.

During the presentation of the draft constitution in the Constituent Assembly, Ambedkar said that the draft constitution envisaged, like the US Federal Constitution, a dual polity. 'Yet the differences that distinguish them are more fundamental and glaring than the similarities between the two.' The difference lies in the absence of rigidity and legalism in the Indian Constitution.[26]

On 18 September 1949, the Assembly finally decided that 'India, that is Bharat, shall be a union of states' (article 1). In view of the integration of Indian states Ambedkar, in the tenth session of the Assembly brought forth a set of new proposals for placing the 'states' almost on the same level with the former provinces.[27] On 14 October 1949, substitution of schedule 1 of the draft constitution was proposed.[28]

Thus, under Part I remained the former British Indian provinces as enlarged by the merger of states: (1) Assam, (2) Bengal (corresponding to West Bengal), (3) Bihar, (4) Bombay, (5) Koshal Vidarbha (corresponding to CP and Berar), (6) Madras, (7) Orissa, (8) Punjab

[25] Ibid., p. 1019.
[26] Ibid., vol. VII, pp. 33-4.
[27] Ibid., vol. X, pp. 154-5.
[28] Ibid., pp. 286-8.

(corresponding to East Punjab), (9) United Provinces. (In the final Constitution they became Part A states.)

In Part II were placed 11 centrally administered areas (under the rule of chief commissioners): (1) Ajmer, (2) Bhopal, (3) Bilaspur, (4) Coorg, (5) Cooch-Behar, (6) Delhi, (7) Himachal Pradesh, (8) Kutch, (9) Manipur, (10) Rampur, (11) Tripura. (Nos. 2, 3, 5, 7, 8, 9, 10 and 11, were states or 'unions' taken over for better administration. They became Part C states in the final Constitution.)

In Part III were nine 'states' and 'unions' under the rule of the Rajpramukhs: (1) Hyderabad, (2) Jammu and Kashmir, (3) Madhya Bharat, (4) Mysore, (5) Patiala and East Punjab States Union, (6) Rajasthan, (7) Sourashtra, (8) Travancore-Cochin, (9) Vindhya Pradesh. (They became Part C states in the final Constitution.)

In Part IV was placed the specially administered territory of the Andaman and Nicobar Islands (Part D states in the final Constitution).[29]

Munshi made it clear that the whole schedule 'has been drafted on the basis of what is existing today'. Yet, in the Assembly quite a large number of amendments were awaiting his proposal, some relating to alteration of the existing names of certain provinces, some suggesting new names that implied the creation of new provinces, while some others relating to change of boundaries. Whereas the first group of amendments sought alterations having only formal bearing, the other two groups had substantive implications, heightened by the mergers of Indian states. President rules out any substantive alteration at that stage.[30]

The Assembly referred to proposals for change of name to the provincial governments for opinions of their legislatures. On Central Provinces and Berar and the United Provinces chose the names of Madhya Pradesh and Aryavarta respectively. On 16 November 1949, the Assembly adopted the first proposal and rejected the other.

Linguistic Provinces

The Congress was committed to the linguistic reorganization of India since 1921. Provincial boundaries, on the other hand, had been drawn and redrawn since the British advent mainly for administrative convenience. The Cabinet Mission's plan, as Rau interpreted, it, recognized

[29] On 10 April 1948, the Special Committee recommended that as far as possible there should be no centrally administered areas except for strategic and defence purposes. the number increased mainly because of mergers of princely states.

[30] *CAD*, vol. X, pp. 311-15.

the existing units as self-contained and inviolable. 'It may, therefore, be urged that the existing boundaries of the several provinces are not to be disturbed under the new constitution, at least initially,' wrote Rau.[31] There were indeed practical difficulties in the creation of a number of new states. When the shackles of the Cabinet Mission plan were removed, there arose political difficulties.

The union and provincial constitution committees were unable to recommend any reorganization. The agitation of Andhra by this time rose to a high pitch. The Government of India made a statement that Andhra might be mentioned as a new state in the draft constitution as Orissa and Sind had been mentioned in the 1935 Act.

The Drafting Committee thought that to mention Andhra in the draft constitution only was not sufficient to bring the state into existence at the commencement of the constitution. For, after the enactment of the 1935 Act, Orissa and Sind had been constituted into separate provinces on 1 April 1936, whereas the Act came into force on 1 April 1937. The Drafting Committee, therefore, suggested the setting up of a commission to go into the question of linguistic reorganization and to take steps to implement its recommendation under section 290 of the Government of India Act, 1935. Indeed, under the new constitution reorganization was possible, but only after the commencement of the constitution.[32]

Following the recommendations, the Government of India appointed the Commission on Linguistic Reorganisation of Provinces with S.K. Dar, retired judge of Allahabad High Court, Pannalal, a retired civil servant, and J.N. Lal, a member of the Constituent Assembly, on 7 June 1948. The report came out on 10 December 1948, being a passionate brief against linguistic reorganization.[33] The result was the passing of the initiative outside the Assembly.

On the demand for creation of new states, Prasad said that there was evident difficulty in naming new provinces in the first schedule before they came into existence. Similar difficulties were involved in mentioning territorial changes before they actually took place. Those changes, he said, 'should be first brought about before they can be incorporated in the constitution; and I would, therefore, suggest to those honourable members who have given notice of such amendments to bring about the change which they want in the actual situation and then ask the Constituent Assembly to incorporate these changes in the constitution'. If such changes

[31] B.N. Rau, *India's Constitution in the Making*, p. 192.

[32] *Draft Constitution of India*, February 1948, p. 159n.

[33] *Report of the Commission on Linguistic Reorganisation of Province*.

did take place before the third reading, the Drafting Committee would take note of them.[34]

Article 391 of the final draft made a provision that 'if at any time between the passing of this constitution and its commencement any new province was created the President would name it under advice of his ministers'. On 15 November 1949, when R.K. Sidhwa pointed out that the implication of the provision was the preclusion of the Assembly members from expressing their views on an important matter like the creation of provinces, the president replied that 'otherwise the creation of provinces has to be held over till after the new constitution comes into force. . . . This new article has been brought in to enable new provinces to be created in which such action becomes possible.'[35] Ambedkar elaborated the legal position as follows:

> With regard to the creation of new provinces between now and the 26th of January, the article that would be operative would be section 290 of the Government of India Act of 1935 and article 391 of the present constitution. Sir, article 319 says that if between now and the 26th of January the authority empowered to take action under the Government of India Act does take action, then the President, under article 319, is empowered to give effect to that order made under the Government of India Act, section 290.[36]

On 24 November 1949, the Government of India Act, 1935 was further amended for enabling the Governor-General to change the names of provinces if their legislatures so desired.[37] The only such change, which took place before 26 January 1950, was the substitution of the name of the United Provinces by that of Uttar Pradesh.[38]

Minor Changes

The amalgamation of certain princely states, which had enclaves spread outside their main territories, created administrative and commercial difficulties. The central government held a series of meetings with representatives of provincial and state governments. 'I was struck, at our meetings', writes Menon, 'by the tenacity with which some of the provincial governments clung to the territories belonging to them.'

[34] *CAD*, vol. X, p. 313.
[35] Ibid., vol. XI, p. 524.
[36] Ibid., p. 582.
[37] Ibid., pp. 923-38.
[38] The United Provinces (alteration of Name) Order, *The Gazette of India Extraordinary*, 25 January 1950.

Finally, 'Exchange of territories where agreed to were effected by orders of the Governor-General or by agreements between the Rajpramukhs concerned.'[39]

During the debate on the new first schedule, however, Munshi assured the members that up to 26 January 1950, it was perfectly open to the Government of India to alter territorial boundaries. Rajendra Prasad noted that the change was possible even after 26 January 1950, in accordance with article 3 of the constitution. In any case, any alteration at the time could be done only by the legislative entity of the Constituent Assembly.[40] Though provincial territories were not altered mergers of states ordered by the Governor-General greatly altered the political map of India.

[39] V.P. Menon, *Integration of the Indian States*, pp. 312-13.
[40] *CAD*, vol. X, pp. 316-18.

CHAPTER 15

Framing of the Constitution (III)

Government Structure

The two most important committees that were responsible for framing the governmental structures of the centre and the units of the Indian union were the Union Constitution Committee[1] and the Provincial Constitution Committee.[2] Of these two committees, again, the Union Constitution Committee was the more powerful and contained almost all the luminaries of the Constituent Assembly except Rajendra Prasad (who was the chairman of the Assembly, and was frequently consulted) and Patel (who chaired the Provincial Constitution Committee). On all important issues the two committees sat jointly. On 5 June 1947 they set up a joint subcommittee with Patel, N.G. Ayyangar, V.T. Krishnamachari, Ambedkar, Munshi, Pant, A.K. Ayyar, Panikkar and Katju. Nehru's absence in this subcommittee is conspicuous; it perhaps indicated his proverbial disinterestedness with details. On some major controversial issues the lead indeed came from the Union Constitution Committee.

On 5 May 1947, the Union Constitution Committee and the Provincial Constitution Committee sat separately and decided to circulate among their members the questionnaire of B.N. Rau[3] which had earlier been sent to all the central and provincial legislators. The date for reply was fixed, in the former case, on 15 June 1947, and, in the latter case, on 20 June 1947. Only one member (Panikkar) of the Union Constitution Committee replied in time, another (K.T. Shah) sent in a body of draft directives and a draft constitution. Of the two belated replies, S.P. Mookerjee's was comprehensive. N.G. Ayyangar and A.K. Ayyar jointly sent a sketchy draft constitution of India. Seven members of the Provincial Constitution

[1] Minutes of the meeting of the Union Constitution Committee are cited from the Union Constitution Committee's File.

[2] Minutes of the meetings of the Provincial Constitution Committee are cited from the Provincial Constitution Committee's File.

[3] B. Shiva Rao, *Select Documents*, vol. II, p. 552.

Committee replied in time. Three other replied late. Rau, therefore, prepared two 'independent' memoranda.[4]

What does this failure to send replies on the part of the members indicate? Lack of time is definitely not an adequate explanation. The questionnaire actually was in circulation for a considerable period of time. Lack of preparedness on the part of the members may be a possible explanation. The questionnaire may, reasonably, appear to have restricted the thinking of the members. Of course, it left some choice for members, but an analysis will show that the patterns were confined to three alternative models—the British, the US and the Swiss. On a rigid scrutiny, it may even appear to be biased. Question about stability of the executive, if a parliamentary system was adopted, and desirability of rotation of the chief executive's office among the different communities may seem suggestive, if the questionnaire is read together with Rau's 'independent' memoranda.

Provincial Constitution Committee

Of the seven replies from the Provincial Committee members at least one (of Phulan Prasad Verma) was a piece of fragmentary directives. Three were for a British-type parliamentary government, two for a Swiss-type composite government and one (Katju) for a US-type presidential government. B.G. Kher, a Congressite and provincial prime minister, who opted for a parliamentary government, made it conditional on the adoption of joint electorates. If separate electorates were to be accepted, on the other hand, he would prefer a Swiss-type executive. Rajkumari Amrit Kaur, a Congressite Indian-Christian, chose the Swiss-type obviously for securing minority representation in the government. All of them wanted the governor to be elected.

Union Constitution Committee

To B.N. Rau's questionnaire on the union constitution, S.P. Mookerjee's reply broadly outlined a 'constitutional' chief executive to head a parliamentary government and to be called 'Rashtrapati'. He would be in office normally for six years, would be eligible for re-election only for three years and removable only be impeachment. There would be a vice-president to substitute him in case of his absence, death or resignation. There would be no rotation of the presidential office and no statutory

[4] Ibid., pp. 454-551.

reservation of executive offices for minorities. Such reservations would have to be through conventions. The ministry could be dismissed only on a show of no-confidence. The legislature was to be bicameral. The upper house would be a permanent body, one-third of its members retiring every two years. The lower house was to be elected by adult franchise. Money bills would generate in the lower house and in case of difference between the houses a joint sitting would decide the issue. To the union legislature should be left the decision on a separate union judiciary. There would be reservation for minorities and no representation of special interests.

Panikkar would have a president with a term of four years, renewable once. The presidential office would go by rotation, a member of the other community would be the vice-president. The president would be a constitutional head with power to dismiss ministry if he thought that it had forfeited support of the house. The legislature would be bicameral, the upper house consisting of three representatives from each unit, one-fourth of the members retiring every two years. Reservation for minorities on the basis of population and representation of special interests of women, labour and universities were prescribed.

The Ayyangar-Ayyar memorandum, circulated on 4 June, declared India to be an independent sovereign republic to be headed by a president elected by the two chambers of the federal parliament. The president's term of office was to be three years, subject to his removal through impeachment. Supreme command of the armed forces was to be vested in the president, whose functions would include representation of the union in external affairs, declaration of war, appointment or dismissal of ministry, grant of pardons and such other powers as conferred on him by the constitution or law. The executive power of the federation would, 'subject to the provisions of the constitution, be exercised by, or on the authority of, a council of ministers' (cabinet), headed by a prime minister. The president would appoint the prime minister from among the members of the federal legislature, and would ordinarily invite the person who was likely to command majority. The other ministers were to be appointed by the president upon the advice of the prime minister and keeping in view the representation of different regions. The prime minister would generally keep the president informed on matters of domestic and foreign policy.

The legislature would be bicameral, the senate not exceeding half the house of representatives in strength. A member of the cabinet could participate in the proceedings of both the houses, but could vote only in the house to which he belonged. The president should have the right to address the parliament. Money bills could originate only in the lower house, recommendation of the cabinet being necessary to move a money bill. In case of disagreement between the houses, the president would convene a joint sitting. The legislative chambers might make rules of procedure subject to the provisions of the constitution. The president would have power, 'if the cabinet is satisfied, at a time when the federal parliament is not in session, that an emergency exists which renders such a course necessary, to make and promulgate any such ordinances for the good government of the federation or any part thereof'. If the president declared, by proclamation, a grave emergency, the federal parliament would have the power to make laws for a unit or any part thereof. The provisions for the judiciary were to be made on receipt of the report of an ad-hoc committee on it.

Rau's Draft

Rau's models of the provincial and union constitution were based on the Government of India Act, 1935. The provincial executive authority was to be exercised by a governor elected for five years, who would be aided and advised by a council of ministers except when he acted in his discretion. The ministers might be appointed and dismissed by the government at his discretion and retained in office during the governor's pleasure or be elected through proportional representation by the members of legislature at the option of the governor. In the former case the relations between the governor and his ministers would be 'as nearly as possible' the same as those between the king and his ministers in England. In the latter case the ministers were removable only by legislative votes. The governor would have special responsibility for the security and maintenance of minority interests.

There would be a provincial legislature (consisting of the governor and one or two chambers), whose procedures would be similar to those under the 1935 Act. The governor would have power to promulgate ordinances when the legislature was not in session. The provincial judiciary would be headed by a high court which might adopt the provisions of the 1935 Act regarding high courts *mutatis mutandis*.

Rau's draft clauses on the union constitution would have a president, elected by the members of the union parliament and to hold office for five years. The president would exercise his executive powers either upon the advice of the council of ministers or in his discretion (in the latter case, being actually advised by a council of state similar to the privy council of Britain). The federal parliament would consist of the president, the house of the representatives and the senate. The first chamber would be constituted on numerical representation, the second chamber would consist of not more than 168 representatives of provinces and not more than 112 representatives of the Indian states. The president would summon and prorogue the houses and dissolve the house of the representatives. In his discretion the president might decline to grant dissolution. In his discretion the president might address the parliament. The president would have special responsibility about peace, security, financial stability of the union or any part thereof and protection of minority interests, which he would discharge in discretion. He would have ordinance-making power when parliament was not in session.

Work of the Committees

In the second meeting of the Provincial Constitution Committee over Rau's memorandum, on 6 June, 'sharp differences' arose over the position of the head of a unit. While some members wanted an elected but 'constitutional' head, some wanted an elected 'presidential' type of chief executive. Still another group wanted a governor appointed by the centre and acting as a liaison between the centre and the units. The question was, therefore, referred to the joint committee, which sat in the afternoon of 7 June 1947. In the morning of the same day the Union Constitution Committee had decided that India would be a 'federation' with a strong centre, that the governors would be chosen by the provinces (directly, by adult franchise, through a special electorate), 'and not by the centre', and that the provincial executive would be parliamentary. The latter decisions were approved by the joint meeting and, on the next day, accepted by the Provincial Constitution Committee. The last-named meeting also dropped the proposal of a deputy governor and decided that temporary vacancies in the governor's office were to be filled up by the president. If such a vacancy was for more than four months, a fresh election was to be held.

On 8 June 1946, the Provincial Constitution Committee decided to have no alternative scheme of a composite cabinet at the provincial level, but the normal parliamentary procedure in matters of the appointment of ministers and their relation with the governors. The final report of the Provincial Constitution Committee, therefore, stipulated that the governors would 'generally' abide by the ministerial advice and in their relation with their ministers would follow an instrument of instructions (after the 1935 model) that was yet to be drafted in the form of a schedule but would have discretionary power in certain special cases. There was no mention of the ministers' responsibility to legislature. The discretionary field of the governor's powers was somewhat curbed but still remained considerably wide.

The Union Constitution Committee adopted a different procedure as, seemingly, the Rau memorandum was disliked by them in principle, particularly in respect of the union executive. The committee first took up Rau's questionnaire (on 6 June 1947). They decided that the head of the state would be called *Rashtrapati* (President), who would be in office for six years, and would be eligible for re-election once. There was to be no rotation of office of the president.

The committee first adopted N.G. Ayyangar's formula that the president be elected by an electorate consisting of a fixed percentage of the population and the members of the lower house of the union legislature. On 10 June a subcommittee, however, recommended the presidential electorate to be composed of the lower houses of the units' legislatures. The Union Constitution Committee, on 11 June 1947, finally accepted the formula of the electorate being composed of the members of the lower houses of the unit legislatures and the two houses of the federal parliament. According to a decision on 6 June 1947, the vice-president was to be elected by members of the two houses of the federal parliament.

The most vital decisions taken by the Union Constitution Committee on 6 June were that the president would (1) act as the commander-in-chief of the armed forces, and have powers (2) to send back a bill to the legislature for reconsideration, within six months, and (3) to grant reprieve and pardon. He would be a 'constitutional' head and would dissolve the federal legislature only upon the advice of the ministers. He would have no special responsibility as suggested by Rau. The president would observe the parliamentary principles in the relationship of his cabinet. Rau's cherished scheme of a council of state was dropped as references to discretionary powers were altogether dropped. There was to be no special formula for a stable executive and no limit on the number of ministers.

In the light of the new decisions, B.N. Rau reviewed his memorandum and practically brought in the Provincial Constitution Committee's new formula of a convention that the president would observe the parliamentary principle (which was to be, further, guarded by a schedule). Even these stipulations were considered unnecessary by the Union Constitution Committee in its meeting on 30 June 1947. All references to discretionary powers of the president were dropped. There was, however, no adequate redrafting of the provision due, perhaps, to a lack of sufficient interest or a clear idea on the part of Rau, who had all along cherished a different picture of the union executive. There only remained a small paragraph providing that there would be a council of ministers to aid and advise the president and that the council would be collectively responsible to the lower house of the union legislature.

The other significant change, made by the committee, on 30 June, was about the 'executive power' of the union which would be 'vested in' the president and not 'to be exercised by' him. The Union Constitution Committee also decided to have two chambers of the federal legislature called the *Rajya Sabha* (Council of States) and the *Lok Sabha* (House of the People). Rau's draft of the constitution twisted the provision, in line with the 1935 Act, to make the executive power exercisable 'either directly or through persons acting under his authority' subject to the provisions of this constitution (clause 53/1). The Drafting Committee, on 3 November 1947, decided to adopt it.[5] After some further revisions the provision appeared in the draft constitution of February 1948 (clause 42/17) without any mention of the exercise of executive power by the president.

A careful study of the above procedure reveals a contradiction between the decision-making and the drafting machineries in the Assembly. The decision-makers indeed had very definite ideas about the constitutional form of the country, fostered to some extent by their bitter experience since 1937. They were generally for a parliamentary executive, a federal bicameral legislature and an independent judiciary. But the drafting part was entrusted to some of the stalwarts of the bureaucracy of the British days, whose orbit of thinking was somewhat confined to the notion of strong governors and a strong Governor-General (who, in the case, was merely 'replaced' by the president). By no canon of justice, however, can the bureaucracy be blamed for this. The political leadership failed to make its mind clear and waited for the bureaucracy to give the lead. When the leadership chose to revise the principles offered by the bureaucracy the redrafting was indeed far from satisfactory. Even there the political leadership failed to comprehend the potential significance of the terms like 'discretion' (for governors) and 'pleasure' (for president as well as for governors). At the end of the committee stage the position of the heads of the union and the units remained considerably powerful.

CONSIDERATION OF THE PROVINCIAL CONSTITUTION

Framing the provincial constitution very much influenced the federal structure of the country. During the presentation of the report of the

[5] B. Shiva Rao, *Select Documents*, vol. III, pp. 335, 337.

committee on the model provincial constitution, Vallabhbhai Patel, on 15 July 1947, told the Constituent Assembly:

The first question we had naturally to consider was whether the provincial constitution shall be of a unitary type or shall be of a federal type, and as there was a little difference of opinion on this question, the committee thought it proper to have a joint session of the Provincial Constitution Committee and the Union Constitution Committee. Both these committees met and they came to the conclusion that it would suit the conditions of this country better to adopt the parliamentary system of constitution, the British type of constitution with which we are familiar.[6]

The Provincial Constitution Committee promptly accepted Rau's draft that the executive authority of the province would (only) be exercised by the governor.

The provincial legislatures would consist of the governor, the legislative assembly and in some provinces, if so desired, a legislative council. There would be one representative in a legislative assembly for one lakh of population, subject to a minimum of 50 (clause 19). Clause 20 provided that

The provisions for the meeting, prorogation and dissolution of the provincial legislature, the relations between the two houses (where there are two houses), the mode of voting, the privileges of members, disqualification of membership, parliamentary procedure, including procedure in financial matters, etc. shall be on the lines of corresponding provisions in the Act of 1935.[7]

The governor would have the right to promulgate ordinances when the assembly was not in session. Till the first general election the existing governors and ministers of provinces would remain in office. (In Rau's draft constitution, however, a uniformity of the patterns of power of the president and the governors was sought to be established by 'vesting' the executive power of the province in the governor as well as making it exercisable by him [article 123/1]. The Drafting Committee adopted it in line with the provision relating to the president, on 24 January 1948.)

Hasrat Mohani, in the Constituent Assembly, on 15 July 1947, opposed the consideration of the Provincial Constitution Committee's report prior to the consideration of the Union Constitution Committee's report, which was indeed already in circulation.[8] Patel and Nehru, however, stressed

[6] *CAD*, vol. IV, pp. 579-80.

[7] B. Shiva Rao, *Select Documents*, vol. II, pp. 637, 671.

[8] Ibid., pp. 581-2.

that the general structure of the Indian government—especially the republican form of it, about which Mohani seemed to be anxious—had nothing to do with the provincial constitution. Mohani's amendment was defeated. Both he moved another amendment, while the clause-by-clause discussion started, seeking to call the chief executive of a province 'president' instead of 'governor'.[9] Patel objected to the move, on ground of confusion between the union 'president' and the provincial 'president'. This amendment was also defeated.

Aziz Ahmad Khan, a Leaguer from UP, moved an amendment seeking to provide for election of the ministers through proportional representation.[10] K.T.M. Ahmed Ibrahim Sahib Bahadur moved an amendment on the above amendment making the ministers responsible to legislature.[11] While Aziz Ahmad's motion was clearly for getting minority representation in provincial ministries,[12] the second motion wanted to clearly lay down separate ministerial responsibilities. Both were, however, defeated.

The India Provisional Constitution Order, 1947, omitted all references to the chief executive's 'special responsibilities' and 'discretion'. According to the draft constitution (February 1948), ministers were to aid and advise the governor, except when he was required by or under the constitution to act in his discretion, and no court could question the governor for acting according to ministerial advice. The governor had 'discretion' in choosing his ministers who would stay in office during the pleasure of the governor (article 144), though the governor would be issued an instrument of instructions (fourth schedule). The other fields of 'discretion' were summoning and proroguing the state legislature and dissolution of the legislative assembly (article 153), returning a bill without assent (article 175), declaration of grave emergency in the state (article 188), appointment of an auditor-in-chief, according to provisions made by the state legislature (article 210), and the chairman and members of the State Public Service Commission (article 285).[13]

[9] Ibid., p. 591.

[10] Ibid., pp. 632-4.

[11] Ibid., p. 634.

[12] See Sitaramayya's speech, ibid., pp. 646-8.

[13] Almost all references to discretionary powers were later dropped at the instance of the high-powered special committee. The provisions about the auditor-in-chief were dropped on 1 August 1949 (in the Assembly) in order to integrate the union and state audit services.

CONSIDERATION OF THE UNION CONSTITUTION

According to the Union Constitution Committee, the federal government was to consist of (i) a president elected by the members of both the houses of the federal legislature through proportional representation by means of single transferable vote, (ii) the two houses of parliament, and (iii) a federal judicature.[14] There would be a vice-president to act as president in contingencies. There would be a council of ministers appointed by the president, who would follow the cabinet principles. There was no mention of ministerial responsibility to the legislature. The tenure of the office of the president was six years. The upper house of the central legislature was based on federal principles, mainly, though not more than ten of its members would be nominated by the president in consultation with the universities and scientific bodies. The other members would be elected by legislatures of units. Of the total strength of this house (Council of States), one-third would retire every two years, making it a permanent body. Its total strength would not be more than half the strength of the lower house (House of the People) elected through universal adult franchise.

While placing the Union Constitution Committee's report in the Assembly, Nehru said that the committee had anxiously thought about the nature of the government at the centre. Direct election of the president, it was thought,

> would not be desirable, first because we want to emphasise the ministerial character of the government, that power really resided in the ministry and in the legislature and not in the president as such. At the same time we did not want to make the president just a mere figurehead like the French president. We did not give him any real power but we have made his position onc of great authority and dignity.[15]

Second, election of the president by the whole people would mean a big waste. So the Committee suggested the indirect election of the president. The president, however, would be elected not only by members of the union legislature but also by members of the provincial legislative assemblies. This system was not evolved solely out of any regard for the federal principle, but also because the president's election by only the central legislature was considered to be on too narrow a basis.

S.L. Saksena had wanted to move an amendment that the president

[14] The Report of the Committee on a Model Union Constitution, *CAD*, vol. IV, pp. 716-36.

[15] *CAD*, vol. IV, p. 734.

should be directly elected, but did not move it as he was 'not free in the matter.[16] T. Channiah (from Mysore state), however, wanted the office to rotate between the North and the South.[17] He was defeated. When the clause about the ministry came, a Leaguer moved for the ministry's election by the National Assembly through proportional representation.[18] Karimuddin wanted a non-parliamentary executive, with the prime minister elected by legislature through single transferable vote, and other ministers through non-transferable vote.[19] Both motions were defeated. Nehru, however, accepted one amendment, moved by K. Chengalaraya Reddy, for inserting 'elected' before 'members' wherever it occurred.[20] To the demand for 'direct election' of the president, Nehru had the answer in the unnecessary delay involved in the process.[21]

There was, however, a background of this issue of the president's election. On 8 June 1947, the Union Constitution Committee decided to have a president—who would be only a constitutional head—elected by the union legislature, and set up a subcommittee to examine the question further, in view of Munshi's opposition to the proposals. The subcommittee consisted of N.G. Ayyangar, Panikkar and Ambedkar. On the same date the Provincial Constitution Committee decided to have the governors—in possession of some discretionary powers—elected by the people directly. Munshi's demand led to a joint meeting of the two committees on 10 June 1947 which recommended, by a majority decision, to the Union Constitution Committee, the election of president by adult franchise through a special electorate. The latter was reluctant to accept the recommendation. On 10 June also the subcommittee of the Union Constitution Committee recommended the inclusion of the lower houses of the units' legislatures into the presidential electorate.[22]

It appears that the majority of the members of the Provincial Constitution Committee backed Munshi in upsetting the decision of the Union Constitution Committee. Munshi claims to have always fought for 'safeguards against unrestricted parliamentary supremacy' in this

[16] Ibid., p. 827. Obviously, he meant a partyship, though no evidence of its issue could be gathered.

[17] Ibid., p. 821.

[18] Ibid., p. 907.

[19] Ibid., p. 908.

[20] Ibid., p. 824.

[21] Ibid., p. 846.

[22] See the Union Constitution Committee's File and K.M. Munshi's *Pilgrimage to Freedom*, pp. 255-8.

country.[23] Munshi's ideological loyalty to Patel, president of the Provincial Constitution Committee, is well known. Though the Union Constitution Committee, under Nehru, ultimately had its way through a rather vague compromise formula, its pressure on the Provincial Constitution Committee for a perfect cabinet type of government at the provincial level was successfully resisted by Patel and his committee. It is also possible that the Provincial Constitution Committee wanted, for the provincial legislatures, a share in the presidential election.

The draft constitution published in February 1948 provided, in the centre, for a council of ministers to aid and advise the president, though the conformity of the president with their advice remained outside the jurisdiction of a court's enquiry. Ministers were to hold office during the pleasure of the president (article 62/2) and were to be entirely responsible to the House of the People (article 62/3). There was no reference to any discretion of the president.

A Cabinet Government at the Centre

Jayaprakash Narayan, outside the Assembly, and a few members within it wanted to substitute clause 2 of article 62 by a specific provision that the ministers would be in office during their enjoyment of the confidence of the House of the People instead of the pleasure of the president. The Drafting Committee in October 1948 decided that, as it was a well-established convention in a parliamentary government that the ministers would be in office so long as they had the support of the legislature, the above proposal was unnecessary. There was also the collective responsibility of the ministry in clause 3.[24] As a solution to any possible confusion, Rau's old idea of an instrument of instructions to the president was revived in the form of a new article (62-A) and a new schedule (III-A). The schedule, requiring the president to act according to the ministers' advice, provided for an 'advisory council' to advise the president on some other appointments to be made by him.[25]

Presenting the draft constitution in the Assembly Ambedkar clearly said that 'What the Draft Constitution proposes is a parliamentary system'.

> In the Draft Constitution there is placed at the head of the Indian Union a functionary who is called the President of the union. The title of the functionary

[23] Munshi, *Pilgrimage to Freedom*, p. 255.
[24] B. Shiva Rao, *Select Documents*, vol. IV, p. 67.
[25] *CAD*, vol. VII, p. 1167; Ambedkar's amendments.

reminds one of the President of the United States. But beyond identity of names there is nothing in common between the form of government prevalent in America and the form of government proposed under the Draft Constitution.[26]

While the provision of the Draft Constitution relating to the union cabinet (article 61) was placed in the Assembly on 30 December 1948, Mahboob Ali Baig moved an amendment which sought to restrict the council of ministers to 15 and to provide that the ministers would be elected through proportional representation by the legislature.[27] K.T. Shah's amendments were extensive and sought to provide, among other things, that 'on every change of the council of ministers' the prime minister or the president would present them in the parliament and seek its confidence in the ministry. The lack of confidence being expressed in one minister or the whole ministry, resignation of the minister or the whole ministry would follow.[28] Baig's amendment was opposed on the floor by Tajamul Husain[29] and rejected. Shah's amendment had the demerit of introducing several responsibility, but sought to make it direct and immediate. The amendments were, therefore, turned down as 'unnecessary' and 'fatal'.[30] Ambedkar, however, assured Baig that schedule III-A would provide for minority representation in the cabinet through conventions. The promise was hardly redeemed as the Drafting Committee finally decided to drop article 62-A and not to move schedule III-A in order to leave the whole thing to conventions.[31]

Mohammad Tahir, on the other hand, sought to grant the president the discretion 'that the governor was given under article 143 of the Draft Constitution'.[32] Ambedkar hinted that a reconsideration about the governor's discretion was possible.[33] Ambedkar commented on Tahir's amendment that he merely 'bodily copied section 50 of the Government of India Act'. But under the 1935 Act, the Governor-General had some discretionary power, whereas the president would not have any:

Under the parliamentary system of government, there are only two prerogatives which the king or the head of the state may exercise. One is the appointment of

[26] Ibid., vol. VII, p. 32.

[27] Ibid., vol. VII, p. 1141.

[28] Ibid., pp. 1144, 1146-7.

[29] Ibid., pp. 1152-5.

[30] Ambedkar's speech. Ibid., pp. 1159-60.

[31] Correspondingly, clause 4 of article 144 and schedule IV-A were dropped. Ibid., vol. X, pp. 268, 275.

[32] Ibid., vol. VII, pp. 1145-6.

[33] Ibid., p. 1158.

the prime minister and the other is dissolution of parliament. With regard to the prime minister it is not possible to avoid vesting the discretion in the president. The only other way by which we could provide for the appointment of the prime minister without vesting the authority or discretion in the president is to require that it is the house which shall in the first instance choose its leader, and then, on the choice being made by a motion or a resolution, the president should proceed to appoint the PM.

If the president made a wrong choice, the legislature could express no-confidence. With regard to the dissolution of the houses, Ambedkar said, 'there again there is no definite opinion so far as the British constitutional lawyers are concerned'.

Ambedkar concluded, 'I think these are purely prerogatives and they do not come within the administration of the country. As such no such provision as Mr. Tahir has suggested in his amendment is necessary to govern the exercise of the prerogatives.'[34]

It is a question of comparative politics whether the concept of 'prerogatives' is not anomalous in a republican constitution. K.M. Munshi actually uses this piece of Ambedkar's speech to establish that the leadership of the Constituent Assembly was not agreed on making the Indian president a mere constitutional figurehead.[35] On the other hand, the 'pleasure' of the chief executive, like the 'discretion' of the governor, may well be regarded as a power granted by the constitution, and not a prerogative.

Bicameral Legislatures

The Union Constitution Committee in early July 1947 at first decided to have 25 members of the Council of States from functional constituencies or panels and other members elected by the lower chambers of provincial legislatures on the basis of the strength of population of provinces (one representative for one million, up to five millions, above which one representative for every two millions, subject to a maximum of 25 representatives). The decision was later revised by the Union Constitution Committee so that the president was authorized to nominate 10 members to the Council of States from distinguished individuals. The Constituent

[34] Ibid., pp. 1158-9. During the tenth session, however, when Santhanam asserted that the president could decline a request of the prime minister for dissolution of parliament, following the British king, Ambedkar denied it categorically, as the practice had ceased in Britain and the dominions. *CAD*, vol. X, p. 270.

[35] K.M. Munshi. *The President under the Indian Constitution*, pp. 8-9.

Assembly, on 31 July 1947, however, through an amendment of Ayyangar, reverted to the original plan of the Union Constitution Committee of having 25 members elected by functional constituencies. Rau, in November 1947, communicated to the Drafting Committee the advice of de Valera that functional representation in the Eire had not worked well. Therefore, the Drafting Committee gave up functional representation of 15 members for presidential nomination from distinguished persons in various fields. Oddly enough, the advice had no effect on the provincial constitution, where the system of functional representation was retained.

The final shape of the Council of States emerged out of an amendment moved by Ambedkar on 3 January 1949 in the Assembly. The wide range of nominational constituencies was reduced to men of 'letters, arts, science and social service', the number of nominated members being reduced from 15 to 12.[36]

Only one of the replies from the Provincial Constitution Committee members (Katju) had required a second chamber for a unit legislature. Rau's draft of the provincial constitution left the scope for bicameral legislatures in some provinces, if the members of the Constituent Assembly from the province so chose. When the Provincial Constitution Committee met, some provinces were found to be demanding two chambers. The committee finally decided to have normally one chamber and two chambers in exceptional cases. The question of the need for a second chamber was referred to a subcommittee, consisting of Kher, Sitaramayya, Subbaroyan and Katju, which recommended that the strength of the second chamber should not exceed 25 per cent of the strength of the first chamber. Representation to the provincial second chamber was to be, on the Irish model, functional, up to a half, the other half being filled up by election from the lower chamber of the provincial legislature and nomination by governors.[37]

In a note with clause 19(2) the Provincial Constitution Committee recommended the abolition of the special representations of the universities, labour and women. In the Constituent Assembly R.K. Sidhwa sought to add to this list trade, industry and commerce, in order to abolish all special representations. J.J.M. Nichols-Roy, a tribal member from Assam, sought the fixing of a lower quota of population per representative in a state legislature for hill tribes. Jaipal Singh, another tribal member

[36] *CAD*, vol. VII, p. 1202. The distribution of seats among the states, however, was determined by an amendment (new schedule III-A) moved on 17 October 1949. *CAD*, vol. X, pp. 406-11.

[37] Provincial Constitution Committee's File.

from Bihar, wanted weightage for all tribes.[38] Patel accepted only two amendments to clause 19 (regarding elections) of Sidhwa and Saadulla, fixing the minimum strength of an assembly at 60 and maximum at 300, respectively.[39]

The draft constitution provided for election of one-half of the total strength of the upper house of a state from five panels of candidates from universities, literature, arts, science, various professions and social service. Special representation of trade, commerce, industry, women and labour was abolished from both the union and state second chambers. The composition of legislative council of a state was finally struck out through an amendment moved by Ambedkar on 19 August 1949.[40] Earlier, on 30 July 1949, another amendment, seeking to leave the election and composition of the legislative councils to parliament, had been declared unsatisfactory.

The whole episode gives an idea of the indecisiveness which the Constituent Assembly suffered from over the question of the second chambers. India inherited the second chamber from the British days. With the introduction of the federal idea into Indian politics, a second chamber had been taken for granted at the central level. Yet, explaining the purpose of the second chamber in the union legislature, N.G. Ayyangar could only say that 'The most that we expect the second chamber to do is perhaps to hold dignified debates on important issues and to delay legislation which might be the outcome of passions of the moment.'[41] But never was the justification of a second chamber in a unit sufficiently established. Ultimately the decision was left to the provincial representatives of the assembly to be taken separately. Even there the decisions were not reached at a stroke. The issue became still more complicated by the question of functional representation involving weightage to certain sections of the people.

Legislative Procedure

The uncertainty of attitude towards a second chamber was also reflected on the changing formula of legislative procedures and relationship of the two houses in the scheme of the Constituent Assembly. In B.N. Rau's memoranda on the union and the provincial constitutions, it had been

[38] *CAD*, vol. IV, pp. 684-6.
[39] Ibid., p. 686.
[40] Ibid., vol. IX, p. 473.
[41] Ibid., vol. IV, p. 927.

suggested that the legislative procedure in the union and provincial legislatures would follow the 1935 model. The Provincial Constitution Committee adopted the suggestion of Rau. The Union Constitution Committee struck down the whole plan and provided that there should be 'usual legislative procedure' in the union parliament. The Constituent Assembly adopted both the plans, with an amendment of Santhanam, that, in the case of a single-chamber provincial legislature, the governor, at his discretion, would have the power to return a bill other than a money bill to the legislature, though, after a second passage by the legislature, the bill must get his signature. While endorsing the amendment Patel said that such power of the governor was unnecessary in a province that would have a double-chamber legislature, as the two chambers would balance each other and their differences would be thrashed out in a joint session.[42] Obviously, the governor's power to return a bill was considered necessary only to check any abuse of power by a single chamber.

But the Union Constitution Committee in its report (Part III, para 15) specified that 'President should have the power of returning the bills which have been passed by the National Assembly for reconsideration within a period of six months'. Santhanam indeed got this power confined to within six weeks and only to non-money bills.[43]

The draft constitution of February 1948 carried both the principles (for the union and the states). The Drafting Committee, however, wanted to bring about a uniformity in the two procedures. Hence Ambedkar on 30 July 1949 moved an amendment to the proviso of article 175 to omit the governor's discretion in returning a bill, to make it applicable even in the case of a bicameral legislature, but to confine it only to non-money bills.[44]

A question, on which a long controversy went on, was that of powers of the two houses at the centre and the units. According to the draft constitution, money bills could generate only in the House of the People and the Council of States could only detain it for 30 days. A non-money bill could generate in either house and, in case of differences between the houses, the president would convene a joint session. At the state level a similar procedure was outlined. In view of strong criticisms of the second chamber, the Drafting Committee in May 1949 reduced the power of the

[42] Ibid., pp. 704, 709.
[43] Ibid., p. 930.
[44] Ibid., vol. IX, pp. 41-2.

union second chamber.[45] The powers of the state second chamber were reduced in July 1949.[46]

An Integral Judiciary

B.N. Rau had asked in his questionnaire if a separate federal judiciary was necessary. Of the Union Constitution Committee members, K.T. Shah, without answering the question directly, gave the impression of favouring an integrated judiciary. Panikkar's was a negative reply, while S.P. Mookerjee wanted the decision to be left to the union legislature. Of the Provincial Constitution Committee members who replied, two gave the answer in the negative. All of them wanted a high court at the head of the provincial judiciary. Three of them wanted the judges thereof to be appointed by the president of the union in consultation with the chief justice of the Supreme Court, the provincial heads and other senior judges. One member wanted the provincial legislature to elect the chief justice of the province, one wanted the chief justice of the union to appoint the chief justice of a province who could again appoint other judges, and one member had no recommendation. Rau's own formula was to incorporate provisions of the 1935 Act in the new constitution. Appointment of judges was to be made by the governor at his discretion.

No formal decision was taken by the two committees on the relation between the union and provincial judiciaries. The joint meeting of the union and provincial constitution committees recommended on 10 June 1947 that high court judges should be appointed by the president of the union in consultation with the chief justice of India, the provincial governors and the provincial chief justices. To appoint the chief justice of a province the president was to consult the chief justice of India, the provincial governor, and other judges of the Supreme Court and the high courts as he deemed necessary. The Provincial Constitution Committee accepted the suggestion.

The Ad-hoc Committee on the Supreme Court, appointed by this committee, whose report was appended to the report of the latter, recommended that, 'A Supreme Court with jurisdiction to decide the constitutional validity of acts and laws was a necessary implication of any federal scheme. This jurisdiction might not, however, belong

[45] Ibid., vol. VIII, pp. 184-5.
[46] Ibid., vol. IX, pp. 13, 43-4.

exclusively to the Supreme Court.' Other courts might enquire into the validity of acts and laws as well.[47]

On the principles and organization of the Supreme Court, the Union Constitution Committee, meeting on 11 June 1947, was guided mainly by the report of the Ad-hoc Committee on the Supreme Court consisting of Alladi Krishnaswami Ayyar, K.M. Munshi, B.L. Mitter, B.N. Rau and S. Varadachariar, except that the judges of the Supreme Court had to be appointed by a panel of eleven members, and not at the president's discretion. The Union Constitution Committee decided that the president would appoint the judges in consultation with the chief justice and other judges.

The Union Constitution Committee accepted the recommendations of the Ad-hoc Committee on the Supreme Court that the Supreme Court would have (1) exclusive jurisdiction over centre-unit and interunit disputes; (2) ultimate jurisdiction on matters arising out of the union government's treatise with foreign states; (3) concurrent jurisdiction with high courts on disputes relating to fundamental rights; (4) appellate jurisdiction similar to that of the Privy Council; and (5) advisory jurisdiction. However, the Ad-hoc Committee's recommendation about a panel of advisers for recommending the appointment of the Supreme Court judges was turned down. The president was given full authority to appoint the judges in consultation with the chief justice and other judges, as necessary. The joint meeting of the union and provincial constitution committees on 10 June 1947 decided that the judges of high courts would be appointed by the president in consultation with the Supreme court judges. The fourth session of the Assembly passed the reports. But, on Ayyar's resolution, the high courts were given the powers to issue writs in cases involving fundamental rights and of superintendence and control of the lower courts.[48] The controversy over the writ-issuing powers was, thus, finally solved. With a view to adding to the dignity of the highest court, another amendment of Ayyar made the Supreme Court judges liable to removal on an address to the President of India by parliament's two houses.[49]

The draft constitution of February 1948 for the first time upheld that the central judiciary would not be separate from the state judiciaries. In the list of union powers it put the 'Supreme Court of India' instead of the

[47] *Report of the Ad-hoc Committee on the Supreme Court.*
[48] *CAD*, vol. IV, p. 889.
[49] Ibid., p. 895.

'federal judiciary'.[50] Following the Ad-hoc Committee's recommendations the Supreme Court was given original, appellate and advisory jurisdictions.

The appellate jurisdiction of the Supreme Court, as laid down by the draft constitution (articles 110, 111, 112) came in for strong criticism. The Supreme Court's appellate jurisdiction extended to cases of civil and criminal nature involving substantial questions of law as to the interpretation of the constitution. Otherwise, disputes over properties worth twenty thousand rupees or above could come under the Supreme Court's appellate jurisdiction.

On 3 June 1949, the Constituent Assembly discussed the question. Several members regretted that the appellate jurisdiction of the Supreme Court did not cover criminal cases not involving the question of interpretation of the constitution. This fact showed, according to them, the constitution's preference for property to life. Thakurdas Bhargava moved an amendment to the effect that cases involving death sentence or transportation could be appealed to the Supreme Court. Finally, Ambedkar moved an amendment authorizing the Supreme Court to entertain appeals on criminal cases where the high courts had awarded death sentence reversing the lower court's judgement. Parliament was given power to confer additional criminal jurisdiction on the Supreme Court.[51]

Provisions for the subordinate courts were made by an amendment moved by Ambedkar on 16 September 1949, adding articles 209A to 209E. The amendments, according to Ambedkar, had two objectives: (1) 'to make provision for the appointment of district judges and subordinate judges and their qualifications' and (2) 'to place this civil judiciary under the control of the high court'.[52]

[50] *Draft Constitution of India*, p. 192n.
[51] *CAD*, vol. VII, p. 40.
[52] Ibid., vol. IX, p. 1571

CHAPTER 16

Framing of the Constitution (IV)

Extra Wheels in the Machine

Considering the intensity of the 'Indian problem', which was very close to explosiveness, one is bound to appreciate the strong and centralized state-structure that the Constituent Assembly of India evolved. In several ways the governmental machinery itself helped this centralization. So did some of the special features of the Indian government.

Discretionary Powers

A significant special feature is the 'discretion' of the governor. The concept of discretionary power of the governor underwent several changes. In B.N. Rau's model provincial constitution, the governor was expected to be working generally according to the advice of the ministers, except on a few occasions, for example the choice of ministers, protection of minorities and maintenance of law and order. If in any case the ministerial advice was disregarded by the governor, the ministers might resign and the governor might be unable to form an alternative ministry. But in extreme cases the governor was advised even to dissolve the legislature and call for another election. The 'discretionary' power would 'in such cases have at least the effect of bringing the issue before the electorate'.[1]

According to clause 9 of the Provincial Constitution Committee's Report, the governor would act in his discretion in the following matters:

'(1) the prevention of any grave menace to the peace and tranquillity of the province or any part thereof,

'(2) the summoning and dissolving of the provincial legislature,

'(3) the superintendence, direction and control of elections,

'(4) the appointment of the chairman and the members of the Provincial

[1] B.N. Rau, *India's Constitution in the Making*, p. 170.

> Public Service Commission and of the Provincial Auditor-General.'[2]

On the question whether a certain subject was within the discretionary powers of the governor, the governor's decision would be final. Patel tried to remove the members' misgivings about the great discretionary authority of the governor even in other respects, by arguing that summoning and dissolving a legislature were the normal powers of governors. The forthcoming Fundamental Rights Subcommittee's report provided for an election commission to be appointed by the governor to conduct elections. In the matter of the few appointments the governor would be guided by the advice of the ministers. 'Therefore . . . practically the only power left to the provincial governor is the power to report to the union President when a grave emergency arise threatening menace to the peace and tranquillity of the province and summoning and dissolving of the provincial legislature.'[3]

In the absence of proper 'proceedings' of the Provincial Constitution Committee's meetings it is not possible to scan the attitude of the committee members towards the question of discretion. But if Patel was voicing in the Assembly the opinion of the committee, it is clear that the committee wanted to do away with frequent use of the discretionary powers under normal circumstances and turn them into something similar to the 'prerogatives' of the British Crown. This impression is strengthened by the decision of the Provincial Constitution Committee over the 'special responsibility' of the governor.

The Special Committee, with Nehru as chairman, which recommended the appointment of a governor[4] rather than election, on 11 April 1948, opined that 'all references to the exercise of functions by the governor in his discretion should be omitted from the Draft Constitution'. From outside the Assembly demand for omission of the governor's pleasure came from Jayaprakash Narayan.

While the Drafting Committee dropped the 'discretion' of the governor in the appointment of ministers, the governor's 'pleasure' to determine their tenure was retained. The Drafting Committee held that such 'pleasure'

[2] B. Shiva Rao, *Select Documents*, vol. II, pp. 158-9, 198.

[3] *CAD*, vol. IV, p. 581.

[4] B. Shiva Rao, ibid., vol. IV, p. 411. The idea that one gathers from interviews with members of the Constituent Assembly and various documents about the intention of the Special Committee, is that the governor, being representative of none, would, appropriately, be a nominal head.

was limited in scope by the confidence of the legislature. The other fields of the governor's 'discretion were retained'.[5]

Paradox of Discretion

It is not easy to explain the turning down of a suggestion of 'policy' from a high-powered body like the Special Committee by the Drafting Committee which sat with Ambedkar, Madhava Rau and Saadulla. Obviously, there was rethinking on the question in the leadership. Possibly, there was the influence of Patel, the remarkable absentee in the Special Committee.

The new trend in the thinking of the Drafting Committee was confirmed when, without removing the discretion of the governor, the Drafting Committee actually moved, on 11 October 1949, for the deletion of the fourth schedule (Instructions to Governors). Ambedkar pleaded that 'the discretion we are going to have with the governor is very very meagre. He has hardly any discretion at all. He has to act on the advice of the chief minister in the matter of selection of members of the cabinet. He has also to act on the advice of the chief minister and his ministers of state with respect to any particular executive or legislative action that he takes.' So the schedules (III-A and IV) were 'useless'.[6]

The strongest attack on 'discretion' came in the form of an amendment from H.V. Kamath to omit the reference to discretion in draft article 143 (1).[7] T.T. Krishnamachari supported the retention of discretion for, after all, article 188 had kept it.[8] But then, there was already the possibility of article 188 being omitted altogether (it was actually omitted later). H.N. Kunzru raised the poignant question, 'Supposing, these words which are reminiscent of the old Government of India Act and the old order are omitted, what harm will be done?'[9] To this Ayyar replied, 'If later on the house comes to the conclusion that those articles which enable the governor to act in his discretion in specific cases should be deleted, it will be open to revise this article.'[10]

One of the paradoxes of the Indian Constitution is that the full significance of the term of 'discretion' has never been examined, either

[5] Ibid., pp. 67, 81.
[6] *CAD*, vol. X, pp. 114-15.
[7] Ibid., vol. VIII, p. 489.
[8] Ibid., pp. 490-1.
[9] Ibid., p. 492.
[10] Ibid., p. 495.

in the Constituent Assembly or in a law court. The President of India has a 'pleasure', but no 'discretion', whereas the governor has both. The Government of India Act left much discretion for the Governor-General as well as the governors, as a 'prerogative'. But 'discretion' in the Indian Constitution is, obviously, a power 'granted' by the Constitution. Ambedkar summed up the position of the Assembly leadership, pointing to the language of the Draft, as follows:

'If the words were 'except whenever he thinks he should exercise discretion against the wishes or advice of the ministers', then I think the criticism . . . would have been valid. The clause is a very limited clause; it says: 'except in so far as he is required by or under the constitution'. Therefore, article 143 will have to be read in conjunction with such other articles which specifically reserve the power to the governor.[11]

He declared that 'the house cannot escape from mentioning, in some manner, that 'the governor shall have discretion'. It is, however, difficult to reconcile this interpretation with article 163 of the final constitution which grants the governor discretion to decide when he is required by or under the constitution, to act in his discretion, beyond the competence of any court to examine.

Legislative Role of the Governor

It was according to the Provincial Constitution Committee's recommendation of the 1935 model for the legislative procedure, ratified by the Constituent Assembly, that the Drafting Committee had laid down that draft article 175 which enabled the governor to give assent to, or withhold it from, or to reserve for the consideration of the president, a bill, passed by the legislature, in his discretion. Santhanam, M.A. Ayyangar, T.T. Krishnamachari (who was not yet in the Drafting Committee) and Shrimati G. Durgabai moved an amendment seeking to make the governor only give his assent to such bills. Jayaprakash Narayan from outside the

[11] Ibid., p. 501. In the case of *Mahavir Prasad* v. *Prafulla Chandra*, Justice B.C. Mitra of the Calcutta High Court gave the interesting rulings that (a) the governor, in appointing the chief minister, acts in his discretion, and (b) the right of the governor to withdraw his pleasure during which ministers would hold office, at his discretion, is unquestionably following from article 163 (2) of the present constitution. According to the judgement, governor's pleasure determining the tenure of the ministers depends, not on the ministers' enjoyment of the confidence of the legislative assembly, but on the discretion of the governor (*AIR* 1969, Calcutta, 198, paragraphs 50, 42 and 41). One wonders if this construction is applicable to the central cabinet.

assembly made a similar demand, while Tajamul Husain wanted the legislature to dissolve itself, in case of the governor's refusal of assent, and to call for an election. The Drafting Committee in October 1948 only agreed to omit the reference to discretion and made a significant comment:

Under Article 175, the powers of the governor to declare that he withholds his assent from or that he reserves the bill for the consideration of the President, will be exercised by him on the advice of his ministers. . . . There may be cases where it might be necessary for the governor to exercise the power of withholding assent even on the advice of the ministers.[12]

At one stage, however, the Drafting Committee had actually proposed to move an amendment to the effect that the governor would withhold his assent from a bill only if, in his opinion, such a bill prejudiced the status of the high court. The idea was not pursued by the committee till the 10th session of the Assembly when an amendment was moved by Krishnamachari, on 17 October 1949, to the rather different effect that the governor shall not assent to but reserve for the consideration of the president any bill which seeks to derogate from the powers and position of the high court. The explanation offered was that the amendment was meant for compensating the non-inclusion of the fourth schedule, which had contained a clause (no. 7) to this effect.[13]

Special Responsibility of Governor and Emergency

Rau's draft of the provincial constitution had suggested the discretionary powers of the governor in cases of grave threats to the peace and tranquillity of a province or to any part thereof to pass emergency ordinances. On 9 June 1947, a question was raised in the Provincial Constitution Committee, whether, in view of the all-India repercussion such ordinances might create, it would not be desirable for the governor to consult the President of India. The question was referred to the Joint Committee which decided that the governor would normally act upon the advice of the ministers. But in cases of emergency, he might, in his discretion, refer the question to the president. The Provincial Constitution Committee on 11 June 1947 accepted the recommendation. 'It was made clear that the only action which the governor may take except on advice is to report to the President.'[14]

[12] B. Shiva Rao, *Select Documents*, vol. IV, p. 125.

[13] *CAD*, vol. X, pp. 392-3.

[14] Minutes of the Provincial Constitution Committee's meetings.

The governor would have, according to the revised decision of the Provincial Constitution Committee, special responsibility for prevertion of grave menace to peace and tranquillity in the territory. In the discharge of this special responsibility, the governor would act in his discretion (clause 15). If the governor in discharging this special duty, needed a legislation by the provincial legislature and failed to secure it, he would have the right to inform the president who would take necessary action. As Patel explained, some members of the committee

> thought that it would be advisable under the present peculiar unsettled conditions in the country to give some limited powers to the governor—eventually the committee came to the conclusion that it would not be workable, that it would create deadlocks and therefore the proper course would be to limit his powers (to sending a report to the President).[15]

What steps the president would take would be determined by the Union Powers Committee.

When clause 15 came in for discussion in the Assembly, Patel further said,

> This question of discretionary powers of the governor is a matter which requires careful consideration. On the one hand it encroaches upon the powers of the ministry.... Again on the other side there is a feeling that, looking to the conditions prevailing in the country, some provision should be made for giving special responsibilities to meet with the difficult situation which has arisen in this country today.[16]

Obviously, the reference was to the existing communal and, to a lesser extent, communist threats in parts of the country. Actually, Patel's speech made it easy for B.M. Gupte to move an amendment to clause 15.

Gupte's amendment sought to authorize the governor to proclaim an emergency and assume all powers of the government except those of the high court, and thereafter make a report to the president. While K.M. Munshi moved an amendment more or less on the same line, H.N. Kunzru's amendment sought to restrict the powers of the governor to merely reporting to the president who would decide upon subsequent actions. Gupte's amendment as modified by Munshi's got the general support. B.G. Kher said, 'If you have a governor elected on adult franchise, do not make him only a figurehead, simply sending telegrams to the President.'[17]

[15] *CAD*, vol. IV, p. 579.

[16] Ibid., p. 707.

[17] Ibid., p. 773.

Patel said that the provincial prime ministers had required such a measure.[18]

The Union Constitution Committee's report, however, did not contain any provision for emergency, except a 'legislative power' of the president. On 30 July 1947, therefore, K. Santhanam and B.M. Gupte moved two amendments which sought to confer upon the president some emergency powers, in case of his satisfaction that the normal functioning of the constitutional machinery was impossible. According to Santhanam's proposal, in such an eventuality, the president could take adequate measures, including (1) suspension of the provincial constitution, (2) promulgation of ordinance to be applicable to the province, and (3) issuing of orders and instructions to the governors and other officers of the province. Gupte's amendment sought to empower the president, under similar circumstances, in consultation with his council of ministers, to issue 'a proclamation assuming to himself all or any of the powers vested in, or exercisable by, any provincial body or authority except the high court, including the power to confirm, modify or remove the proclamation issued by the governor'.[19]

The Union Constitution Committee had not, obviously, yet made up its mind. N.G. Ayyangar, on behalf of the committee, felt the need for further examination of the suggestions and proposed that the drafters of the constitution be left with the task of formulating the provision. He said:

> The net result of what I have indicated is that while I am not prepared to hand over the entire administration of a province into the hands of the President even in an emergency of that sort, I am prepared to concede the position that he should have certain emergency powers in order to decide what appropriate action should be taken for dealing with a particular emergency and no more.[20]

Santhanam and Gupte withdrew their amendments.

The governor's role in constitutional emergency (draft article 188) remained a major subject of controversy. The Drafting Committee in October 1948 was not sure of its necessity in view of the elaborate emergency provisions in Part XI of the Draft. Jayaprakash Narayan demanded its substitution by another article declaring that states were autonomous units. If, however, law and order really broke down, the president with the aid of the armed forces would have the power to maintain order. The state machinery might even be suspended in grave emergency.

[18] Ibid., pp. 780-1.
[19] Ibid., p. 949.
[20] Ibid., p. 952.

Such steps would be immediately communicated to the central legislature. Tajamul Husain wanted the governor to have power only to communicate an emergency to the president, on advice of his ministers. The Drafting Committee did not accept either of the proposals, as the former was unnecessary in view of other emergency provisions and the latter was an impossible position. A governor could not possibly be advised by his ministers to admit a constitutional breakdown. The implication was that the governor in a constitutional emergency must act in his 'special responsibility', if not in his discretion.[21]

Jayaprakash Narayan had a comprehensive formula to deal with emergency as such which he wanted as a replacement of articles 277 and 278 of the draft constitution. The Drafting Committee in October 1949 accepted only a part of it, according to which the federal government would be declared responsible for the protection of every state from external aggression and internal violence. The committee rejected his suggestion that in case of a war the centre could exercise concurrent jurisdiction on state subjects and the president could take over the administration of such parts of the state as were necessary for the purpose. The committee had doubt about the propriety of taking over a state's administration during a war. The other kinds of emergency could not also be tackled by this formula. Another amendment proposal on behalf of the rulers of some states for declaring the centre's responsibility for protection of the Indian states was accepted. At this stage the Drafting Committee also proposed to amend the president's power to suspend constitutional remedies by reducing the period of such suspension from 'six months after the withdrawal of emergency' to the period of 'the continuation of emergency'.[22]

A Nominated Governor

When B.N. Rau prepared a model provincial constitution for consideration of the Provincial Constitution Committee, he pointed out that under the Cabinet Mission's proposals the union government would not have the power to appoint the governors of provinces. As the governors were, however, expected to depend upon the advice of the ministers, he advised the election of the governor by the state legislature.[23] The Provincial Constitution Committee decided on a popularly elected governor, as an

[21] B. Shiva Rao, *Select Documents*, vol. IV, pp. 364-5.
[22] Ibid., pp. 365-71.
[23] B.N. Rau, *India's Constitution in the Making*, pp. 141-2.

elected governor would be able to 'exert considerable influence on the popular ministry'.[24] The Constituent Assembly ratified the decision.

The draft constitution prepared by the Drafting Committee in February 1948 (article 131) suggested choice of the governor either by direct vote of all persons who have the right to vote at a general election for the legislative assembly of the state or by the presidential nomination 'from a panel of four candidates to be elected by the members of the legislative assembly of the state or, where there is a legislative council in the state, by all the members of the legislative assembly and legislative council of the state assembled at a joint meeting'.[25]

The second alternative was a new suggestion of the Drafting Committee to meet the point of view of some members who considered 'that the coexistence of a governor elected by the people and a prime minister responsible to the legislature might lead to friction and consequent weakness in administration'.[26] The Special Committee, in April 1948, endorsed this viewpoint desiring to turn the governor into a nominal head.[27]

When the article came up for discussion in the Constituent Assembly (during the second reading), Brajeswar Prasad moved, on 30 May 1949, the amendment to the effect that, 'The governor of a state shall be appointed by the President by warrant under his hand and seal.'[28] Speakers like Jawaharlal Nehru, Ambedkar and Alladi Krishnaswami Ayyar gave full support to the resolution, Ayyar said:

> In the consideration of this question the main points to be remembered are that this Assembly has accepted the introduction of responsible government in the states, that the governor is merely a constitutional head of the province and that the real executive power has been vested in a ministry responsible to the lower house in the different states. The question for consideration before the House is whether under these circumstances there is any point in going through an expensive and elaborate machinery of election based upon universal suffrage.[29]

Ayyar's explanation may sound unconvincing to many. The governor's powers of legislative veto and in emergency—particularly that of declaring constitutional breakdown—when placed in an elected person would mean something very different from that when they were placed in an appointed

[24] Report of the Committee on a Model Provincial Constitution.

[25] B. Shiva Rao, *Select Documents*, vol. II, p. 658.

[26] *The Draft Constitution of India*, p. 57.

[27] B. Shiva Rao, *Select Documents*, vol. III, p. 409.

[28] *CAD*, vol. VIII, p. 426.

[29] Ibid., p. 431.

official. In several other speeches, at the same time, the governor's role as a link between the centre and the states was emphasized.

The most forceful speaker to point out the danger of turning the governor into an agent of the president through appointment was the moderate League member of the Constituent Assembly, Saadulla, V.S. Sarawate (Madhya Bharat) pointed out the distinction made between the governors and Rajpramukhs in the matter of their appointment. The amendment was, however, adopted. So was adopted another amendment of Ambedkar for substitution of article 132 of the Draft by 'The governor shall hold office during the pleasure of the President'.[30]

Modification of the Emergency Provisions

While H.N. Kunzru gave his limited support, he pointed out that the new situation called for the amendment of the draft articles 175 and 188, to avoid conflict between the governor and the popular ministers in a parliamentary government. He suggested the amendment of article 175 in such a way as to grant the president the power to disallow a provincial bill within a certain period. Instead of article 188 he suggested, 'The President of the republic can under another article be enabled to take action where the peace of the country is threatened because of anything happening in a province or where a province is found to face with a situation which if not firmly handled may lead to a conflagration.'[31]

T.T. Krishnamachari, on behalf of the Drafting Committee, hinted that the amendment of article 175 was under consideration, though he could not make any commitment about article 188. Ultimately, as already seen, article 175 was substituted and article 188 was dropped on 3 August 1949. This called for a revision of the emergency provisions. Article 277-A was, therefore, introduced and article 278 was substituted by new articles 278 and 278-A on the same day.[32] Article 277-A sought to declare the union's responsibility to protect the states against external aggression and internal disturbances and ensure that the government of every state is carried on in accordance with the provisions of the constitution. The long-term significance of the new article was further strengthened by the new article 278 which empowered the president, if he was satisfied, on a report from the governor or the ruler of a state, or otherwise, that the government of the state could not be carried on in accordance with the provisions of

[30] Ibid., p. 470.
[31] Ibid., p. 441.
[32] Ibid., vol. IX, pp. 131-2.

the constitution, to take upon himself all or any of the functions of the state executive, to enable the union parliament to take over the functions of the state legislature and to take other incidental and consequential steps. Article 278-A sought to provide for efficient functioning of the union government during such an emergency. The two moves were interdependent.

This was the major stroke by which the centre was made responsible for constitutional government in the units and was enabled to act even without a report from the chief executive therein.

GOVERNOR'S REPORT

As Santhanam said, articles 278 and 278-A were in some respects the most important articles of this constitution. 'There is no doubt that at first sight they look rather unpleasant as they appear to be a re-entry of the old and hated section 93.' But the distinction lay in the governor's discretionary power, which was absent in the new emergency provisions. Neither could the president act in his discretion.

> In themselves, they are unobjectionable and they are essential. But, of course, if the centre acts upon the strict letter of the law, anything may be deemed to constitute a breakdown of the constitution, and it is possible that interference of the centre may be frequent and objectionable. . . . The only remedy is through the growth of healthy conventions.[33]

There was, however, a contradiction in the terminology of the articles 278 and 278-A. Would the governor act in his discretion in making the report? The Drafting Committee, it has already been seen, was of an affirmative opinion. Then why was it necessary to add 'otherwise'? Thakurdas Bhargava's speech brings into relief this paradox:

> The words 'on report or otherwise' do denote a state of things in which the governor may not be doing his duties, or may give a wrong report. Suppose there is a conflict between the governor and the ministers, and the ministers and the houses pass a resolution to the effect that the centre should intervene . . . and this state is not reported by the governor. What would happen?[34]

On the other hand, a few members complained that if the governor represented the union president, how could he be disloyal to him? The paradox is that, if the governor was an agent of the centre, he was expected

[33] Ibid., pp. 152-4.
[34] Ibid., p. 168.

to report a breakdown, either at his discretion or on ministerial advice. Why was then the provision for satisfaction of the president 'otherwise'? No official spokesman—Ambedkar, Ayyar and Krishnamachari—answered the question whether the governor would act in his discretion.[35] It was for Kamath to demand a revision of the draft article 143 (2) suitably, to remove the reference to the governor's discretion.

Kamath also sought to remove the reference to 'the satisfaction' of the president, and especially 'otherwise'. 'It is a constitutional crime', said Kamath, 'to empower the President to interfere not merely on the report of governor or ruler of a state, but otherwise. "Otherwise" is a mischievous word. It is a diabolical word in this context and I pray to god that this will be deleted from this article.'[36]

Another amendment of Kamath was to substitute 'internal insurrection or chaos' for 'internal disturbance', which was vague and might clash with the state subject of 'public order'. When Shibbanlal Saksena endorsed Kamath's first-mentioned point, Brajeswar Prasad, a second-ranker in the official group, asked a question which gives the idea of the extent of the 'new thinking': 'Sir, I would like to have elucidation on one point. If the governor of a province is forcibly arrested by some people, then how can he ever inform the centre?'[37]

The amendments of Ambedkar (new articles 277-A, 288 and 288-A), however, got general approval (except that of Kunzru, who thought them unnecessary, in view of articles 275 and 276, and Nazimuddin Ahmed, who was afraid of undue encroachment of the centre on states' autonomy).

STRUCTURAL ANOMALIES

In his *Constitutional Precedents*, Rau had compared the democratic executive set-up of ten countries, six of which were of the British type. A major feature of the dominion constitutions, Rau wrote, 'stated broadly, is that though the written constitution distinguished functions to be exercised by the Governor-General-in-Council from those to be exercised by him individually, in practice the distinction has ceased to exist . . . conventions have grown up whereby the Governor-General almost always

[35] The apparent paradox may be resolved only if Santhanam's interpretation—that in reporting to the centre the governor would have no discretion—is accepted. As such a report would be a ministerial report, the President would also have to depend upon information secured 'otherwise'.

[36] *CAD*, vol. IX, p. 140.

[37] Ibid., p. 143.

acts on advice'.[38] It was, in fact, this shadow of the dominion constitutions over the larger section of the constitution-makers of India that was responsible for a number of incoherences in the executive structures of the union and the states. Yet, in the whole constitution the governor was specifically required to act in his discretion only in revenue disputes between the Assam state government and district councils and as the agent of the President of India in administering the Part B tribal areas (within Assam).

Emergency and Rights

The House discussed the president's power of suspension of constitutional remedies for the violation of rights (Part III) on 4 August 1949. Kamath and Kunzru moved for restriction of the scope of this suspension to a few articles relating to freedom. On Ambedkar's request, the article was held over[39] and placed on the day on which an amendment to article 277 (requiring the president to lay before parliament every proclamation of emergency as soon as possible) was passed. The modified draft article restricted the scope of suspension to only those rights which might be mentioned in the proclamation (an amendment very close to Kamath's) and required the suspension order to be placed in parliament as soon as possible. The suspension might also be operative 'in the whole of the territory or a part of it'.[40] A number of amendments were still moved but defeated. Ambedkar's amendment formed part of the Constitution.[41]

Financial Emergency

The provision for financial emergency was presented in the form of an amendment, moved by Ambedkar, on 16 October 1949, almost at the fag end of the second reading of the draft constitution, 'having regard to the present economic and financial situation in this country'.[42]

It is in Rau's draft of the union constitution that one finds mention

[38] B.N. Rau, *Constitutional Precedents*, 1st series, p. 45.
In the Assembly when demands were made for making the ministers removable only by a no-confidence motion in the legislature, Ayyar's advice was against writing down the details of such relations, which would create crisis as in the Third Reich. Basing upon conventions, he said, Canada and Australia succeeded. *CAD*, vol. X, pp. 270-1.

[39] *CAD*, vol. IX, p. 186.

[40] Ibid., vol. X, p. 523.

[41] Ibid., pp. 553-4.

[42] Ibid., p. 361.

of the president's 'special responsibility' to act in case of financial emergency.[43] With the removal of all 'special responsibilities' of the president from the Union Constitution Committee's report the provision for financial emergencies was also removed from it. The worsening economic situation of the country till the end of 1949 caused the revival of the said provision.

The attendance in the House was poor, the discussion on such a vital amendment still poorer. The official side was represented by two short speeches of Ambedkar and Munshi, supported by Brajeswar Prasad and Sidhwa, and the opposition by passionate but strong arguments of Kamath and Kunzru. 'I feel that this contingency of danger to economic stability or credit of India or any part thereof ought not to be regarded as adequate ground for the proclamation of emergency', said Kamath. 'To invest the President with such wide powers in the event of the financial stability or the credit of India, or of a province or state thereof, being threatened is going much too far.'[44]

Contradicting Ambedkar's comparison of the financial emergency provisions with the National Recovery Act of the USA,[45] Kunzru doubted that there was anything in this amendment that would enable the Government of India to deal with a future economic depression in the same way in which President Roosevelt had tried to deal with it. 'The whole object of the amendment seems to be to reduce expenditure and to prevent the provincial governments from giving up any of their existing sources of revenue.' The fact that this matter had not been dealt with along with the other financial provisions contained in the constitution 'shows that there was no general need felt at the time the financial articles were considered for enabling the central government to exercise complete budgetary control over the provinces'. A province could hardly do anything to jeopardize the financial stability of India. There were indeed difficulties with some of the provinces on the question of the latter's revenue earnings. But such differences did not call for such a drastic step. This amendment enabled the president to declare financial emergency in case of any conflict over revenues, Kunzru held.

Munshi, in reply, referred to the debates in parliament which 'clearly showed that the country is on the brink of a precipice'. 'The attitude', he said, 'is that the centre will step in at the time when there is a breakdown

[43] B.N. Rau, *A Model Union Constitution*, Draft clause 15.

[44] *CAD*, vol. X, p. 363.

[45] Ibid., pp. 368-70.

in the financial structure of the country.'[46] Ambedkar's amendment was carried.

The Last Stroke

The last stroke of emergency provisions on the state's autonomy came in the revised and renumbered draft constitution that was placed in the House in November 1949. A new article (365) declared that non-compliance of a state government with the directions of the centre would be considered a 'failure' of the state, following which, by implication, the president would have the power to declare 'constitutional breakdown'. On 15 November 1949, Kunzru raised the point of order that the incorporation of the new article was beyond the competence of the Drafting Committee,[47] as it amounted to a substantial change. Ambedkar admitted that the change was more than 'consequential' of articles 280-A and 306-B which had been adopted by the House during the second reading. Article 280-A, which considered the non-compliance of states with union directives as a 'failure' related to financial emergency only, and article 306-B related only to the Part B states. Obviously, the Drafting Committee had expanded their scope.

Thakurdas Bhargava wanted the deletion of the article. Kamath moved an amendment. After a long battle, the issue was closed by the president. Article 365 was approved the next day, presumably through party mandate.[48]

Amendment Procedure

All the replies of the Union Constitution Committee members recommended a rigid type of constitution. Rau's memorandum on the draft union constitution also recommended the amendment to be carried by a two-thirds majority of the union legislature and of the legislatures of the units. For the first three years, however, the amendment should be possible by parliament, through an ordinary majority for the removal of difficulties in enforcing the constitution.[49]

The question of the amendment of the constitution proved to be quite ticklish. The Union Constitution Committee, while accepting the formula

[46] Ibid., p. 371.
[47] Ibid., vol. XI, pp. 506-9.
[48] Ibid., p. 588.
[49] B.N. Rau, *India's Constitution in the Making*, p. 96.

of Rau, appointed a subcommittee to examine the question further. The subcommittee met on 11 and 12 July 1947 and recommended changes in the procedure, that came in the supplementary report of the Union Constitution Committee dated 13 July 1947.

The subcommittee at first recommended, as the amendment procedure, the initiation of a bill by either House of the federal parliament and, on its passage by two-thirds of the members of each house present and voting, its ratification by one-half of the units of the federation (i.e. the provinces, 'states' and groups of 'states') and finally the president's assent. In the subsequent meeting the necessity of the units' ratification was considered unnecessary except on the proposals for any change in (a) the federal legislative list, (b) representation of units in the federal parliament, and (c) powers of the Supreme Court.[50] Consideration of this part of the committee's report was held over on 31 July 1947 on N. Gopalaswami Ayyangar's request as the committee was still considering, in view of large number of amendment proposals, the extent of share that could be given to the units in the amending process.

Rau's draft constitution adopted the subcommittee's report but provided for a simple amendment procedure of the constitution for the initial three years after the commencement of the constitution.[51] The plan was corroborated by de Valera, according to the report of Rau. The Drafting Committee, however, did not accept the suggestion and made the constitution amendable generally by a two-thirds majority. But amendment of the provisions which related to '(a) the lists in the seventh schedule, (b) the representation of states in parliament, or (c) the powers of the Supreme Court' would require the endorsement of one-half of the state legislatures. A simple amendment procedure was, however, proposed for the provisions relating to the choice of the governor, number of the houses of state legislatures if such moves were initiated in the state legislatures. The provision for reservation of seats for the minorities would, in any case, remain unalterable for 10 years.[52] Indeed, a long list of temporary and transitional provisions was incorporated in Part XVII of the Draft.

But the pressure for making the constitution amendable in a simple way, at least for some time, continued, and the Drafting Committee, while considering the suggestions on the draft constitution, proposed to move an amendment to the effect that:

[50] Citations from the Union Constitution Committee's File.

[51] B. Shiva Rao, *Select Documents*, vol. III.

[52] *Draft Constitution of India*, articles 304 and 305.

Notwithstanding anything contained in clauses (1) and (2) of this article (304) any of the provisions of this Constitution except the provisions of this article and article 305 may be amended by parliament by law whether by way of variation, addition and repeal, within a period of five years after the commencement of this constitution.

In support of the proposal, the Drafting Committee, interestingly, advanced three arguments: First, the position of the states in the new union was not yet clearly determined. Second, the Constituent Assembly was not a body elected through universal adult franchise. Third, de Valera had favoured a simple amendment procedure as in the Irish Constitution. Hence, 'the process of amending the constitution during the first 10 years should be made easier than is provided in this constitution'.[53]

But, by the time the articles were considered in the Assembly the Drafting Committee changed its position, and an amendment proposed by P.S. Deshmukh to ensure the flexibility of the constitution for the first three years was turned down by the Assembly.[54]

The final provision about the amendment procedure came as an amendment moved by Ambedkar on 17 September 1949. The new plan additionally required the ratification by one-half of state legislatures on amendment proposals with regard to legislative relations of the union and states, extent of executive powers of the union and the states, election of the president, powers of the high courts, and the amendment procedure itself. Provisions about the governor and houses of the state legislatures were now redundant, as the governor was now merely a nominee of the president and as reservation of legislative seats for the minorities was not partly dropped and partly provided temporarily. Article 305 was withdrawn.

During discussion on the amendment provisions, further criticisms were levelled against the rigidity of the constitution. Amendments were moved by P.S. Deshmukh, Brajeswar Prasad and H.V. Kamath, but by no 'socialist'. No one suggested that any part of the constitution was unalterable.[55] In his reply, Ambedkar firmly denied the allegation and said that all articles were subject to amendment in a reasonably easy way by parliament.[56] Ambedkar said:

[53] B. Shiva Rao, *Select Documents*, vol. IV, pp. 374-5.

[54] *CAD*, vol. V, pp. 1644, 1665.

[55] Indeed an amendment moved by P.S. Deshmukh to 'protect' the rights from amendments was withdrawn by the mover as it was not favoured by the Assembly. Ibid., vol. IX, pp. 1644, 1665.

[56] Ibid., pp. 1659-62.

We divide the articles of this constitution under three categories. The first category is the one which consists of articles which can be amended by parliament by a bare majority. The second set of articles are articles which require two-thirds majority. . . .

Now, we have no doubt put certain articles in a third category where for the purpose of amendment the mechanism is somewhat different or double. It requires two-thirds majority plus ratification by the states.[57]

Only the third category of articles was referred to as 'fundamental'. At the end of the third reading of the constitution Ambedkar again refuted the charge of its inflexibility in the following words:

One has only to examine the provision relating to the amendment of the constitution. The Assembly has not only refrained from putting a seal of finality and infallibility upon this constitution by denying to the people the right to amend the constitution as in Canada or by making the amendment of the constitution subject to extraordinary terms and conditions as in America or Australia, but has provided a most facile procedure for amending the constitution. I challenge any of the critics of the constitution to prove that any Constituent Assembly anywhere in the world has, in the circumstances in which this country finds itself, provided such a facile procedure for the amendment of the constitution.[58]

[57] Ibid., p. 1661.
[58] Ibid., p. 76.

Conclusion

What I do say is that the principles embodied in the constitution are the views of the present generation, or if you think this to be overstatement, I say they are views of the members of the Constituent Assembly. Why blame the Drafting Committee for embodying them in the constitution? I say, why blame even the members of the Constituent Assembly?—B.R. Ambedkar in the Constituent Assembly.[1]

If we investigate the origins of modern constitutions we find that, practically without exception, they were drawn up and adopted because people wished to make a fresh start, so far as the statement of their system of government is concerned—K.C. Wheare.[2]

The idea of a written constitution, achieved through a representative assembly, was very much of Western origin. It marked either the collapse of an old power relation involving the admission of new classes to power or structural changes in the body politic, both more or less sudden in nature. According to some people, a written constitution first emerged in England in 1653 (namely the Instrument of Government of Cromwell), though it was promptly scrapped by the restoration of Charles II. The name—Constituent Assembly—was, however, for the first time adopted by the French National Assembly in 1789.

C.F. Strong found in the movement for a written constitution, in the continental countries as well as the British North American colonies since the latter part of the eighteenth century, an attempt at 'seeking the means of circumventing the despotism under which the continent lived', adopting as a model the British Constitution which had grown over centuries. Besides, there is an element of 'social contract' in such a constitution.[3]

The thesis of this volume is that the Constitution of India, like any other constitution, is essentially a human document worked out by people motivated by a particular historical condition. As every human endeavour is subject to limitations, a constitution is liable to be criticized, as much

[1] *CAD*, vol. XI, p. 975.
[2] *Modern Constitutions*, pp. 8-9.
[3] C.F. Strong, *Modern Political Constitutions*, pp. 33-7.

as adored, amended and even scrapped. It is ironical that France, which has had five republican constitutions since the Revolution, intermitted by despotic or semi-despotic rule, inserted in each of them a provision that the republican form of government was not subject to amendment. No constitution, however, makes provision for its scrapping.

A Unique Assembly

In India, the Cabinet Mission plan first set up the Constituent Assembly; the 3 June 1947 statement of Mountbatten then split it and the Indian Independence Act finally gave it not only the status of a sovereign Constituent Assembly, but also the power to control a provisional government. The Constituent Assembly, in its final form, was, therefore, very much different from the Constituent Assembly that had been anticipated by the Cabinet Mission within the dominion pattern.

Born with a peculiar stigma, it was confronted not only with the task of drafting a constitution for India, but also with the odd job of making the most important political decision for the country, namely the state's structure. No other constituent body in the world has had to make such an important decision in as much as each of them merely recorded the achievements of the revolution through which the major political decisions had already been reached.

Yet, the Constituent Assembly was given no freedom to act. It was fettered by the legacies of 'the Indian problem'. Independence was made conditional upon a so-called communal solution which, by far, was impossible to attain. Sovereignty of the Constituent Assembly was achieved only at the cost of India's unity. The Constituent Assembly of India was able to register a very limited success of the Indian national movement. It was the promulgation, not the drawing, of the constitution which was, strictly speaking, an act of revolutionary significance.

A comparison between the Indian Constituent Assembly, on the one hand, and the other revolutionary assemblies like the Philadelphia Convention (1787) and the French National Assembly (1789-91), on the other, is, therefore, patently inadequate. Both the Philadelphia Constitutional Convention and the French National Assembly were convened at the height of two major national revolutions. The Constituent Assembly of India, on the other hand, came through a deal, that was backed by the strength of a mass movement, but was not exactly a product of it. Such a deal had been foreseen by Jawaharlal Nehru as early as 1940:

Ordinarily, such sovereign assemblies come into existence after a successful revolution in a country. But it is certainly a possibility, if not a probability, that the shadow of the coming events and world changes might lead to an agreement that such an assembly should function as formulated. The demand for such an assembly is ultimately a declaration of what we want to do whenever we have the power to do so. That power may conceivably come to us by agreement without a conflict or it may come after a conflict.[4]

It came without a conflict, but not without a price.

The Philadelphia Constitutional Convention met for 'revising the Articles of Confederation', but decided to frame a federal constitution. In France the States General met as a legislature, but turned itself into the National Assembly and framed a constitution. Both of them, due to historical reasons, went beyond the terms of reference attached to them.

The Constituent Assembly of India indeed crossed the limit originally set around it by the statement of the Cabinet Mission. Yet, whereas the liberty that the Philadelphia delegates took was of their own choosing and the members of the French National Assembly earned their freedom by their successful struggle against the king, the change of the status of the Constituent Assembly of India was very much a product of the developments which were beyond the control of the House. The freedom of the Indian Constituent Assembly had to be earned from the British at a very high cost—its own and the country's integrity. The Indian Constituent Assembly not only recorded the inevitable misfortune of partition but also was instrumental to its occurrence.

A Sense of Direction

Nevertheless, partition of the country gave the Assembly a sense of direction which its earlier sessions lacked. If the partition was the result of circumstances that developed outside the Constituent Assembly of India, the other major decisions were also taken according to the several political notions that had taken shape in the course of the national movement, particularly on the platform of the Indian National Congress which commanded on overwhelming majority in the Constituent Assembly. Those notions, in 1947-9, crystallized into a strong federation and a parliamentary government. It was left to the changing political situation in the country to determine how 'strong' the centre of this federation would be. The rather long duration of the Constituent Assembly was

[4] Nehru's foreword to Y.G. Krishnamurti's *Constituent Assembly*.

contributory to the emergence of this strongly unified political organism. Beginning with the hazy idea of a loosely federated India, the members of the Constituent Assembly moved a long way to reach a tangible unity, effectively mitigating all local aspirations.

It was the imperative of the social forces of the time that India would emerge into a strong and organized political entity. Ambedkar effectively stressed this social imperative when, during the presentation of the Draft to the Constituent Assembly, he severely criticized the orthodox demand for a village-centred policy: 'I am glad that the Draft Constitution has discarded the village and adopted the individual as its unit.'[15]

That the application of the principle of parliamentary government was somewhat crippled at the unit level, was due to the 'strong centre' growing stronger. But, when it was a question of the nature of the union government, the decision of the leadership was firmly for a parliamentary government. On the details, however, the leadership had no clear picture, except the somewhat bitter memory of the provincial administrations in the short period before the Second World War. The formulation of the details was initially left to one of the ablest Indian bureaucrats, B.N. Rau, whose acquaintance with the Indian constitutional development was more through the Reforms Office, than through the judiciary. Rau's premises for the constitution-making, as already noted, were (1) the Government of India Act, 1935, (2) the dominion constitutions and, to a lesser extent, (3) other constitutions, for example, of the USA and Switzerland.

The original drafts of the union and provincial constitutions formulated by Rau were almost wholly based on the models of the Government of India Act, 1935, and the dominion constitutions. Some of their basic assumptions, therefore, inevitably clashed with the republican and anti-executive notions of the Congress leaders. The result was the intervention of lawyers like Ayyar and Ayyangar in the question of the Union Constitution and a somewhat unsatisfactory compromise on the question of the provincial constitution. On the question of minority representation to the legislature and the executive the Swiss constitutional precedent was, for a while, considered. But, as the minority problem took a new turn, the scheme was dropped.

Besides the minority question, the states formed almost the only element of the 'Indian problem'. Here, the Constituent Assembly had very little part to play. It only registered whatever the states ministry worked out in its 'negotiation' with the rulers.

[15] *CAD*, vol. VII, p. 89.

On the question of rights, both Rau's and the Congress leaders' knowledge appears to have been chiefly academic, except for the somewhat vague commitment to socio-economic reforms and the bitter memories of the suppression of individual freedom during the British raj on the part of the Congress. Here also lawyers, like Ambedkar and Ayyar, brought about the compromises, between individual freedom and executive exigencies, right to property, religion, etc., and the need for reforms.

The synthesis brought about was not always quite satisfactory. For instance, the retention of the terms 'pleasure' and 'discretion' (the latter in reduced frequency) was not accompanied by proper explanation.[6] The Assembly, after rejecting the qualification of 'reasonableness' on the restrictions on fundamental rights, brought it back. Many of the now-apparent 'puzzles' of the Constitution are in fact due to the drafting anomaly, arising out of the cross-purposes of the politicians and the administrators.

The First Principles

N.V. Gadgil, a member of the Constituent Assembly, complained in October 1948:

> There has not been a sufficient discussion of first principles or any attempt to lay down the theoretic foundation of the constitutional structure either in the proceedings of the Constituent Assembly or in the press or public during or after the work of the Assembly. On a close study the Draft Constitution would appear to be a structure erected primarily under the influence of the 1935 Act and secondarily that of the British dominions.[7]

It was shortly after the Constituent Assembly started the discussion of the draft constitution that Jennings gave his first critical appreciation of the Draft, though in a different tone from Gadgil's.[8] 'The most remarkable feature of the Draft Constitution of India', about which Jennings complained, was its length. Yet, the constitution was not complete and needed detailed legislation. An offshoot of this complication was relative inflexibility of the constitution. But deeper than these criticisms of the 'form' there is a major complaint. 'Though the constitution proposed is

[6] *The Report of the Administrative Reforms Commission on Centre-State Relations* (June 1969) stressed that the governor's discretionary powers may be 'either expressly stated in the constitution or can be inferred therefrom'. The validity of such an assertion needs examination in the light of the Constituent Assembly's intentions.

[7] N.V. Gadgil, *Some Observations on the Draft Constitution*, preface.

[8] *The Hindu*, 26, 27, 29, 30 November 1948.

fundamentally British in its machinery, the constitutional law derives its inspiration from the United States of America, and perhaps rightly so, for the Indians tend to be legalistic in their outlook, whereas English constitutional lawyers are interested mainly in machinery.'[9]

A more considerate British thinker, W.H. Morris-Jones, commenting on some legacies of India, wrote: 'If the new Indian rulers received a legacy from their own immediate past, they assuredly carried over also a legacy from their experience of the nationalist movement'.[10]

The claim to originality of any constitutional formula has long been recognized as futile. For a constitution of the mid-twentieth century India the expectation of originality is perfectly irrelevant. Yet India in 1949 certainly went much ahead of her constitutional position in 1937. A number of constitutional principles and practices that were adopted in the republican constitution could not be supplied by the Government of India Act, 1935. Republicanism was unknown in the Commonwealth. The bill of rights (with the extraordinary appendage of the directive principles) was adopted almost wholly from outside the framework of the 1935 Act. The new federalism was definitely different from, though influenced by, the 1935 formula. The relation of the executive and the legislature was greatly modified at the federal level.

Decision-making in the Assembly

Granville Austin thinks that the original contribution of the Constituent Assembly of India was 'decision-making by consensus'.[11] Referring to the 'non-partisan character of the discussion' on the draft constitution, B. Shiva Rao writes that the Congress Party 'never yielded to the temptation of attempting to carry any of its provisions or of imposing any of its ideas through the weight of its part-majority'.[12] Shiva Rao has cited the solution of the problems of the political minorities and national language. The present study, on the contrary, has shown that the first question was not solved to the satisfaction of all minority groups. Solution of the second question was, in the language of Austin himself, a 'half-hearted compromise'.[13] The socialists were simply cold-shouldered, even

[9] *The Hindu*, 26 November 1948.

[10] W.H. Morris-Jones, *The Government and Politics of India*, pp. 25-6.

[11] Granville Austin, *The Indian Constitution*, pp. 311-17.

[12] Shiva Rao, *The Framing of India's Constitution*, vol. V, p. 839.

[13] Austin, *The Indian Constitution*, Chapter 12.

occasionally snubbed. Complaints were often heard of the Congress Party steam-rollering the Constituent Assembly.

Members of the Muslim League, on more than one occasion, referred to the Constituent Assembly being a 'packed house'. During the third reading of the draft constitution, Shibbanlal Saksena, himself a Congressite, observed that the meetings of the Constituent Assembly only registered the decision already taken in the meetings of the Congress Party.[14] Ambedkar himself observed on the floor of the Assembly that 'they had to go to another place to obtain a decision and come to the Assembly'.[15] 'Accommodation' is, therefore, possibly the more appropriate word than 'consensus' to describe the process of decision-making in the Constituent Assembly. On fundamentals, there was little concession.[16]

Promises and Fulfilment

The leaders of the Indian Congress recognized their debt to the training in constitutionalism that Britain had imparted them. Behind the drafting of the articles was the skill of the brilliant civilian B.N. Rau, an intellectual bred in the atmosphere of English law. As early as in 1945 Ambedkar felt satisfied that in order to have the Constitution of Independent India it was only necessary to modify certain provisions of the Government of India Act, 1935. Thus, besides recording the political fact of transfer of power, the Constitution did not bring about much of fundamental change.

The 'limited' and 'political' achievement of the Constituent Assembly in India consisted in stalling the disintegrationist forces of India which grew during the latter part of British rule and got encouraged by the fact of partition. It consolidated the unity of India including the native states. It put an end to the cancerous problem of minorities. In short, it cut the Gordian knot of the classical 'Indian problem', though the merit of the

[14] *CAD*, vol. XI, p. 704.

[15] Ibid., p. 1094. Shiva Rao asserts that, 'on a number of controversial issues, efforts were made to eliminate or at least to minimise differences through informal meetings of the Congress Party's representatives in the Constituent Assembly. Of such meetings no authentic reports were kept and only some speculative statements appeared in the newspaper reports'. Shiva Rao, *The Framing of India's Constitution*, vol. V, p. 835.

[16] F.G. Bailey, a leading political sociologist writes: 'Let us be clear, at the outset, that a decision by consensus cannot be reached in a council where active members number more than about fifteen'. Bailey, 'Decisions and Consensus in Councils and Committees', *Political System and the Distribution of Power*, ASA monograph, No. 2, p. 2. Policy-making bodies, Bailey thinks, cannot act through consensus.

surgery appears to be dubious. In any case, the present political map of India was drawn in the Constituent Assembly and a parliamentary democracy was set up to preside over it.

Writing the 'foreword' to a Socialist Party publication on the work of the Constituent Assembly of India, in 1947, Jayaprakash Narayan regretted that the Constituent Assembly's 'deliberations have been dominated by cool and sedate lawyers who give no evidence that they comprehend the significance of the turmoiled birth of a nation'. He warned that 'The Indian Constitution is not likely to be, unless drastically amended, an instrument of full political and social democracy.'[17]

This was bound to be so. Right from the beginning the makers of the constitution had no illusion about their aim. On several occasions they made it clear in the Assembly that the constitution was going to be nothing more than a political document. While criticizing the draft of the constitution, K.T. Shah, a radical Congressite, observed, 'The constitution's aim, as explained by Dr. Ambedkar, or, as can be derived from the wording of the Constitution itself, is almost entirely political and not at all social or economic.'[18]

Truly, the work of the Constituent Assembly was the reflection of the political developments that took place in the national political arena. Yet, the national revolution of India was not complete in the period of work of the Assembly. As a result, the Constituent Assembly was found to be doing a balancing act between the claims of stability and adaptability. Placed between its own commitment to widespread socio-economic reforms, repeatedly though rather vaguely promised, and the pressure of the propertied class, it upheld the claims of property and at the same time confirmed its promises for socio-economic reforms through the directive principles and left the door open for land reform in certain states where the programme had already been initiated.

Political unification of a diverse territory, paradoxically facilitated by its partition, abolition of communal political rights and assertion of individual rights, while retaining the concern for people's welfare, contributed to the building of a liberal bourgeois democracy that can work in a post-colonial situation. Except for a miniscule, albeit vocal, minority nobody spoke of socialism. The only class agendum that was unfolded was land reform, not socialization of land.

There is a certain paradox in the leadership's cold-shouldering of the

[17] Socialist Party, *Draft Constitution of Indian Republic*, p. 5.

[18] *CAD*, vol. VII, p. 345.

demand of declaring India a secular state, made by K.T. Shah and Hasrat Mohani, in view of the loud, repeated and honest assertion of the virtues of secularism and communal amity. The Constitution, as it was framed, granted religious freedom and equality and prohibited taxation for promotion of any particular religion. There is, however, nothing in the Constitution which prevents the state from spending money out of the Consolidated Fund of India for the same purpose. In fact, article 238(10) (ii) (now article 290A) charged Rs 51 lakh on the Consolidated Fund of Travancore-Cochin (now Kerala) for the benefit of the *devaswom* funds. V.P. Menon reports that this provision owes its origin to the negotiations he conducted between the Government of India and the princely state of Travancore over their merger.[19]

A number of important developments took place during the rather prolonged functioning of the Constituent Assembly and were reflected in the Constitution. As a result, the Constituent Assembly members were taken along routes of which they were only vaguely and indistinctly aware at the beginning.

Yet, a very important feature of the Constitution was the transitional character of several provisions, among which those relating to the units of the federation are most remarkable. The parliament got absolute power to change the territorial boundaries of states. Integration of princely states was not obviously complete. The problem of linguistic reorganization of states was unsolved. One notes the various adaptation and removal of difficulties orders that had to be passed to make the Constitution applicable to the still fluid condition of the country.

The social forces of the time permitted exactly this much and no more. The stable and independent political order that was most urgently needed for the full flowering of Indian economic prosperity was ensured by the two epoch-making incidents of transfer of power and framing of the Constitution. Right to property was ensured to the extent that a welfare state could afford to ensure.

In his reply to the debate on the third reading of the Constitution, Ambedkar, however, showed his awareness of the shortcomings of the Constitution:

> On 26th January 1950, we are going to enter into a life of contradiction. In politics we will have equality and in social and economic rights we will have inequality. In politics we will be recognising the principle of one man and one vote, one value. In our social and economic rights we shall, by reason of our social and

[19] V.P. Menon, *The Story of the Integration of Indian States*, pp. 269-73.

economic structure, continue to deny one man one value. . . . We must remove this contradiction at the earliest possible moment or else those who suffer from inequality will blow up the structure of political democracy which this Assembly has so laboriously built up.[20]

Rajendra Prasad, in his concluding speech on the third reading, also said, 'The Constitution has provisions in it which appear to be objectionable from one point or another. We must admit that the defects are inherent in the situation in the country and the people at large.'[21]

If the Constitution has great omissions, the mistakes of commission are not quite insignificant. Complaints of complicating details in the Constitution have been raised very often and by many, including Jennings. In the constitutional documents several provisions are overlapping; some may even be considered superfluous.[22] Understandably, the radicals of the country, specially the socialists, demanded the Constitution to be amendable by an ordinary legislative procedure. Ambedkar answered these demands by citing the American and Australian Constitutions in comparison to which the Draft Indian Constitution laid down 'the simplest' amendment procedure.[23] His answer on this point is interesting from the theoretical point of view:

The Constituent Assembly in making a constitution has no partisan motive. Beyond securing a good and workable constitution it has no axe to grind. In considering the articles of the constitution, it has no eye on getting through a particular measure. The future parliament, if it met as a Constituent Assembly, its members will be acting as partisans seeking to carry amendments to the Constitution to facilitate the passing of party measures which they have failed to get through parliament by reason of some article of the Constitution which has acted as an obstacle in their way. . . . That is the difference between the Constituent Assembly and the future parliament. That is the reason why the Constituent Assembly though elected on limited franchise can be trusted to pass the Constitution by simple majority and why the parliament though elected on adult suffrage cannot be trusted with same power to amend it.[24]

The claim is valid as far as it goes. For, every Constituent Assembly has a mind which can be understood in the light of the concrete political

[20] *CAD*, vol. XI, p. 979.

[21] Ibid., p. 993.

[22] D.N. Sen, a leftist academician, thought that the Indian Constitution was 'a copy-book text borrowed indiscriminately from alien sources'. D.N. Sen, *The Paradox of Freedom*, p. 8.

[23] *CAD*, vol. VII, p. 43.

[24] Ibid., pp. 43-4.

and socio-economic forces of the time and place. The limitations of these forces, therefore, are bound to be attached to the constitution it produces, and to be exposed gradually with the passage of time. It is for this reason that comments like, 'no amendment may be required at all for many decades to come' (Santhanam) appear naive.[25]

However, within the Assembly all parties, except the extremist sections of the League, the Akali Sikhs and the socialists gave their support to the Constitution, full-hearted or qualified. Outside the Assembly the Communist Party was the only considerable political group which decried it for long. Of the total strength of 308 members 275 signed the final Constitution, 28 did not. At the end of the Assembly's life there were five vacancies (four Muslim seats from East Punjab and one from Rajasthan). No conclusion can definitely be drawn about the members' attitude towards the Constitution by this statistics; for the absent names include those of some known critics as well as supporters of the Constitution.[26] Yet, the missing signatures appear somewhat mysterious to those who recall that the final Constitution was ceremonially carried to Patna to obtain the signature of a member who was then in sickbed.

Trends of Amendments

Seventy-eight amendments in course of 50 years make an average of one and a half per year. The impact of this statement is, however, reduced if one remembers that several of the amendments are routine or minor in nature. Thus, seven amendments,[27] five exclusively,[28] relate to the ninth schedule listing the legislations secured against fundamental rights (vide article 31B, itself a product of the first amendment that created the ninth schedule). Four amendments,[29] three exclusively[30] relate to the decadal

[25] Ibid., vol. IX, p. 719. (Before the completion of a quarter century of the republic, the Constitution was amended thirty-one times.)

[26] There were five vacancies on the last date of the Assembly. Some of the members who did not sign the Constitution are (1) Perumalaswami Reddi, (2) S.H. Prater, (3) Ramkrishan Ranga Rao, (4) T.A. Ramalingam Chettiar, (5) P.M. Velayudhapani (Madras); (6) M.R. Masani, (7) S. Nijalingappa, (8) S.K. Patil (9) Abdul Kadir Mohammed Shaikh, (10) Aziz Ahmed Khan (Bombay); (11) Damodar Swarup Seth, (12) Govind Ballabh Pant, (13) Harihar Nath Shastri, (14) Jagannath Baksh Singh, (15) J.P. Srivastava, (16) Hasrat Mohani, (17) Rafi Ahmed Kidwai (UP); (18) Hukam Singh, (19) Bhopinder Singh Mann (E. Punjab); (20) Sarangadhar Das (Orissa state).

[27] Amendments 1, 4, 29, 34, 47, 76, 78.

[28] Amendments 29, 34, 47, 76, 78.

[29] Amendments 8, 23, 45, 62.

[30] Amendments 8, 45, 62.

extension of the reservation of legislative seats for the scheduled castes and scheduled tribes (article 334). Raising the upper age limit of the members of State Public Service Commissions from 60 to 62 was made by the 41st Amendment while the 60th Amendment raised the limit of profession tax from Rs 250 to Rs 2,500.

Several amendments were necessitated by fast changing political situation. Confrontation of the government and the judiciary during Mrs Indira Gandhi's period produced a large number of amendments and cancellation of amendments, the climax being reached during the Keshavananda Bharati case and the Minerva Mills case resulting in the laying down of the theory of 'basic structure' and invalidation of two constitutional amendments. Emergency (1975) has produced a number of amendments. The seventh schedule has been amended five times. But the credit for the largest number of amendments goes to the states reorganization. At the macro-level, that is creation, union, partition of new and old states and alteration of their boundaries, there have been 17 amendments[31] while, at the micro-level, namely the autonomous districts of north-east India, there have been eight amendments.[32]

Intra-governmental problems have caused a few amendments. In the wake of the Gujarat agitation calling for the resignation of an elected legislature the 33rd Amendment (1974) required the speaker or the chairman of a House to satisfy himself that a resignation was really voluntary. The relation between the president and the prime minister has not always been cordial. The 42nd Amendment (1976), therefore, sought to spell out that the president shall act according to his cabinet's advice. The Janata Party government retained the position but opened a leeway for president by allowing him to refer an advice back to his cabinet for reconsideration. But, if the cabinet returned the advice, the president must act according to it (44th Amendment).

The 42nd Amendment enhanced the duration of president's rule, after legislative approval, from six months to one year. The 44th Amendment brought this duration back to six months. Violence in Punjab, however, led to the raising of the total period of emergency, only for that state, from three years to five years through amendment numbers 59 (1988), 63 (1990), 64 (1990), 67 (1990) and 68 (1991).

Up to the end of the 1950s there were seven amendments; between

[31] Amendments 7, 9, 10, 12, 13, 14, 18, 22, 27, 32, 35, 36, 43, 44, 53, 55, 56.

[32] Of these only one was a formal amendment, the 49th. The rest were made through parliamentary acts. Of course, the creation of states is done through parliamentary acts. But there are consequential amendments.

1960 and 1969 there were 15 amendments; between 1970 and 1979 there were 22; between 1980 and 1989 there were 17 and between 1990 and 1995 there were 17. Statistically, the period of six years between 1990 and 1995 is the most crowded. Considering the fact that this was a period when no party had a two-thirds majority in the parliament, one is tempted to jump to the conclusion that consensus is the key to smooth amendments. One is further tempted to contrast this statistics with the 44 amendments that took place between 1966 and 1989 of which only two amendments (43rd and 44th) were sponsored by the Janata Party government. Yet, it was only in the first phase of Mrs Indira Gandhi's prime ministership that amendments became most contentious. During the period between 1966 and 1975 (10 years) 25 amendments took place, two of them (the 24th and the 26th) having been subjected to a kind of plebiscitary election in 1971. The two issues of this election were the privy purses and the right to property. Privy purses were abolished through the 26th Amendment (1971). But the 24th Amendment unleashed a tussle with the judiciary that was over only after the removal of right to property from Part III of the Constitution.

If the Golaknath and Keshavananda cases are seen as the first crises of confidence, the second came with the emergency of 1975 which culminated in a proposal to set up a De Gaulle-type republic in India.[33] This emergency had started with a bang but ended with a whimper producing the first dethronement of the Congress Party at the centre and changing the contours of the party system in India for good.

The current phase of politics may be seen as the third crisis of confidence. It is marked by a continuous corrosion of the stated values of the Constitution. It can be traced to the emergency when the 42nd Amendment put the words 'secular, socialist' in the Preamble. It may be noted that, on 25 June 1975, when the emergency was proclaimed, Mrs Indira Gandhi released a 21-point programme, the first point of which was 'no more nationalization'. Two days later the programme was renamed as the 20-point programme, omitting the first point. It was also at this time that India's prime minister was found frequenting religious places.

The Congress Party's return to power in 1980 saw the beginning of the process that later came to be called 'liberalization and globalization'. At the social level obscurantist communal and caste forces raised their head demanding regimentation of the polity on the one hand and its fragmentation on the other. Interestingly, all these demands seek to by-

[33] See *Mainstream*, 3 January 1976.

pass the Constitution or seek its bending rather than amendment. In the 1980s there was an effort to stress that what the government was doing was actually socialism. Secularism was sought to be interpreted as equal treatment of all religions. Now 'socialism' has become a dirty word not to be mentioned in public. There is a sedulous effort at distinguishing between 'pseudo-secularism' and 'genuine secularism'. On the other hand, there is the theory that caste is a secular weapon for fighting communalism with.

The structural resilience of the Indian Constitution is demonstrated by the fact that, notwithstanding the impressive number of amendments, the basic structure of the Constitution is preserved. Two kinds of class challenges have been coped with. First, the challenge of feudalism has been dealt with by means of amendments. The various land reform measures and the abolition of the privy purses and princely privileges testify to this assertion. The second challenge—that of the communists—was dealt with by means of the constitutional provisions. Until 1978[34] the Supreme Court of India stood by the view it had adopted in the Gopalan case of 1950 sanctioning preventive detention.[35] In 1959, article 356 was, for the first time, applied to impose president's rule in the first communist-ruled state in India, namely Kerala. The secessionist demands in various parts of the country, too, have been met by force. The 16th Amendment in 1963, however, constitutionally prohibited secessionist politics.

A Structural Anomaly

The most persistent structural problem, created by the Constituent Assembly, relates to the role of the governor, making that office the most controversial one. The governor was, deliberately, made the centre's agent but was authorized to act according to the advice of his council of ministers except when he is required by the Constitution to act in his discretion. The Constitution, originally, required the governor to act in his discretion in two specific cases, both under the sixth schedule: (1) According to paragraph 9(2) any dispute between a district council and the state government over share of royalty on mining leases would be decided by the governor acting in his discretion; (2) According to paragraph 18(3) the governor would administer the Part B tribal areas, as the agent of the president, in his discretion, i.e. without the advice of his council of

[34] See *Maneka Gandhi* v. *Union of India*, AIR 1978 SC 597.
[35] *A.K. Gopalan* v. *State of Madras* (1950) SCR 88.

ministers. After the reorganization of north-east India this second discretion has disappeared. But, in practice, the governors enjoy unlimited discretionary power in state administrations.

Thus the governors reserve bills for assent of the president at their discretion and send reports, including reports recommending president's rule in the states, without consulting their councils of ministers. This logically anomalous position results from a stretching of the provisions of the Government of India Act, 1935. Under that Act the governor had three kinds of power;[36] powers exercised according to the advice of his council of ministers, powers exercised in his discretion and powers exercised in his individual judgement in the discharge of special responsibilities in which cases he would consult his ministers but would not be bound by their advice. According to section 50(3) of the Act, the governor had discretion to decide whether a certain matter fell within his discretionary field or his individual judgement. The discretion to decide, thus, was confined between two poles, i.e. his specified discretionary field and his specified field of special responsibility. Even B.N. Rau's first draft allowed no special responsibility to the governor. But discretion was there. By a sheer grammatical coup, however, the Rau draft laid down that the governor would have unquestionable discretion to decide as to when he was required by the Constitution to exercise his discretion. To put it mathematically, the 1935 Act gave the governor a choice between A and B—a limited choice. The Rau draft, which remained intact through all the stages of the Constituent Assembly's work gave the governor a choice between A and non-A, an unlimited choice. The governor, of course, is accountable to the union government and he may need an amount of discretionary power. It may, however, be salutary for India's federal structure to specify the governor's discretion, particularly because the special responsibilities of the governor have now appeared in the Indian Constitution.

The 7th Amendment to the Indian Constitution (1956) provided for the governors' special responsibilities in the states of Andhra Pradesh, and Bombay. The Bombay Reorganization Act of 1960 substituted the word 'Bombay' by the words 'Maharashtra and Gujarat'. No individual judgement was granted to the governors in these states.[37] When the state of Nagaland was created, the governor was granted special responsibility, for the state's law and order, to be exercised in his individual judgement.[38]

[36] Section 50 of the Government of India Act, 1935.

[37] Article 371.

[38] Article 371A.

In 1971 special responsibility without individual judgement was granted to the governor of Manipur.[39] In 1975 the governor of Sikkim was granted special responsibility for peace and equitable arrangement for ensuring the social and economic advancement of all sections of the people to be discharged, subject to the direction of the president, in his discretion.[40] In 1987, when Arunachal Pradesh was granted statehood, the governor was granted special responsibility with regard to law and order to be exercised in his individual judgement.[41]

In this maze of discretion and special responsibility a return to the language of the 1935 Act can render some clarity. The governor's power of dismissal of ministry and dissolution of legislature is inconsistent with his power to recommend president's rule except for the purpose of preventing the dislodged political party from return to power through a fresh election. Reservation of bills for the president's assent, at personal discretion of the governor, is inconsistent with the federal as well as the parliamentary principle particularly when a Supreme Court functions to prevent a transgression of the limits to the states' power.

[39] Article 371C.
[40] Article 371F.
[41] Article 371H.

Bibliography

I. Official Records Relating to the Constituent Assembly

Most of these records are now available in B. Shiva Rao's *Select Documents*. The other important records are:

Constituent Assembly Debates, 12 vols., Delhi: Manager of Publications.

Constituent Assembly Debates, Report of the Two in-Camera Sessions, confidential but printed, Indian National Archives.

Files Relating to the Constituent Assembly of India, Ministry of Law, Indian National Archives, Government of India.

Orders of the Day, 7 vols., issued by the Constituent Assembly Secretariat, cyclostyled, Indian National Archives.

II. Journals and Newspapers

The All India Reporter, 1967 (Supreme Court), 1969 (Calcutta High Court).

The Anglo-Indian Review, New Delhi, 1947-50.

The Economist, London, 7 June 1947.

The Free Press Journal, Bombay, 1947-50.

The Eastern Economist, New Delhi, 1940-50.

The Indian Journal of Political Science, 1946-51 & 1965 (published by the Indian Political Science Association).

The Hindu, Madras, 1945-50.

The Hindusthan Standard, Calcutta, 1945-50.

The Hindusthan Times, Delhi, 1945-50.

The Times, London, June 1922.

III. Year Books

The Hindusthan Year Book, Calcutta, 1946-50.

The Nalanda Year Book, Calcutta, 1946-50.

The Statesman Year Book, London, 1945-50.

The Times of India Directory, Bombay, 1946-50.

IV. Secobdary Sources

Adams, George B., *Constitutional History of England*, revised by R.D. Schuyler, New York: Holt, 1934.

Administrative Reforms Commission, *Report on the Çentre-State Relationships*, Delhi: Manager of Publications, 1969.

Agarwal, Shriman Narayan, *Gandhian Constitution for Free India*, Allahabad: Kitabistan, 1946.

Alexandrowicz, C.H., *Constitutional Developments in India*, Bombay: Oxford University Press, 1957.

All Parties Conference, *Report of the Committee Appointed by the Conference to Determine the Principles of the Constitution* (in short, *Report of Committee*), Allahabad: The Indian National Congress, 1928.

Ambedkar, B.R., *Pakistan or Partition of India*, Bombay: Thacker & Co., 1929.

———, *States and Minorities*, Bombay: Thacker & Co., 1947.

Anstey, Vera, *The Economic Development of India*, London: Longman Co., 1929.

ASA (Association of Social Anthropologists of the Commonwealth), Monograph No. 2, *Political System and the Distribution of Powers*, London, Tavistock Publications Ltd., 1965.

Austin, Granville, *The Indian Constitution: Cornerstone of a Nation*, London: Oxford University Press, 1966.

Azad, Abul Kalam, *India Wins Freedom*, Calcutta: Orient Longman Ltd., 1957.

Balaram, N.E., *A Short History of the Communist Party of India*, Trivandrum: Prabhath Book House, 1967.

Banerjee, Anil Chandra, *Indian Constitutional Documents*, 4 vols., 3rd revd. edn., Calcutta: A. Mukherjee and Co., 1961-5.

Banerjee, Binoyendranath, *Muslim Politics in India*, Calcutta: Orient Book Company, 1946.

Banerjee, D.N., *Some Aspects of the Indian Constitution*, Calcutta: World Press, 1962.

Basu, Durga Das, *Commentary on the Constitution of India*, 8 vols., 5th revd. edn., Calcutta: S.C. Sarkar and Sons Private Limited, 1965.

Beard, Charles A., *An Economic Interpretation of the Constitution of the United States*, 16th print, New York: Macmillan & Co., 1959.

Bombawall, K.R., *The Foundations of Indian Federation*, Bombay: Asia Publishing House, 1967.

Bose, Nirmal Kumar, *Studies in Gandhism*, 2nd edn., Calcutta: The Indian Associated Publishing Co. Ltd., 1947.

———, *My Days with Gandhi*, Calcutta: Nishana, 1953.

Bose, Subhas Chandra, *The Indian Struggle, 1920-1942*, Compiled by Netaji Research Bureau, Bombay: Asia Publishing House 1964.

Brecher, Michael, *Nehru—A Political Biography*, London: Oxford University Press, 1959.

Carr, E.H., *A History of Soviet Russia: The Bolshevik Revolution, 1917-1923*, 3 vols., London: Penguin, 1966.

Carter, G.M. and Herz, J.H., *Government and Politics in the Twentieth Century*, New York: F.A. Praeger, rpt., 1967.

Chanakya, *Indian Constituent Assembly*, Bombay: Bombay Book Depot, 1947.

Congress Party, *Bulletins*, 1946-50, published from Allahabad and New Delhi.

Coondoo, R., *The Division of Powers in the Indian Constitution*, Calcutta: Bookland Co., 1964.

Coupland, Reginald, *The Constitutional Problem in India*, 3 parts, London: Oxford University Press, 1944.

———, *India—A Restatement*, London: Oxford University Press, 1945.

Deakin, Alfred, *The Federal Story*, Melbourne: Robertson and Mullens Co., 1944.

Deshmukh, C.D., *Economic Developments in India, 1946-1956*, Bombay: Asia Publishing House, 1957.

Deva, Acharya Narendra, *Socialism and the National Revolution*, Bombay: Padma Publication, 1946.

Dutt, Rajani Palme, *India Today and Tomorrow*, revised and abridged edition of *India Today*. London: Lawrence, 1956.

Emerson, Rupert, *Representative Government in South-East Asia*, Harvard: Harvard University Press, 1955.

Farrand, Max, *The Framing of the Constitution of the United States*, New Haven: Yale University Press, 1955.

Finer, Herman, *The Theory and Practice of Modern Government*, London: Methuen & Co. Ltd., 1954.

———, *Governments of Greater European Powers*, London: Methuen & Co. Ltd., 1956.

Gadgil, N.V., *Some Observations on the Draft Constitution*, Bombay: Gokhale Institute, 1948.

Gandhi, M.K., *Hind Swaraj*, rpt., Ahmedabad: Navajivan Press, 1958.

———, *Letters to Sardar Vallabhbhai Patel*, Ahmedabad: Navajivan Press, 1957.

The Gazette of India, Extraordinary, Nos. of 26 November 1949-26 January 1950.

Ghosh, Ramesh Chandra, *The Government of the Swiss Republic*, Calcutta: The World Press, 1953.

Gledhill, Allan, *The Republic of India*, London: Stevens and Sons, 1951.

———, *Pakistan, the Development of Its Laws and Constitution*, London: Stevens and Sons, 1957.

Gooch, R.K., *Parliamentary Government in France: Revolutionary Origins, 1789-1791*, Ithaca: Cornell University Press, 1960.

Government of India, Ministry of States, *White Paper on Indian States*, Delhi: Manager of Publications, 1949.

Griffiths, P.J., *The British in India*, London: Robert Hale Ltd., 1946.

Gupta, Madan Gopal (ed.), *Some Aspects of the Indian Constitution*, Allahabad: Central Book Depot, 1960.

Gwyer, Maurice and A. Appadorai, *Speeches and Documents on the Indian Constitution*, London: Oxford University Press, 1957.

Harrison, Selig, *India, The Most Dangerous Decades*, Princeton: Princeton University Press, 1960.

Hicks, U.K., *Federalism and Economic Growth in Underdeveloped Countries*, London: George Allen & Unwin, 1961.

Hindu Mahasabha, *Constitution of the Hindusthan Free State*, Poona, 1944.

Indian Statutory Commission. *The Report and Recommendations*, in vols. 1 & 2, published by the Government of Great Britain, 1930.

Jain, P.C., *The Industrial Problems of India*, Allahabad: Kitabistan, 1944.

Jennings, W. Ivor, *Some Characteristics of the Indian Constitution*, Madras: Oxford University Press, 1953.

———, *The Constitutional Problems in Pakistan*, Cambridge: Cambridge University Press, 1957.

———, *The British Commonwealth of Nations*, 4th revd. edn., London: Oxford University Press, 1963.

Karunakaran, K.P., *Continuity and Change in Indian Politics*, Delhi: People's Publishing House, 1964.

Keith, A.B., *Speeches and Documents on Indian Policy, 1750-1920*, London: The Word Classics, 1922.

———, *A Constitutional History of India, 1600-1935*, Allahabad: Central Book Depot, 1936.

Khan-Durrani, F.K., *The Meaning of Pakistan*, Lahore: Sh. Muhammad Ashraf, 1944.

Krishnamurti, Y.G., *Constituent Assembly*, Bombay: New Book Company, 1940.

Lenin, V.I., *Selected Works*, vols. 5 & 6, London: Lawrence and Gispert, 1936-9.

Livingston, William S., *Federalism in the Commonwealth, A Bibliographical Commentary*, London: Cassel, 1963.

Lumby, E.W.R., *The Transfer of Power in India*, London: Allen & Unwin, 1954.

Luthera, V.P., *The Concept of Secular State and India*, Bombay: Oxford University Press, 1964.

Maitland, Frederic W., *The Constitutional History of England*, New York: Macmillan, 1908.

Markandan, K.C., *Directive Principles in the Indian Constitution*, Bombay: Allied Publisher, 1966.

Masani, M.R., *The Communist Party of India*, London: Derek Verschoyle, 1954.

Mashruwala, K.G., *Some Particular Suggestions for the Constitution of India*, Bombay: Hamara Hindusthan Publications, 1946.

McCracken, John Leslie, *Representative Government in Ireland 1919-1948*, London: Oxford University Press, 1958.

Mehta, Asoka, *Socialism and Gandhism*, Bombay: Congress Socialist Publishing Co., 1935.

Mehta, Asoka, *The Political Mind of India*, Bombay: Socialist Party Publication, 1952.

———, *Democratic Socialism*, Bombay: Chetan Prakashan, 1954.

Mehta, Asoka and Achyuta Patwardhan, *The Communal Triangle in India*, Allahabad: Kitabistan, 1942.

Menon, V.P., *The Story of the Integration of the Indian States*, Calcutta: Orient Longmans Co., 1956.

———, *The Transfer of Power*, Calcutta: Orient Longmans Co., 1957.

Mishra, Panchanan, *The Making of the Indian Republic*, Calcutta: Scientific Book Agency, 1966.

Mitra, N.N., *The Indian Annual Register, 1917-1947, June* (published as *The Indian Quarterly Register from 1924 to 1929*), Calcutta: Annual Register Office.

Moon, Penderel, *Divide and Quit*, London: Chatto and Windus, 1961.

Morris-Jones, W.H., *Parliament in India*, London: Longmans Green & Co., 1957.

———, *The Government and Politics of India*, London: Hutchinson, University Press, 1964.

Muir, Ramsay, *A Short History of the British Commonwealth*, 2 vols., 5th edn., London: George Philip & Sons, 1934.

Munshi, K.M., *The President under the Constitution of India*, Bombay: Bharatiya Vidya Bhavan, 1963.

———, *The Changing Shape of Indian Politics*, 2nd edn., Poona: Deshmukh & Co., 1946.

———, *Pilgrimage to Freedom*, Bombay: Bharatiya Vidya Bhavan, 1967.

Myers, Charles A., *Industrial Relations in India*, Bombay: Asia Publishing House, 1958.

Narayan, Jayaprakash, *Towards Struggle*, Bombay: Padma Publication, 1946.

Nehru, Jawaharlal, *The Unity of India*, 3rd edn., London: Lindsay Drummond, 1948.

———, *An Autobiography*, rpt., London: Bodley Head, 1958.

Nehru, Jawaharlal, *A Bunch of Old Letters*, London: Asia Publishing House, 1959.

Overstreet, G.D., M. Windmiller, *Communism in India*, Bombay: Perennial Press. 1960.

Palmer, Norman D., *The Indian Political System*, London: George Allen & Unwin, 1960.

Punjabi, K.L., *The Indomitable Sardar*, Bombay: Bharatiya Vidya Bhavan, 1962.

Parikh, N.D., *Sardar Vallabhbhai Patel*, 2 vols., Ahmedabad: Navajivan Press, 1953.

Park, R.L., and I. Tinker (eds.), *Leadership and Political Institutions in India*, Princeton: Princeton University Press, 1959.

Prasad, Rajendra, *India Divided*, Allahabad: Hind Kitab, 1946.

———, *At the Feet of Mahatma Gandhi*, Allahabad: Hind Kitab, 1955.

———, *Autobiography*, Bombay: Asia Publishing House, 1957.

Pylee, M.V., *Constitutional History of India, 1600-1950*, Bombay: Asia Publishing House, 1967.

Quraishi, Z.M., *The President of India*, New Delhi: New Literature, 1962.

Rao, B. Shiva, *The Framing of India's Constitution*, vols. I-IV: *Select Documents*, vol. V: *A Study*, New Delhi: The Indian Institute of Public Administration, 1966.

Rao, K.V., *Parliamentary Democracy in India, A Critical Commentary*, 2nd edn., Calcutta: The World Press Pvt. Ltd., 1965.

Rau, B.N., *Constitutional Precedents*, 1st, 2nd and 3rd series, Delhi: Manager of Publications, 1946-7.

———, *India's Constitution in the Making*, ed. B. Shiva Rao, Calcutta: Orient Longmans Co., 1960.

Rose, Saul, *Politics in Southern Asia*, London: Macmillan Co., 1963.

Roy, N.C., *Towards Framing the Constitution of India*, Calcutta: The World Press, 1948.

Saksena, R.C., *Labour Problems and Social Welfare*, 4th edn., Meerut: Jaiprakash Nath & Co., 1955.

Salvemini, Gaetano, *The French Revolution*, London: Jonathan Cape, 1950.

Santhanam, K., *Union-State Relations in India*, Bombay: Asia Publishing House, 1960.

———, *Transition in India and Other Essays*, Bombay: Asia Publishing House, 1964.

Sapru, Tej Bahadur, *The Indian Constitution*, Madras: The National Secretary's Office, 1926.

Sapru, Tej Bahadur et al., *Constitutional Proposals of the Sapru Committee*, Bombay: Padma Publications, 1945.

Sarkar, R.N., *Government of India Acts, 1858, 1915 & 1935 with Indian Independence Act (and the India Provisional Constitution Orders) 1947*, Calcutta: S.C. Sarkar and Sons Private Ltd., n.d.

Sen, Dhirendra Nath, *The Problem of Minorities*, Calcutta: The University of Calcutta, 1940.

———, *Revolution by Consent?* Calcutta: Vidyodaya Library, 1947.

———, *From Raj to Swaraj*, Calcutta: Vidyodaya Library, 1954.

———, *The Paradox of Freedom*, Calcutta: Vidyodaya Library, 1958.

Setalvad, M.C., *The Indian Constitution, 1950-1965*, Kashinath Trimbak Lectures, 1st series, Bombay: University of Bombay, 1967.

Sharma, B.M. and L.P. Choudhury, *Federal Polity*, Bombay: Asia Publishing House, 1967.

Shukla, B.D., *A History of the Indian Liberal Party*, Allahabad: The Indian Press, 1960.

Sitaramayya, Pattabhi, *The History of the Indian National Congress*, rpt, Bombay: Padma Publications, 1946.

Spann, R.N., *Constitutionalism in Asia*, Bombay: Asia Publishing House, 1963.

Spear, Percival, *India*, Ann Arbor: University of Michigan Press, 1961.

Srinivasan, N., *Democratic Government in India*, Calcutta: World Press, 1963.

Strong, C.F., *Modern Political Constitutions*, 4th revd. edn., London: Sidgwick and Jackson, 1963.

Tendulkar, D.G., *Mahatma*, 8 vols, Fort, Bombay: Publications Division of *The Times of India*, 1953.

Thompson, E.J. and G.T. Garrat, *Rise and Fulfilment of the British Rule in India*, Allahabad: Central Book Depot, 1958.

UNESCO, *Contemporary Political Science, Survey of Methods, Research and Training*, Paris, 1950.

Wasi, S.M., *President Prasad—A Biography*, Calcutta: Thacker Spink, 1962.

Weiner, Myron, *Party Politics in India*, Princeton: Princeton University Press, 1957.

Wheare, K.C., *Federal Government*, London: Oxford University Press, 1956.

———, *Modern Constitutions*, London: Oxford University Press, 1958.

———, *Constitutional Structure of the Commonwealth*, Oxford: Clarendon Press, 1960.

Zurcher, A.Z., *Constitutions and Constitutionalism Since World War II*, 2nd revd. edn., New York: University Press, 1965.

Index